Sherlock Holmes FAQ

Series Editor: Robert Rodriguez

Sherlock Holmes FAQ

Everything Left to Know About the World's Greatest Private Detective

Dave Thompson

APPLAUSE
THEATRE & CINEMA BOOKS
An Imprint of Hal Leonard Corporation

Copyright © 2013 by Dave Thompson

Published in 2013 by Applause Theatre and Cinema Books
An Imprint of Hal Leonard Corporation
7777 West Bluemound Road
Milwaukee, WI 53213

Trade Book Division Editorial Offices
33 Plymouth St., Montclair, NJ 07042

The FAQ series was conceived by Robert Rodriguez and developed with Stuart Shea.
All Photographs are from the author's collection unless otherwise indicated.
Printed in the United States of America

Book design by Snow Creative Services

Library of Congress Cataloging-in-Publication Data

Thompson, Dave, 1960 January 3–
    Sherlock Holmes FAQ : all that's left to know about the world's greatest private detective / Dave Thompson.
        pages cm
    Includes bibliographical references and index.
    ISBN 978-1-4803-3149-5 (pbk. : alk. paper)
1. Doyle, Arthur Conan, 1859–1930—Characters—Sherlock Holmes. 2. Holmes, Sherlock–Miscellanea. 3. Sherlock Holmes films. 4. Sherlock Holmes television programs. I. Title.
    PR4624.T44 2014
    823'.8—dc23
                                                                    2013041890

www.applausebooks.com

To Mick Farren, who solved every mystery life flung at him.
Thanks for Willy's Rats!

Contents

Acknowledgments

Thank you to everyone who lent a hand, offered an opinion, or threw in an utterly unreasonable demand as I wrote this book, but especially to Amy Hanson, for her tireless championing of Peter Cushing's BBC Holmes, and permission to quote from her extensive knowledge of Ripperana; to Chrissie Bentley, for introducing me to Ambrose Horne; to Vincent O'Neil, for sharing his thoughts on Arthur Conan Doyle and Harry Price; and to Chloe Mortensen, for reminding me that Moriarty is not quite as bad as he is painted. Well, not always.

To John Cerullo, Marybeth Keating, Jaime Nelson, and Angela Arcese for bringing the project to life.

And finally, to all the other people who threw something strange into the casebook, even if it was just bad jokes. Karen and Todd, Linda and Larry, Betsy and Steve, Jo-Ann Greene, Jen, Dave and Sue, Gaye and Tim, everyone at Captain Blue Hen in Newark, Oliver, Trevor, Toby, Barb East, Bateerz and family, the Gremlins who live in the heat pump, and John the Superstar, the demon of the dry well.

Introduction

There are probably as many books about Sherlock Holmes as there are words in all of the stories. Or at least different words.

That may be an exaggeration, but only marginally. There is no single character in western fiction who has inspired more authors to write about him than Sherlock Holmes, with even James Bond and Doctor Who—the two that come closest—lagging far, far behind in terms of simple shelf filling. A complete Sherlock Holmes bibliography could fill a small library, a vision that is made all the more remarkable when one considers that the original stories that inspired this phenomenal outpouring would take up barely six inches of shelf space.

Just four novels and fifty-six short stories constitute the complete adventures of Sherlock Holmes. To this there can be added a dozen or so other writings by Sherlock Holmes's creator, Arthur Conan Doyle, whose inclusion in, or exclusion from, "the canon" (as the primary series of tales is known) has fired a debate that might never end. But they would add no more than another inch of published paper, tucked away in a room that is already stuffed with so many other books that it would take a lifetime to read them all. "Never," one might say, "has so little given birth to so much."

Neither does this outpouring look like it is ending. The massive success of *Sherlock*, the BBC's twenty-first-century reimagining of Holmes has inspired a whole new generation of writers and researchers to immerse themselves in the world of Holmes, and an older one to reacquaint themselves. Indeed, one of the most popular fiction serials of the modern age, Douglas Preston and Lincoln Child's Agent Pendergast, closed 2013 with the publication of *White Fire*, a thoroughly modern detective tale rooted in a near century-old Sherlock Holmes mystery.

Sherlock's triumph, however, transcends all of these—that triumph itself being defined not by viewing figures (which themselves are massive) or popularity (ditto), but by the skill with which we are invited to enter a world in which the "real" Sherlock Holmes, the classic Holmes whom we have spent the past century-plus enjoying, never existed. Until today.

The original Holmes was a child of his times, the last years of the Victorian era and the first of the twentieth century. The modern Holmes is likewise a child of *his* times, the first decades of the twenty-first century. That is, more than one hundred years after Conan Doyle's original stalked the streets, the intervening century has shaped the modern Holmes just as thoroughly as the prototype was shaped by the years that preceded him. Culture creates the heroes it requires.

Conan Doyle's Sherlock Holmes fit his era like a glove. British writers and TV creators Steven Moffat and Mark Gatiss's is equally well proportioned.

Conan Doyle's Holmes studied newspapers and magazines. The modern one harnesses the Internet. The original Holmes was addicted to opium. His successor is addicted to nicotine. The original was partnered by an army doctor, John Watson, recently returned from what was then Britain's most recent war, far away in Afghanistan. Today's Holmes is partnered by a man of the same cut and same name, fresh from what is still Britain's most recent war . . . far away in Afghanistan.

Parallel after parallel pile up, but the fact is, the modern television Holmes is as unique a televisual character as the original was a unique literary creation. The fact that they share the same DNA, investigate the same mysteries, and sometimes speak the same lines binds them, of course. But it also defines their individuality. Were they ever to meet face to face, the nineteenth-century Holmes and his twenty-first-century doppelgänger, they probably wouldn't even say hello.

Yet while the twenty-first-century Holmes was this book's original inspiration, it is the nineteenth-century Holmes who dominates it—as, of course, he should. For, while it is true that the work of Moffat and Gatiss would never have existed without the Conan Doyle prototype, it is equally true to say that we would not have cared about its existence without the century of other writings, and other Holmeses, that divide the two.

For many viewers of the modern TV show, such tales as *The Hound of the Baskervilles*, *The Sign of Four*, and *The Final Problem* are as familiar as their own biographies. Yet have they ever read these tales in their original printed form? Probably not. They have seen the movies, devoured the comics, watched the myriad past TV adaptations.

Names like Holmes's brother Mycroft and his nemesis Moriarty, his adversary Irene Adler and his favorite policeman, Inspector Lestrade, are as familiar as Holmes's and Watson's own. But could the majority of fans tell you how many tales these characters originally appeared in? Again, probably not. A landscape has developed around Sherlock Holmes, and a mythology, too, that stretches far beyond anything that Conan Doyle ever envisioned. And it is the mythology that this book is interested in.

The "Frequently Asked Questions" that title this book may or may not be those that immediately come to mind when considering Sherlock Holmes. "What is his middle name?" "Where was he born?" "Did he ever marry?" "Does he really have a glass eye?"

Many of these will be answered as this book unfolds (nobody knows; nobody knows; nobody knows but it seems unlikely; and how on earth do you come up with these questions?), but just as many may not. Rather, we concentrate on the kind of questions that arise *around* the stories, as opposed to directly *within* them—presuming a certain knowledge of Sherlock Holmes on the part of the reader, and assuming, too, a certain curiosity to stretch beyond the canon, and the most familiar movies and TV adaptations, into the deeper reaches of both Holmes's existence and that of his creator.

Opinions will be voiced. While chroniclers of modern pop culture insist that the Internet has democratized the art of criticism, allowing every user to voice his or her own in a public forum, the truth of the matter is somewhat different. Rather than voice a personal opinion, many people regard the net as a place to insist that theirs is hard fact; will not acknowledge any contrary viewpoint, and actively spend their time trolling other sites in order to harshly dismiss any they might find.

For those people; for those whom society has pegged as sad and lonely middle-aged men who still live with their mothers, whose website is the center of the universe for a few dozen sad and lonely other, similarly positioned acolytes whose own view of the world is formulated by the last thing their goldfish brain registered, the following is for you:

Sherlock Holmes is brilliant. Every sentence he speaks is brilliant. Every deduction he makes is brilliant. Every actor who has played him is brilliant. Every word in every book is brilliant. Et cetera.

For the rest of us, those who see the world in shades beyond black and white, and for whom an opposing opinion is something to encourage with debate, as opposed to damn with crass insult, the *Sherlock Holmes FAQ* is a roller-coaster ride through a ghost train of dark corners, forgotten imagery, unusual interpretations, and more idiosyncratic investigations than you could shake a deerstalker hat at.

We will meet Holmes's extended family, and then extend beyond that to encounter some of the myriad contemporaries, successors, followers, and imitators whom he has spawned over the decades.

We will go to the movies, where Sherlockian cinema itself now celebrates over 110 years' worth of history; tune in to oldtime radio; and sit enraptured in front of the television.

We will journey beyond the veil with Arthur Conan Doyle; we will visit the city that Holmes called home; we will fight on foreign fields alongside the indefatigable Doctor John Watson. (Whose middle name begins with H but was never revealed by Conan Doyle. Another FAQ succinctly answered.)

And all along the way, we will celebrate the phenomenon that is Sherlock Holmes.

Sherlock Holmes
FAQ

The Adventure of the Artist as a Young Whelp

In which we meet the Family, despair of the Youth, and investigate the Greatest Mystery of them all. Do we call him Arthur Conan? Or Mr. Conan Doyle?

It is one of literature's most piquant ironies. One of the greatest-ever figures in the entire history of the English language, one of the most iconic characters in the history of English culture, and certainly one of the best-known residents of the English capital city, was the creation of a Scotsman.

A Scotsman who had barely visited London when he first put Holmesian pen to Sherlockian paper. Who was no more familiar with the city's rhythms, rookeries, and riverside than any other reasonably well-read denizen of the lands that the average Londoner thinks of as "the provinces"—which equates to any part of the British Isles that is *not* London.

Home for Arthur Conan Doyle and his wife Louisa at the time when Holmes was conceived was in Southsea, close by the naval town of Portsmouth on the English south coast, where he ran a not especially successful medical practice. Prior to that, he lived for a short time in Plymouth, in the English southwest; worked in Aston and Sheffield in the midlands; and traveled to Greenland and Africa as a shipboard doctor. But he was born and bred in Edinburgh, at 11 Picardy Place, on May 22, 1859, and therein lies that aforementioned irony, one that continues to tickle proud Caledonians to this very day.

His family were no strangers to either the metropolis or its brighter lights. Grandfather John Doyle may have been of Irish birth, but his abilities as an artist drew him to London in 1822, at the age of twenty-five, and he would stay there for the remainder of his life.

So would the majority of his children, three daughters and four sons: Richard (1824–1883), a talented cartoonist whose work was very familiar to readers of

Just knock on the door . . . .   © *Steve and Betsy Mortensen*

the popular press of the day (both Richard and his father were among the earliest contributors to *Punch* magazine); James (1822–1892), an artist and an expert on heraldry; Henry (1827–1892), an art critic and painter who later became the director of the National Gallery of Ireland. Only the youngest, Conan Doyle's father, Charles Altamont Doyle, (1832–1893), broke the mold. He moved to Edinburgh at the age of seventeen and might well have regretted it forever more.

Charles Doyle was an aspiring artist but a confirmed alcoholic, his life scarred by discord, depression, and disappointment. True, he married well—Mary Foley, five years his junior (they wed when she was seventeen) was beautiful and very well educated; her passion was reading and storytelling, and the worlds to which she transported her children were a far cry from the increasing poverty and discomfort of the family's reality.

"In my early childhood," Conan Doyle would write years later, "as far as I can remember anything at all, the vivid stories she would tell me stand out so clearly that they obscure the real facts of my life."

Mary spoke of her own landed family back in Ireland and convinced Arthur that they were descended from aristocrats, to whom chivalry and manners were the keys to success. She taught him to read and, by the age of five, prodigiously early for the era and the family's status, the boy was devouring the best-sellers of the day—Scots icon Sir Walter Scott, adventure spinners Robert Michael Ballantyne, Captain Maine Reade and Captain Marryat, the supernatural histories of Harrison Ainsworth.

Even the lad's name bespoke dignity; or at least, it would come to. Arthur Ignatius Conan Doyle took the second of his middle names, the "Conan," from his paternal grandmother's family. It was never intended to convey any suggestion of a double-barreled nomenclature, at least by his parents.

Feeding upon the fruits of his mother's tales of past majesty, however, young Arthur readily sensed the soupçon of grandeur that such a distinctive combination would offer him. In referring to himself as Arthur Conan Doyle, he forced future biographers and many more to decide for themselves how he should be addressed. Many, and this book is no exception, chose to indulge his own subterfuge. Conan Doyle became his surname, Arthur his sole Christian name. Except when he was feeling especially vitriolic. What fun to remind people that your full set of initials is an anagram of "acid."

As a child, of course, he was simply Arthur Doyle, but even then he stood out from the crowd. According to legend, he read so fast that at one point the local lending library was forced to remind him that borrowers were forbidden to exchange books more than twice a day. This tale suggests that he either did not read entire novels at a time, and merely skipped around the most exciting points, or, more likely, that he concentrated his intentions upon the weekly or monthly installments in which many novels were debuted before being bound into collected editions.

His escape into fiction—and, by the age of six, he was composing his own—was probably merciful. The family was wracked by father Charles Altamont's inability to deal with the disappointments that his career as an artist seemed set to deal him. Though competent enough, he was seldom fortunate in obtaining commissions or publications, condemned forever to dwell in the shadow of his contrarily successful brothers and father—and, through the final years of his life, his son.

Drunken, violent, riven by depression, his impact on the lives of his children—of whom, ultimately, there were nine, although several struggled to reach adulthood—would indeed have required something powerful to blot it from the mind, and mother Mary's literary encouragement supplied that. At the same time, doubtless, as she endured a hellish existence of her own, bound to such a brute.

Today, pop culture sees the word "Altamont" and applies it instantly to the disastrous free concert that the Rolling Stones played at the speedway of that name in December 1969. There the murder of one fan and the untrammeled violence of the Hell's Angels security forces ensure Altamont remains instantly recognizable shorthand for violence and chaos. A century earlier, Charles Doyle's family might have been excused for viewing it in much the same light.

An older Conan Doyle allowed such memories to slip from his mind. But he never forgot his first attempts to write a story that might be filed alongside the greats that already populated his library. For hidden terror stalked every sentence.

He used foolscap paper, writing "in what might be called a fine bold hand—four words to the line—and . . . illustrated by marginal pen-and-ink sketches by the author. There was a man in it, and there was a tiger, I forget which was the hero, but it didn't matter much, for they became blended into one another about the time when the tiger met the man."

It was, he realized at that early age, very easy to lead a fictional character into danger. "And very hard to get them out again . . . . On this occasion the situation was beyond me, and my book, like my man, was engulfed by the tiger."

Neither would education offer him any solace. Aged seven, Conan Doyle entered Newington Academy, a school that he later compared to the very worst that Charles Dickens could ever have imagined, presided over by one particular teacher whose pockmarked face and single staring eye seem to have been as terrifying as his love of beating the boys in his charge.

Conan Doyle was no longer living at home. Claiming it would make life easier for him were he to be boarding close to his school, mother Mary sent him to live with family friends, the lawyer and historian John Hill Burton, his wife, Mary, and their son, William.

Again it would seem that she viewed this as an escape for her favorite child, separating him from the grueling poverty and fear that now haunted the family home, and it would be two years before Conan Doyle returned to live with his parents, who now occupied a mean top-story apartment in what had once been a grand old Edinburghian townhouse, but which rapacious landlords had long since converted into grim tenements for the city's poor.

There, on mean city streets as gritty and dangerous as any of those he may have read about in Dickensian London, the young Conan Doyle became as adept with his fists as he was with his mind, an educated brawler who devoured English and French literature on the one hand (his godfather and great-uncle Michael Conan regularly sent him gifts of French books), then sallied forth as a street fighter on the other.

The Uplifting Adventure of the Catholic Scholarship

It was Uncle Michael who first suggested that the boy be extracted altogether from this grim environment and sent away to boarding school; Uncle Michael, too, who recommended that the school should conform to both the Doyles' and the Conans' Roman Catholic faith.

There were two choices, the Benedictine Downside, and the Jesuit Stoneyhurst; the decision was made, it seems, by the latter's willingness to offer the young lad a scholarship that obliterated the traditional annual fee of £50. Therefore, in September 1868, aged just eight and bawling his eyes out the whole journey through, Conan Doyle was admitted to Stoneyhurst's preparatory establishment Hodder House, a boarding school in Lancashire, northern England, close by the town of Clitheroe. The first person he met when he left the train at Preston was the black-robed monk who had been sent to collect him.

It was an august institution. Stoneyhurst could (and still can—it remains a going concern today) trace its origins back to 1593, to a time when Catholicism itself was illegal in England. It is no surprise whatsoever to discover among the school's alumni no fewer than twenty-two martyrs, executed for their faith by Protestant persecutors. Three of this number (Philip Evans, Thomas Garnet, and John Plessington) were subsequently canonized; twelve more were beatified.

Charles Carroll, the sole Catholic signatory to the U.S. Declaration of Independence, and Philip Calvert, who occupied that most remarkable-sounding of all colonial American post-ings, the Keeper of the Conscience of Maryland, were Stoneyhurst old boys; so was the poet William Habington; and so was the magnificently named Ambrose Rookwood, one of the primary archi-tects of the Gunpowder Plot.

Arthur Conan Doyle from an early 19th century cigarette card.

Despite his early misgivings, Conan Doyle settled swiftly into the school rou-tine. Perhaps he sensed, especially as he grew older, that his life had taken a very definite turn for the better. Remaining in Edinburgh, and what passed for the school system there, would never have pulled him out of the gutter that his father's dissolution was driving the family toward, and any intellectual intentions that he may have nursed would surely have been knocked out of him in the fight, the literal fight, for survival.

Now the bucolic Lancashire countryside was his home. Just six weeks a year would be spent back in Edinburgh, as the school broke for the summer vacation; he would even choose to spend Christmases at Hodder. But he and mother were devout letter writers, and they remained in constant contact throughout the eight years that he would ultimately be away; first at Hodder House before he passed on to Stoneyhurst College, where he remained until the age of sixteen, in 1875.

He was not an especially remarkable student, despite his keen intellect. One of his contemporaries, the cartoonist Bernard Partridge, captured a glimpse of young Arthur Doyle in a memory preserved by the inestimable Richard Lancelyn Green Archive in Portsmouth, England. He was "a thick-set boy, with a quiet manner, and a curious furtive smile when he was visited with one of the school penalties . . . . He was, I fancy, rather lazy in his studies, never taking a prominent place in his form: but his brain was very nimble, and he was constantly throwing off verses and parodies on college personalities and happenings."

Stoneyhurst was strict. Not, perhaps, in the precise manner immortalized by such earlier paeans to English school life as *Tom Brown's School Days*, where boys could be roasted as readily as chestnuts and both bullying and torture were regarded as legitimate means of toughening a young man up for adulthood.

But the school certainly adhered faithfully to the strictures of Catholic discipline, a set of laws under which any transgression could be punished with either humiliation or physical pain. Both of which, naturally, were masked beneath the need to instruct the rule breaker in the need to consider his actions and repent his sins.

Celibacy was especially strictly enforced. Single-sex boarding schools, after all, have a reputation that is not always too far from the truth, and though modern eyes look back upon the Victorian era as one of tightly closed legs, cold showers, and ironclad morality, a quick glance at the underground literature of the age reveals the Queen's most loyal subjects to have been no less rambunctious in that department than in any other.

Certainly the authorities at Stoneyhurst were in no doubt that what they perceived as the growing dissolution of society was hatched wholly in the nocturnal predilections of young men left unsupervised in the other boarding schools of Britain. Monks and prefects alike, then, were charged to keep their eyes open for even the merest whiff of untoward behavior, and the punishments meted out to transgressors probably don't need to be described.

Further health and hardiness was encouraged by a strict regimen of being awoken at five every morning by the harsh, deafening cackle of a policeman's wooden rattle (the predecessor of the piercing whistle); and by the almost absolute absence of heating from the dormitories. Even in the dead of winter, nothing more than the most meager fire would be permitted, and when cracks were discovered in the walls and windows of those long, dark rooms, rumor would circulate that they had been created purposefully by one of the monks for the sheer delight of increasing the pupils' discomfort.

Under those conditions, two young men huddling in the same bed together would doubtless have been more motivated by trying to keep warm than by any form of adolescent sexual curiosity, but the punishments would have been the same.

By his own autobiographical confession, Conan Doyle was a regular recipient of monkish justice. He misbehaved constantly, he wrote, simply to prove that his spirit remained unbroken no matter how harsh the regime. Indeed, he recalled almost proudly the most brutal punishment that awaited any perceived miscreant, a beating that was known as "twice nine." That is, nine blows to the palm of each hand by an instrument called a *ferula*, a flat rubber paddle around the size of the sole of a work boot, delivered with such force that a single blow caused the palm to swell and bruise. Nine was absolute torture—and nine was the minimum number of blows that would be delivered.

Conan Doyle reported, presumably from bitter experience, that even "turn[ing] the handle of the door to get out of the room in which he had suffered" was beyond the ability of a punished pupil. Presumably any other form of manual activity would prove equally difficult.

Sports proved another outlet for Conan Doyle's youthful exuberance. As with many schools of the mid-nineteenth century, Stoneyhurst had created its own rules around the basics of sports that today's fan might think have been codified forever. Soccer, for example, is so established in sporting history, after all, that it seems incredible to think that it was just 150 years ago, in 1863, that anybody sat down to actually firm up the game's laws on a universal basis, and even then, rival codes, or laws, continued to flourish around the world—a process that gave rise to rugby, Australian rules, Gaelic football, and, of course, American football.

Stoneyhurst's version of the game during Conan Doyle's years there was especially unique. A smaller ball was there to be kicked, thrown, or otherwise bashed by any number of players. Teams had no set size limit, nor was there a rule that demanded equal numbers on either side. Goals were tiny, just seven feet wide, and the ensuing free-for-all was essentially a mad melee of wheeling arms and kicking legs that made its way from one end of the playing surface to the other. And then back again.

Conan Doyle, who would later distinguish himself as at least an adequate soccer player (as we shall see in a subsequent chapter), was no fan of Stoneyhurst football, describing it as a "freak game" that, in common with the similar pastimes played at other public schools, did much to hamstring the development of players genuinely talented at what became the "real" game.

Likewise, Stoneyhurst's take on cricket had developed along its own unique lines, although a more recognizable version of the sport, known as London Cricket in honor of its southern codification, moved into the school curriculum during Conan Doyle's time there, and he went on to captain the school team.

Sports, and his still voracious appetite for reading and writing aside, Conan Doyle's early ambitions appear to have been modest.

He recalled in his autobiography once informing a monk that he fancied a career as a civil engineer, to which the monk responded that he might become an engineer but he would never be civil—a poke at the boy's incessant misbehavior and, presumably, rudeness. He was a keen participant in the school's amateur dramatics, and when an aunt invited him to spend the Christmas of 1874 with her family in London—his first-ever visit to that city—he ensured that a couple of West End plays, *Hamlet* and *Our American Cousin*, were on the agenda.

Other highlights of that three week break included a visit to the circus; a ride out to the Crystal Palace in Sydenham, where "life size dinosaurs" were a major attraction; trips to the Tower of London and Westminster Abbey; and, although nobody, not even Conan Doyle himself, could have perceived its significance at the time, a tour around Madame Tussaud's legendary Waxworks Museum at its original premises on Baker Street.

There he thrilled to the exquisite tableaux that preserved for all time (or at least until they were recycled into other figures) the great and good of both recent and lingering history, lifelike in every aspect, astonishing in their

A thoroughly modern Sherlock—Benedict Cumberbatch.   *Photofest*

attention to detail. Then, leaving at the end of the visit, perhaps he glanced farther along the street, the long parade of once-handsome buildings that were only gradually being converted into flats, or apartments: flat A on the ground floor, flat B on the first . . . .

It was during his final year at Stoneyhurst that Conan Doyle first became aware that his youthful love of storytelling had grown into a teenaged ability to captivate audiences. While editing the school magazine, he also threw himself into the composition of serial stories, lengthy epics of adventure and derring do more appropriate, perhaps, to the pages of a penny dreadful than the august halls of a Jesuit college.

Penny dreadfuls were the bane of the faculty's existence, cheap (as their name implies), lurid (ditto) magazines into which the most sensational, shocking, and horrifying fiction imaginable was shoehorned, in bite-sized quantities, and every installment ending upon a new note of cliff-hanging calamity, to ensure the reader had no alternative but to return for more in the very next issue.

Fifty years on, radio and movie serials would seize upon a similar notion to keep their audience coming back; today, television offers the same diversion. Different crimes for different climes. In 1870s England, with radio and television still far off in science-fiction land, penny dreadfuls were *the* public enemy number one. And Conan Doyle discovered that he had a rare talent for writing them.

He read his tales aloud to his audience, seated on a desk while they crouched on the floor around him, spinning out sagas so suspenseful that he would occasionally threaten to end a tale early because he knew his anxious audience would not hesitate to bribe him with apples and cakes, if only he'd read another page.

Still in his teens, Conan Doyle had discovered for himself the secret of great storytelling (if not necessarily great stories). "When I had got as far as . . . 'slowly, slowly, the door turned upon its hinges, and with eyes which were dilated with horror the wicked Marquis saw . . . ' I knew that I had my audience in my power."

Conan Doyle returned to London in spring 1875 to sit the matriculation examination for London University, becoming one of fourteen Stoneyhurst pupils to be selected for that prestigious institution. He passed with honors, but before taking his place at London he had one further test to undertake, one further year of Catholic education far away in Austria, at the Stella Matutina, a Jesuit school in Feldkirch.

There, as Uncle Michael insisted, he learned to speak German and generally opened his mind to other academic possibilities; there, too, he edited the school newspaper, the *Feldkirchian Gazette*—a handwritten (in violet ink) publication that he subtitled "a scientific and literary magazine" and populated with verse, stories, news, and, inevitably, controversy. In one issue, in November 1875, he took the school authorities to task for their insistence upon reading every pupil's personal mail before it was delivered to its rightful recipient. The authorities, unaccustomed to being challenged over what they believed was fit and proper behavior, responded by closing down the newspaper.

Feldkirch, however, offered the young man one treat that—like the unsuspecting visit to Baker Street the previous Christmas—would remain on his mind for years to come. It was there that he discovered the writings of the American author Edgar Allen Poe: the classic horror of "The Pit and the Pendulum," "The Tell-Tale Heart," and, most poignant of all, "The Murders in the Rue Morgue"—a tale of ratiocination," Poe improvised, in which a brilliant and bafflingly idiosyncratic detective named C. Auguste Dupin devised methods of criminal detection that were far beyond the abilities of the flatfooted policemen around him.

When Conan Doyle left Feldkirch to return to Edinburgh (via a short trip to Paris, where Uncle Michael was now living), Dupin's methodology—the triple sciences of observation, intuition, and deduction—were firmly at the fore of his mind. Which was handy, because a veritable mystery awaited him.

The Strange Case of the Solicitous Lodger

Conan Doyle arrived in Edinburgh to discover—or at least suspect—that his mother had taken a lover.

Doctor Bryan Charles Waller was nominally a lodger in the family home, but father Charles's continued abandonment of all but a physical presence in the household had allowed the newcomer to essentially become the man

Benedict Cumberbatch, 2010   *Photofest*

of the house, a role in which Mary seemed happy to cherish him with all the respect and support that she should surely have been offering her husband.

In all truthfulness, one would have required a very hard heart to begrudge her the obvious happiness that the interloper provided. Waller was everything that Conan Doyle's father was not. Wealthy, educated, and professional, he hailed from precisely the same chivalrously historic background with which Mary used to entertain her son, a descendent of brave knights at Agincourt and noble warriors in the English Civil War. A Royal poet flowered in his family tree, and a famous author, too. And he was young. He was just six years Arthur Conan Doyle's senior, although in terms of worldly wisdom, he might have been decades ahead.

Nevertheless, society had a word for women in Mary's apparent situation, and it was not a particularly pleasant one. She was a cuckold. Conan Doyle was mortified.

But there were advantages, too. Waller's family owned an estate in Yorkshire, Masongill (that's where she was when Conan Doyle arrived home, visiting Waller's mother); and the rent that he paid for room and board had permitted the Doyles to move, for the very first time, into a far higher standard of living than they had ever known before.

Home now was a large apartment at 2 Argyle Park Terrace, a bright and breezy corner of Edinburgh's well-to-do New Town development. Where, for certain, the curtains twitched and the neighbors gossiped, all wondering why such a handsome young doctor, whose family fortune could have afforded him a mansion of his own, had chosen to live instead with a woman the same age as his mother, her permanently drunken husband, and the five (now six, with Conan Doyle's return) children who had not themselves fled the nest.

Conan Doyle shared their suspicions, but whereas the neighbors appear to have kept their own counsel, he was less well mannered. Letters to those absent siblings were alive with his suspicions and disgruntlement. He certainly dismissed his mother's explanation that Waller was in fact enamored by his sister Annette.

If that was the case, why did she move out shortly (as far away as Portugal, where she now worked as a governess) after he moved in, whereas he had stayed put in her former home?

Further fuel was poured on those furrow-browed fires when Waller paid for the entire family to move once again, this time to a two-story apartment in one of Edinburgh's most well-appointed neighborhoods, 23 George Square. There he established his medical practice; and there Mary, Charles, and their children lived rent free at the good doctor's expense. At least until Waller's concerns for Charles's mental health finally saw the older man institutionalized.

At that point, the doctor drove a brutal stake through Conan Doyle's relationship with his mother when he moved her out of Edinburgh altogether, to a cottage on the Masongill estate. She would remain there for the next thirty years, until 1917, ignoring the entreaties of her son to come live with him as ruthlessly as Waller ignored those of his own wife (he wed in 1896) when she begged him to show her even a fraction of the attention he lavished upon Mary Doyle.

Conan Doyle had no love, then, for Waller. But he was also an opportunistic young man, and when Waller suggested the boy study medicine (and doubtless pointed out that there were many wheels he could grease to facilitate that ambition), Conan Doyle agreed. He abandoned his original plans of studying at the London University and agreed to remain in Edinburgh—home to one of the finest medical schools in the kingdom. In October 1876, Arthur Conan Doyle enrolled at the University of Edinburgh Medical School.

2

The Adventure of the Unexpected Medical Student

In which the Vagaries of Indecision cast our Hero to at least a few of the Seven Seas, before embroiling him in the Easily Solved Adventure of the Syphilitic Sailors

Conan Doyle was not a natural doctor. That is to say, he viewed medicine as a career as opposed to a vocation, and even there he was less than committed to devoting his entire life to treating bunions, dropsy, and gout, or any of the other conditions that generally constituted the daily routine of a doctor's private practice at the time.

Sports and literature consumed far more of his mind than scalpels and lances; he far preferred dramatic theater to the operating theater, and while he proved himself more than capable of learning all that he needed to, absorbing the lessons that would allow him to set himself up as a general practitioner, always he believed that medicine was simply a means to an end.

Which, at this point in his life, was largely predicated around money, and the lack thereof. No matter that Waller's largesse seemed to know no bounds at home. Conan Doyle was determined to accept as little as he needed to from the family benefactor, avoiding anything that could be construed as establishing a debt between them.

He acknowledged Waller's aid in setting him up at university and repaid him with his academic progress. But less than two years after enrolling, he was seeking an escape route, accelerating his academic career to the point where a full year's worth of classes could be completed in six months, and then setting out into the wider world as a doctor's assistant.

It was not a well-starred move. Three weeks into his first job, with a Doctor Richardson in the English city of Sheffield, Conan Doyle was summarily dismissed for reasons that appear unclear but which undoubtedly included his arrogant insistence that he already knew everything worth knowing; his irrepressible high spirits; his penchant for playing practical jokes; and his seemingly insatiable need to take up an opposing argument on any subject that was raised. A typical young man, in fact. But not so typical that the doctor was willing to overlook the lad's faults. Conan Doyle was sent packing without a single penny in payment for whatever work he had done.

Distraught but not distracted, he accepted an invitation to spend time in London with his uncle Richard. He wound up living with the family at their Chelsea home for the next two months, but any lessons he might have absorbed in Sheffield had clearly been left unlearned. Soon, Conan Doyle's own kinfolk found themselves in absolute sympathy with Doctor Richardson and were practically begging their guest to leave.

He finally did so, taking up an offer to assist at a small practice in the tiny Shropshire village of Ruyton-of-the-Eleven Towns, where the incumbent Doctor Elliott was all the locals required to keep sickness and disease at bay.

Or so it seemed. For four months, Conan Doyle waited for his employer to summon his medical skills into action; and for four months, he spent his time reading, and walking in the beautiful local countryside. Just once, Conan Doyle recalled, was he permitted to show off his medical knowledge, when he was called to the scene of . . . of all things! . . . an exploding cannon.

Celebrating at a village fête, a group of locals had taken it into their heads to fire a piece of ancient military ordnance and were repaid by an explosion and a shower of vicious shrapnel, one shard of which was now embedded in an onlooker's skull.

Doctor Elliott was elsewhere at the time, so Conan Doyle raced to the scene alone. There, he extracted the shrapnel, sewed up the wound, and left his employer looking utterly redundant by the time he arrived, which did not serve to endear the young man to the older practitioner.

Four months had passed, and Elliott declared it was time for Conan Doyle to move on. He was . . . too arrogant. Too high-spirited. Too prone to practical jokes. Too argumentative. And when Conan Doyle demanded either wages or expenses for all the weeks he had spent in the middle of nowhere, the doughty old doctor simply shrugged. "Consider yourself a gentleman traveling for his own improvement," Elliott told him as he pushed the penniless boy out of the surgery door.

Conan Doyle would eventually find paid employment, assistant to Dr. Reginald Ratcliffe Hoare at a large practice in Aston, on the outskirts of the midlands city of Birmingham. There, his duties largely comprised filling prescriptions, and one can gauge the prosperity of the practice from Conan Doyle's recollection of often handing out a hundred or more in the course of a single evening. It was very much a working-class-and-below neighborhood, and the shilling-and-sixpence cost of the scripts, he knew, took more than a small bite from the average family's resources. But those 1/6ds added up, and for the first time in his life, Conan Doyle found himself not only making a living wage, but also with the time on his hands—or, perhaps, less worry on his mind—to pursue a few of his other fascinations.

The Strange Case of the Struggling Author with a Taste for Gelseminum

In early 1879, Conan Doyle dashed off a short story, "The Haunted Grange of Gosthorpe," twenty-four handwritten pages long, and mailed it to *Blackwood's Edinburgh Magazine*, one of the oldest and most established of all the era's literary periodicals. Of which there were many, which meant that when *Blackwood's* failed to even reply, his next effort was sent to *Chamber's Journal*, another Edinburgh-based publication.

There his writing found a welcoming home. "The Mystery of the Sassassa Valley" not only cast his name into print for the first time, it also earned him a check for three guineas (three pounds and three shillings). More than he earned in a month in Aston.

Chamber's did not accept any of the other tales he sent them. But *London Society*, a magazine held in high esteem during his childhood as one of those that occasionally published his father's illustrations, accepted "The American's Tale," a horror story set in the wild west of Montana, in a town aptly known as Flytrap Gulch. Where there lurked a flesh-eating plant capable of devouring a human being whole.

Conan Doyle received for this tale thirty shillings and a letter from the editor that suggested he might consider abandoning medicine altogether and setting out as a full-time author. Conan Doyle might have taken his advice, too, had the magazine only paid him more for his story. But it didn't, and so he labored on.

His medical leanings were not wholly overlooked. In September 1879, the same month as *Chambers Journal* gave him his fiction debut, the *British Medical Journal* published Conan Doyle's letter discussing the properties of the drug Gelseminum (a popular remedy for neuralgia, derived from dried rhizome and yellow jasmine) and its potential to become a poison.

Experimenting upon his own body, Conan Doyle spent a full week gradually increasing his daily dosage until he reached ten milliliters—double what the medical profession then considered to be a fatal dose.

Admittedly, he was suffering from diarrhea, headaches, dizziness, vision problems, and severe depression, but he was still alive. The experiment was his first published journey into the science of observation and deduction. Needless to say, it would not be his last.

In the meantime, he was tiring of medicine. Or, at least, tiring of the sheer mundane monotony of the medicine that he practiced. He craved adventure, and an idea was germinating.

The Adventure of an Informative Diversion Around the London Dockyards

Throughout his most recent visit to London, ill-fated though it was, Conan Doyle had spent much of his time in the city's east end, a hotbed of crime, vice, and poverty that was nevertheless dominated by one of the industrial jewels in the British Empire's crown, the vast networks of docks into which flowed all the wealth of the world.

Visiting the area today, stripped of all significance, first by years of decay and then by the last two decades' worth of redevelopment, gentrification, and so-called modernization, it is impossible to imagine the sheer magnitude of the docks as they were in Conan Doyle's day. The mile upon mile of foreboding brickwork that constituted the warehouses, into which all of the things that the modern era transports by train, plane, truck, or even Internet would be stacked; spices from the east, cotton from the west, iron from here, rubber from there, if there was a demand for it in the United Kingdom, its first port of call was the London docks.

Conan Doyle visited the docks at what might be described as a historically propitious time, on the very eve of the opening of one of the greatest architectural and technological undertakings of the age, the Royal Albert Dock. And a few years later, in the adventure of "the Five Orange Pips," Sherlock Holmes would tap into Conan Doyle's memories of the place by paying his own visit to a dock so massive that, among many other breathtaking statistics, it stretched out over three miles of quay.

London had always been a major port, but the Victorian era established the city as perhaps the premier one in all of the world, and the Royal Albert Dock was a major contributor to that grandiosity. Encompassing eighty-seven acres of land, six years in the building, and still in use today (albeit for purposes considerably less glamorous—it is now a watersports park), the completion and operation of the Royal

Gordon's. It's how the English keep their gin up!

Search no more! Gordon's is undeniably the driest, most delicately flavoured gin you can find. The clue? Elementary, my dear connoisseur: it is still based on Alexander Gordon's brilliant discovery in 1769. Would we change even one drop of that precious formula? Tamper one bit with the biggest seller in England, America, the world? Never! Perfection is good enough for us.

Gin and Lemon-entry, my dear Watson.

Albert Dock was a major point of pride for east Londoners; a major point of entry and exit for ships and people from all over the world; and a major lure for criminals of every persuasion.

Meat and tobacco imports were the dock's primary interest, with the very latest in haulage technology designed to accommodate the enormous fifty-five-gallon hogsheads in which American tobacco was packed.

Electric lighting illuminated the work areas, the first dock ever to be so equipped, but it was no safeguard against the thieves—who themselves ranged from the merest light-fingered individual opportunist, to the dyed-in-the-wool crime organization—for whom so much tobacco was an irresistible siren. And the lure was ever-lasting. The docks closed for the final time in 1981, dilapidated and ruinous. But right up until the end, British police and detective drama rarely let the docks out of their sight.

Thus we might be surprised that Holmes seems to have visited the dock only that once, to ascertain the whereabouts of the American barque *Lone Star*. But Inspector Lestrade and his Scotland Yard colleagues would certainly have been familiar with its pathways and warehouses, machine shops and hidey-holes; and with all the manifold misuses to which the criminal class put the vicinity. It was here that Lestrade apprehended the murderous steward James Browning, as he sat "rocking himself to and fro" in his berth aboard the SS *May Day* ("The Adventure of the Cardboard Box"), but he would have paid countless other visits to the dock in pursuit of every other color of criminal.

The east end surrounded the docks and was, in turn, supported by them—inasmuch as the new wave of Victorian entrepreneurs allowed their workers anything approaching a living wage in return for their labors. A small city within a city, there was barely a household in the east end that was not in some way linked umbilically to the docks, with crime and industry marching hand in hand through alleyways that remained in darkness even when the sun was bright.

The opium trade started here, and smuggling, larceny, and prostitution set up homesteads. Murder was common, assault endemic. It was no place for any respectable gentleman, unless he had both business and protectors in the area.

Conan Doyle had neither, but he spent his time there regardless, and he dreamed of abandoning the vagaries of landlocked medicine and finding himself a position at a ship's surgeon. That November of 1878 would see the outbreak of the Second Afghan War (an inevitable successor to the First, fought almost forty years previous), and both army and naval recruiters were out in force, in both the east and west ends of London. Conan Doyle had even stopped to speak with them once, but ultimately he decided against signing up. The dream of a life at sea remained strong, however, and shortly after Conan Doyle returned to Edinburgh, his Aston adventures at an end, a friend, Claude Currie, made him a remarkable offer.

The Adventure of the Shipboard Sawbones

Currie had recently accepted a post as surgeon aboard a whaling ship, the SS *Hope*, set to steam out of Peterhead, Scotland, in just two weeks' time, bound for the waters of the Arctic. He had already bought the clothing he would need for the journey when his personal situation changed and it was no longer possible for him to go. Would Conan Doyle like to take his place? The two men were of a similar size, so the clothes would fit. And they were clearly of similar inclination, too.

The money was good—fifty shillings a week, plus a three-shilling bonus for every ton of whale oil with which the vessel returned. The journey would be cold, it would be wet, it would be brutal. She may have been a steamer, but the SS *Hope* was barely better equipped to deal with the hostile waters of the Arctic than anything Captain Ahab might have mustered in the *Moby Dick* adventure that Conan Doyle devoured as a child.

He agreed immediately.

Conan Doyle worked aboard a whaler for just six weeks, but later years, as he wrote his autobiography, saw him reflect his time aboard the *Hope* with romance and nostalgia . He saw a part of the world that few of his contemporaries could imagine, "the great Greenland flows," as he noted in his journal. The "genial and kindly" icefields. The sea at rest, and the ocean in storm.

No matter that the journey scored just two whales; nor that the modern reader might (and should) be outraged that Conan Doyle (like most of his contemporaries) viewed the slaughter of these beautiful creatures as mere sport, albeit one in which the death of a whale eclipsed "any other triumph that sport can give."

The journey, he insisted, had transformed a gawky youth into a full-grown man.

A man who now needed to place all of that behind him as he prepared to sit his finals at university.

Conan Doyle graduated in August 1881, a bachelor of medicine and a master of surgery, and set about applying for any position that seemed suitable. The armed forces again felt like a serious proposition, but ultimately he selected a more peaceful station, ship's medical officer aboard the *Mayumba*, a 1,500-ton passenger, cargo, and mail steamer operated by the African Steam Navigation Company.

There, his early days at sea were largely dedicated to treating the passengers for seasickness as the vessel rocked and rolled through a storm in the Bay of Biscay, while hoping that the weather would abate sufficiently for his flooded cabin to drain. Later, he himself was the patient after he succumbed to what was probably a mild case of malaria (one of his crewmates was less fortunate and died of the disease while Conan Doyle was bedridden).

He spent much of the rest of his time fraternizing with the passengers and learning to operate the camera that he had purchased specifically for the voyage. He envisioned, and would ultimately succeed in, publishing an account of his journey, and he knew that visual documentation would be crucial to the endeavor. The piece was eventually published in the *British Journal of Photography*.

The *Mayumba* remained at sea for three months, finally returning to Liverpool in January 1882, following a voyage that took her down the coast of Africa to Old Calabar in Nigeria (stopping at Freetown, Sierra Leone; Monrovia, Liberia; Ghana and Lagos on the way) and whose only other highlight was a shipboard fire that came close to destroying the entire vessel. Stepping onshore, Conan Doyle resolved never again to work at sea. The climate was atrocious, he complained to his mother, and the wages were "less than I could make with my pen." That latter may or may not have been an optimistic projection, but the *Mayumba* experience certainly set his mind toward making the dream come true.

Meanwhile, the real business of work remained a pressing concern. An attempt by his family in London to help out was doomed to failure the moment Conan Doyle admitted that he no longer felt any kinship with the Catholic faith that had sustained so many previous generations of Doyles; and by spring, he was back in Aston, filling scripts for Doctor Hoare and submitting short stories to whichever magazine would accept them. Which, right now, was a depressingly small number.

Would that be Ms. Moriarty?

The (Lack) of Adventure of an Easily Distracted South Coast Medical Practitioner

Conan Doyle's next move was, at least from his mother's perspective, his most ill-advised yet. A friend and fellow doctor named George Turnavine Budd had recently opened a practice in Plymouth, a naval town perched on England's southwesternmost peninsula, which his letters insisted was so riotously successful practice that Conan Doyle simply *had* to come down and help him.

In fact, the practice turned out to be more chaotic than successful, although Budd put up such an ostentatious front that even the naturally suspicious Conan Doyle could not help but throw himself into the madness.

In modern terms, Budd operated what could almost be described as a cross between outpatient rehab and a full-blooded intervention. Patients were not treated for what ailed them, they were cajoled into giving up whatever bad habits caused them to ail in the first place.

One woman was forced to forego her daily intake of tea, in favor of cocoa—and Budd had her swear that she would keep to the regimen with one hand on one of his medical textbooks.

An old man was told to stop eating and drinking so much before he even got to detail his complaints, which were indeed the symptoms of his natural predisposition toward gluttony. Another was thrown down the stairs after he and Budd got into an argument about the true nature of the patient's condition.

Budd distributed drugs seemingly at random, partly because his practice charged not by the visit (which was free) but by the prescription, but also because he seemed genuinely to know what the patient's true ailment was and delivered a cure no matter how unlikely it may have seemed. Conan Doyle soon found himself in the bizarre situation of implicitly trusting Budd's instincts, at the same time as his faith in Budd himself began to ebb.

It transpired, with shadows of Conan Doyle's experiences at Feldkirch, that Budd and his wife were in the habit of reading Conan Doyle's mail before handing it over and had taken offense at some of the remarks Mary Doyle was making about them.

She did not trust the couple as far as she could spit. She saw Budd as a charlatan, a con man, a ne'er do well who would receive his comeuppance sooner rather than later. It was clear to the Budds that, for as long as this insufferable harpy had Conan Doyle's ear, they would never truly be able to trust him, so they set about distancing him instead.

They manufactured arguments that he could never win and complaints that he could never answer, until finally Conan Doyle had had enough. He resigned from the practice, only to spend the next three weeks running it singlehandedly while Budd recuperated from a sudden illness. (Budd would later be immortalized in the short story "Crabbe's Practice," an unstinting study of an unscrupulous medic who sets up shop in a provincial English town.)

Conan Doyle's next halt was Portsmouth, another naval town, but much larger than Plymouth, and its size was its premier attraction to him. Any night of the week saw the streets packed with sailors, with all the attendant drinking and fighting that image provokes. A well-placed doctor's surgery could not help but take advantage of such passing trade.

Conan Doyle wound up, however, in Southsea, a suburb of Portsmouth that was in fact doing its level best to distance itself from the rough and tumble of its neighbor by establishing itself as a seaside resort. There, Conan Doyle's patients were more likely to be ailing old ladies and gout-ridden retired colonels, but he rented premises at 1 Bush Villas, on a street called Elm Grove, a three-story house nestled between a hotel and a Baptist church.

He furnished and stocked the surgery; he ordered a brass name plate to adorn the outside wall; he advertised his services in the local newspaper. Then he waited.

His first visitor was a local curate, welcoming him to the neighborhood and inviting him to attend his church. The second was a man from the gas board, demanding arrears left unpaid by a previous tenant. The third was the neighborhood hypochondriac, come to check out the new man; the fourth was a woman who required a vaccination that cost Conan Doyle 2/6d to purchase, at which point he discovered she could afford to give him only 1/6d.

Facing ruin already, he had no choice but to contact his mother to ask her to lend him some money. She gladly handed it over, on condition that he would take in his nine-year-old brother Innes. Conan Doyle agreed, and while he probably spent less time seeing patients than he did at the pawnbroker's store, either pledging or redeeming sundry household items, the practice muddled by. Besides, the enforced idleness did have one redeeming quality. Again, it gave him time to write.

The Adventures of the Now Not-Quite-So-Struggling Author

He revisited Goresthorpe Grange, the haunted home of his first-ever piece of (unpublished) fiction, and was rewarded when this new tale was published in *London Society*.

Reflections of his time in the Arctic were expanded for "The Captain of the Polestar," a chilling (in both senses of the word) tale of love on the ice floes, published in *Temple Bar*.

"Life and Death in the Blood," for *Good Words* magazine, predicted the miniaturized human surgeons who are injected into an injured man's bloodstream in the 1966 movie *The Fantastic Voyage*; other Conan Doyle tales appeared as far afield as the *Boy's Own Paper*, a hearty digest of responsible fiction and fascinating facts aimed at the young Victorian gentleman; and *All the Year Round*, a journal founded by Charles Dickens in 1859 and still going strong a dozen years after his death in 1870.

Delving into what, a decade or so earlier, had become one of the most enduring maritime mysteries of them all, Conan Doyle even reinvented the strange case of the *Mary Celeste*, found drifting deserted off the coast of Portugal, and portrayed it as a tale of mutiny and murder.

"J Habakuk Jephson's Statement" was published in *Cornhill Magazine* and was rewarded with a payment of 29 guineas, which effectively paid his rent for a year. The *Illustrated London News* compared the tale to the best of Edgar Allen Poe, a viewpoint that thrilled Conan Doyle as much as the check. But it was the response of such dignitaries as the U.S. consul to Gibraltar (whose authorities oversaw the inquest into the original mystery) and the island's attorney general that most delighted him, as Conan Doyle found himself

Are you ready to enter *House of Fear*?   *Photofest*

embroiled in the first literary scandal of his career. The "just-the-facts" manner in which the tale was written convinced many readers that it was a true confession and unleashed a storm that did not hurt Conan Doyle's reputation as a writer, or his self-esteem, in the slightest.

Slowly, too, his practice began to turn around. Early in 1883, Conan Doyle was able to hire a housekeeper who, doubling as an appointments secretary, proved herself capable of increasing his workload even further, simply by convincing would-be patients that the doctor was in demand. There was, it seemed, nothing so effective at drumming up business as pretending you already had a waiting list of patients and scheduling appointments days into the future.

More traffic, Conan Doyle realized, could be encouraged by merely socializing. He joined the Portsmouth Literary and Scientific Society, presided over by a fellow (if far more accomplished) contributor to the *Boys' Own Paper*, Major

General Alfred W. Drayson. He became a member of the local Lawn Bowls club, and the friendly doctor who proved such a boon to the team soon numbered several of his fellow enthusiasts among his patients.

He reawakened his college years' love of cricket by joining (and eventually captaining) the Portsmouth Cricket Club, and, noting the growing popularity of soccer—Association Football as it was more properly known—in the area, he was among the local businessmen who in 1884 founded the town's first club, Portsmouth AFC (Association Football Club).

Not to be confused with the later (and still flourishing) Portsmouth FC, founded in 1898 by local brewery owner John Brickwood, Portsmouth AFC was an amateur side best remembered today for the secret identity of its first goalkeeper, a certain A. C. Smith. Conan Doyle, as his colleagues knew him.

From all accounts, he was a handy player to have around. According to the local paper, the *Portsmouth Evening News*, he ranked among "the safest Association backs" in the entire county of Hampshire; no mean feat at a time when nearby Southampton's local team, St Mary's Young Men's Association FC, was on the cusp of becoming the regional powerhouse of the next twenty years. Portsmouth AFC survived until 1896.

In the midst of so much activity, Conan Doyle continued writing. He completed his first novel, *The Narrative of John Smith*, only to be left shattered and reeling when he ignored the most essential law for any writer, of always keeping a copy to hand, and entrusted his manuscript to the mails. It was lost in the post en route to the very first publisher he mailed it to. It would be over a century before those four handwritten exercise books suddenly resurfaced in an auction at Christie's in 2004, and seven years after that before it finally appeared in print. True to Conan Doyle's own memories of the story, it was not worth the wait. "My grief at its loss," he once wrote, "would be nothing to my horror if it were suddenly to appear again."

Recovering from the mortification of losing his literary firstborn to the vagaries of the post office, Conan Doyle set to work on what we might term his second first novel, *The Firm of Girdlestone*, a semi-autobiographical journey from medical school to Africa. He also maintained a gradual but steady flow of correspondence to the leading medical journals of the day, *The Lancet* and *Medical Times*, where he campaigned for a better understanding of gout and for widespread vaccinations against smallpox and typhoid, before defiantly courting controversy when he advocated the reinstatement of the Contagious Diseases Act, whose recent (spring 1883) suspension was widely believed to have caused a major upsurge in cases of venereal disease (VD) around the port towns of Chatham, Plymouth, and of course Portsmouth.

The law, when it stood, permitted the authorities to undertake a compulsory and, by definition, humiliating examination of any woman suspected of suffering from VD. It had taken years of campaigning to have it struck down, but Conan Doyle was in no doubt as to whom the true beneficiaries of the enlightenment were—the germs that the "harlots and prostitutes" (his words) harbored. His own practice, like many others in the port towns, was already tired of treating the victims of this plague, not only the sailors whose first port of call upon reaching dry land tended to be a prostitute, but also anybody else with whom that man came in contact—his wife or girlfriend, his newborn child . . .

Conan Doyle's logic, of course, was impeccable. Holmesian, even. If a problem exists, seek out the facts and eradicate it at its source. But, like Holmes's logic, it also overlooked perhaps the most crucial factor of all: human nature. Many respectable women who were absolutely innocent of harlotry and prostitution had been rounded up for examination as potential carriers, and many, too, had complained about the nature and possibly even the intentions of the exam and the examiner. The law remained struck down.

Conan Doyle met his wife Louisa—Touie, to her friends—in March 1885. She was the elder sister of one of his patients, a young man named John Hawkins who was in the final stages of cerebral meningitis. Certainly he was beyond whatever care could be administered at the lodging house where he lived and past the attentions of any hospital, too. A compassionate Conan Doyle agreed to let the suffering man live with him for his last days on earth.

It was an inauspicious beginning for any romance, and Conan Doyle chivalrously waited until Hawkins's funeral was past before asking the grief-stricken Louisa if he might call upon her one day. Haste, however, does not seem to have been an issue. The couple became engaged in mid-May, less than two months after John Hawkins's death and around the same time as Conan Doyle received the news that his father had been formally certified a lunatic and committed to the Royal Lunatic Asylum in Montrose. He would never see release and died at Crichton Royal Institution in Dumfries on October 10, 1893.

In early August 1885, Conan Doyle and his fiancée made the long journey up to the Waller family estate at Masongill to be married at the local parish church of Thornton-in-Lonsdale. The ceremony on August 6 was small—Mary Doyle and Louisa's mother, Emily, were present, as were the ubiquitous Waller (who gave the bride away) and his mom, and just two of Conan Doyle's siblings, Innes and Connie. The couple honeymooned in Dublin (where, not at all coincidentally, Conan Doyle's college old boys' cricket team, the Stoneyhurst Wanderers, were on tour), then returned to Portsmouth.

It was marriage, Conan Doyle later mused, that convinced him to cast his entire being into his ambition of becoming a novelist. It quickened his brain, he said, and sharpened his imagination and his range of expression.

"I realized that I could go on [writing] short stories for ever and never make headway," he wrote. He threw himself into completing *The Firm of Girdlestone* and was already hard at work on a third novel when the first rejection slips began arriving on the doormat.

Later, he realized how much cause he had to thank those short-sighted publishers who dismissed his earliest efforts. For it was this third novel that would completely realign his life.

3

The Sometimes Shocking Case of the Sherlockian Precursors

In which an American author, a Scottish Surgeon, a French Thief-taker and a Veritable Shelf of Adventurous Fiction conspire to birth an Immortal Legend

Who was the original Sherlock Holmes? Who, of all the myriad names, faces, and reputations that Conan Doyle undoubtedly read about, researched, or simply remembered, was the prototype for the world's most legendary detective—and, of course, his faithful companion, John Watson?

Well, according to *The Snowmen*, the 2012 Christmas edition of the long-running science fiction show *Doctor Who*, it was, in the character's own words, "a lizard lady from the dawn of her time," and her wife.

Which is absolutely absurd, even if those lines were written by the same man, Steven Moffat, who co-created television reinvention *Sherlock*. *Doctor Who*'s Madame Vastra is green and reptilian, a survivor of a race that dwelled on Earth before humankind evolved, now established as a detective in late Victorian London; Jenny is her assistant and lesbian lover. But she also has a second assistant, a potato-shaped alien (a Sontaran) named Strax, and frankly it is all getting way too bizarre to even continue this sentence.

Let's forget I even mentioned it.

Who was the original Sherlock Holmes? Who, of all the myriad names, faces, and reputations that Conan Doyle undoubtedly read about, researched, or simply remembered, was the prototype for the world's most legendary detective?

Of them all, none made so great an impression upon him as Doctor Joseph Bell.

Thirty-nine years old when they met, tall and prepossessingly lean, possessed of sharp nose and sharper eyes, with the fingers of a musician and a chin that thrust determinedly out, "Joe" Bell, as he was commonly known, was one of the tutors at Edinburgh while Conan Doyle was a student. He was also, or would soon become, Queen Victoria's personal surgeon whenever she visited Scotland, a Justice of the Peace, and a great-grandson of Benjamin Bell, one of the pioneers of forensic surgery.

And, one day, he would be Sherlock Holmes.

Which is not to say he was a detective, although perhaps, in many ways, he was. Clinical, analytical, thoughtful, observant, he taught the young students in his charge that they should *never* jump to conclusions. That they should study the patient as intently as they studied the patient's symptoms. Too many doctors, then and now, all but removed the sufferer from the condition, overlooking the unique minutiae of a case in favor of diagnosing the larger picture. Contrary to the oft-quoted wisdom of Emil Mazey, just because something walks like a duck and talks like a duck, that doesn't mean it *is* a duck.

Lung cancer misdiagnosed as an eating disorder. Influenza mistaken for a minor cough. Shingles written off as a staph infection. A century and a half later, doctors are still overlooking the telltale specifics and sending patients on their way with an absolutely erroneous diagnosis; and that is with all the technological assistance that the modern medic can call upon. In 1875, a doctor had just one thing that he could truly rely upon, and that was vision—the ability to see, and the ability to understand what he was seeing.

Vision was Joe Bell's talent.

It was a process that Conan Doyle's former friend George Budd had both absorbed and practiced, albeit with considerably more haphazard and even careless results than Bell would have tolerated. Bell himself, on the other hand, was an expert, hammering again and again at the need to always pay attention, to look out for every detail, to regard nothing as inconsequential until immutable fact revealed it to be so. The general state of medical care today suggests that few of Bell's lessons ever became enshrined in the annals of the profession, except perhaps in reverse . . . it is the patient who needs to be observant and attentive, and the doctors who give their secrets away. But no student who passed through Bell's classes was likely to do so without taking some part of the master's methodology with him.

In those students' memories of Bell, we see many of the qualities with which Conan Doyle would imbue Sherlock Holmes.

There was the patient who visited the doctor to complain of an ailment but who patently proffered a false name. Bell studied the man for a moment, then wrote the correct name on the prescription. He'd spotted it, he explained to the incredulous patient, inscribed on the man's shirt band.

"In teaching the treatment of disease and accident," Bell wrote, "all careful teachers have first to show the student how to recognize accurately the case. The recognition depends in great measure on the accurate and rapid appreciation of small points in which the diseased differs from the healthy state. In fact, the student must be taught to observe. To interest him in this kind of work we teachers find it useful to show the student how much a trained use of the observation can discover in ordinary matters such as the previous history, nationality and occupation of a patient."

Thus Bell could detect a patient's recent travels from the nature of his illness. He could discern a man's upbringing from the way he dressed and conducted himself. A civilian would remove his hat upon entering the surgery. A military man would not even think of such a thing.

He could sniff the air and know to a reasonable degree of certainty the kind of environment in which a man lived or worked. He could glance at a visitor's hands and comprehend his profession, displaying his own fingers, ink and chemical stained as they were, as proof. Clearly, he would say, these are not the hands of a laborer or a craftsman. Nor do they belong to an office worker or a store owner.

Conan Doyle discussed Bell in an 1892 interview he gave with *The Bookman*. There he described Sherlock Holmes as "the literary embodiment, if I may so express it, of my memory of a professor of medicine at Edinburgh University, who would sit in the patients' waiting room with a face like a Red Indian and diagnose people, as they came in, before they even had opened their mouths. He would tell them their symptoms, he would give them details of their lives, and he would hardly ever make a mistake.

"'Gentlemen,' he would say to us students standing around, 'I am not quite sure whether this man is a cork-cutter or a slater. I observe a slight callus, or hardening, on one side of his forefinger, and a little thickening on the outside his thumb, and that is a sure sign he is either one or the other.' His great faculty of deduction was at times highly dramatic."

An undisguised Bell appeared again in the short story "The Recollections of Captain Wilkie," published in the magazine *Chambers's Journal* in 1895.

"I had the advantage of studying under a master . . . who used to electrify both his patients and his clinical classes by long shots, sometimes at the most unlikely of pursuits; and never very far from the mark.

"'Well, my man,' I have heard him say, 'I can see by your fingers that you play some musical instrument for your livelihood, but it is a rather curious one; something quite out of my line.' The man afterwards informed us that he earned a few coppers by blowing 'Rule Britannia' on a coffee-pot, the spout of which was pierced to form a rough flute."

Perhaps the most famous memory of Bell, however, was delivered in an essay titled "The Original of Sherlock Holmes," by Dr. Harold Emery Jones.

Producing a vial of liquid one day, Bell declared, "This, gentlemen contains a very potent drug. To the taste it is intensely bitter. It is most offensive to the sense of smell. But I want you to test it by smell and taste; and, as I don't ask anything of my students which I wouldn't be willing to do myself, I will taste it before passing it round."

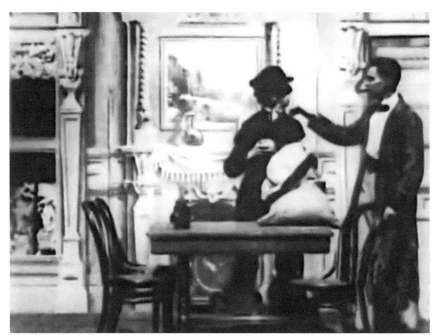

Still from the 1903 movie *Sherlock Holmes Baffled*   *Wikimedia*

With this, wrote Doctor Jones, "he dipped his finger in the liquid, and placed it in his mouth. The tumbler was passed round. With wry and sour faces the students followed the Professor's lead. One after another tasted the liquid; varied and amusing were the grimaces made. The tumbler, having gone the round, was returned to the Professor.

"'Gentlemen,' said he, with a laugh, 'I am deeply grieved to find that not one of you has developed this power of perception, which I so often speak about; for if you watched me closely, you would have found that, while I placed my forefinger in the medicine, it was the middle finger which found its way into my mouth.'"

Holmes could not have demanded a more subtle tutor.

L'étrange affaire du policier français

When and why Conan Doyle decided that his next novel would be a detective yarn is uncertain. Certainly his love of Edgar Allen Poe's contributions to what was at that time still a newborn niche would have played a major part in it. But so was his affection for the writings of Eugène François Vidocq, a real-life French adventurer whose multitudinous careers as smuggler, soldier, and circus performer were simply the preface to his crowning glory, the position of first-ever chief of the Brigade de la Sûreté, or the Security Brigade, an experimental plain-clothes police unit whose successes in fighting crime in Paris saw the practice adopted nationwide.

In both instances, the real-life Vidocq and Poe's fictional Chevalier C. Auguste Dupin, detection was a matter of cunning, stealth, and keeping open a very sharp eye. Even the most fastidiously careful criminal makes mistakes, they believed, and the key to solving the crime was to find those errors. Remember, this was an age before fingerprinting, blood samples, hair analysis; before all of the modern shortcuts that have supposedly lightened the detective's load; an age when a burglar could leave the scene of the crime literally littered with dabs and DNA and nobody would have been any the wiser.

Nobody, that is, aside from the keen-eyed detective who might notice that the footprints left in the muddy soil were clearly those of a well-built man with one lame leg; that the scratches on the window ledge showed the burglar was left-handed; that a single hair caught on a piece of broken glass belonged to a blond; and so on and so forth.

Keen-eyed and patient, Vidocq made it his business to fraternize with the very people he was supposed to be arresting, with his own criminal past a faultless character witness. Nobody he spoke with doubted that here was a man who really had escaped the prisons in Douai and Toulon, and in listening to his tales, they felt compelled to tell their own.

"In so populous a capital as that of Paris," Vidocq wrote, "there are usually a vast many places of bad resort, at which assembled persons of broken fortune and ruined fame; in order to judge of them under my own eye, I frequented every house and street of ill fame, sometimes under one disguise and sometimes under another . . . till the rogues and thieves whom I daily met there firmly believed me to be one of themselves . . . . Not only had I acquired their fullest confidence, but their strongest regard [as well]."

That, too, was a lesson that Holmes would learn.

The birth of the detective novel was slow. Through the nineteenth century, it struggled into life, but even the best-wrought investigative story would be but a subplot within another. In his novel *Bleak House* in 1852, Charles Dickens introduced the world to Inspector Bucket. The epitome of the methodical, slow-but-sure detective, Bucket was in no way capable of the imaginative leaps that Dupin and Vidocq (and another grand French detective, Emile Gaboriau's Inspector LeCoq) took for granted. But he persevered and got there in the end.

Then there was Wilkie Collins, a close friend and protégé of Dickens, who delivered in 1868 *The Moonstone*, a gripping tale that T. S. Eliot later insisted was "the first, the longest and the best of English detective novels." And now came the deluge, a veritable flood of further such writings churned out by a small industry's worth of blood-and-thunder hacks. By the time Conan Doyle set himself to writing a detective tale of his own, he needed less to match himself to the masters than to raise himself above the inky braying of the common herd.

Yet Conan Doyle's fascination lay not only in his sympathy with the sleuth and his fascination with methodology. The criminal mind, too, intrigued him, and as germane to the creation of Sherlock Holmes as Poe, Vidocq, and Collins might have been, Conan Doyle also looked back to another stream of literature that had thrilled him as a youth and to which he might have boasted some familial connection.

Grandfather John Doyle lived in what was is now Sussex Gardens, close by London's Hyde Park but which was then known as Cambridge Terrace. There, at number 17, John, his wife Marianne, and their seven children regularly entertained the likes of Sir Walter Scott, Benjamin Disraeli, Dante Gabriel Rossetti, William Harrison Ainsworth, Charles Dickens, and William Makepeace Thackeray, the cream of London literati.

It was a fascinating environment in which a young mind could develop, and for all his later battles with alcohol and anger, Charles Doyle—Arthur Conan Doyle's father—at least chose wisely when he wed Mary Doyle, a woman whose own love of literature was as pronounced as that which had once been expounded around the Cambridge Terrace dining table. Family tradition insists that Thackeray visited the Edinburgh Doyles at least once, and bounced the baby Arthur on his knee; hardly surprising, then, that the growing child's reading inevitably leaned toward the authors whom his parents described as the friends of the family.

Most of these writers, to the absolute delight of any growing lad, had specialized in some truly gripping tales of blood and guts and mayhem. Many centered around a single location whose name remains sacrosanct in the annals of criminal detention. Rykers, Dartmoor, Devil's Island, Alcatraz, all could claim to be the world's most notorious prison. But none, not even then, cast such a shadow across the criminal underworld as did the granddaddy of them all.

Newgate Prison.

The Chilling Tale of the Ultimate Gaolhouse

Sited at the west end of Newgate Street, in the area now bounded by Holborn and Clerkenwell, the precise year in which the gates of Newgate Prison yawned wide to swallow their first inmates has been lost to history. It was certainly in use by 1190, however, and it benefited considerably from funds left by Sir Richard ("Dick") Whittington, thrice Lord Mayor of London.

Most walled cities of the period used gates as prisons—Ludgate and Cripplegate in London served a similar function; Newgate, or Chamberlain's Gate as it was originally known, however, swiftly grew in notoriety as the authorities deemed it suitable for housing only the worst possible criminals, those whose lives were valued so little, or whose crimes were so great, that confinement within that dank, stagnant, overcrowded jail, rife with corruption and disease, was considered almost as severe a penalty as the execution that awaited them at the end of their stay. Indeed, two lord mayors of London died of jail fever contracted during sessions at the neighboring Old Bailey courthouse!

Up alongside to Bethlehem Royal Hospital—the "Bedlam" of popular imagery—and more so than any other prison operating in the country at that, and perhaps any other, time, Newgate looms larger in England's history than any other single building could.

With the exceptions of royalty and aristocracy, there is barely a well-known name in the annals of London crime who was not at one time an inmate of Newgate. And barely a nineteenth-century novelist who, having inserted into his cast of characters one that was destined for jail, would not then invoke the name of Newgate at some point, and the sympathetic reader would know where the felon was destined from there. The long drop.

The speed with which the Great Plague decimated Newgate's inmates in 1665, and the near riot that ensued as interested parties attempted to save its inmates from the Great Fire a year later, served as a centerpiece of Harrison Ainsworth's *The Old St Paul's*. A subsequent burning of the prison, during the Gordon Riots of 1780, featured in Charles Dickens's *Barnaby Rudge*. Newgate was newsworthy, even when it was history.

No accurate record of the original prison's appearance, prior to the Great Fire, survives. A second construction, completed in 1672 on a similar plan to its predecessor, likewise perished in flames during the aforementioned Gordon Riot. The edifice most familiar to readers and criminologists alike, then, was that built by George Dance in the late

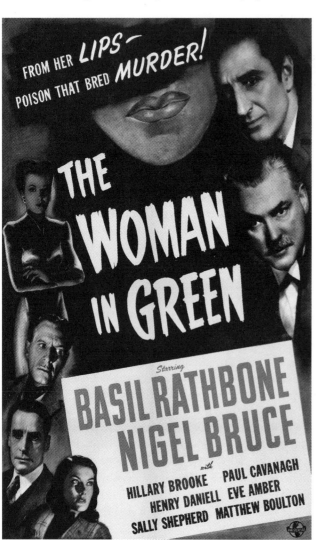

Can even Holmes unravel this latest mystery?

eighteenth century, a dignified, severe building ornamented with fetter-garlands in place of the emblematic figures of Liberty, Peace, Security, and Plenty that once adorned the west side, Justice, Prudence, and Fortitude the east.

Expansions to the prison, necessitated by its constantly increasing population, were carried out below the pavement and, above ground, in the form of small yards and cells that spread out haphazardly in all directions.

Dominating the prison, the tall tower of St. Sepulchre's Church—a survivor of the Great Fire, the flames having burned themselves out at the very walls of the church—jabbed towards the heavens.

Here was housed the curfew bell, rung to mark the beginning and end of each workday, and the more ominous Great Bell, whose mournful tolling marked the departure of a condemned man for the gallows and called for the immense crowds that accompanied these parades—and who hung from every available pillar and post in the hope of getting an unobstructed view of the proceedings—to gather, either along the route to Tyburn (opposite the modern Marble Arch) or, following the authorities' decision in 1783 to stage all subsequent executions outside Newgate itself, in the streets and buildings around the prison.

Sherlock Holmes had no qualms whatsoever about the use of the death penalty as the ultimate deterrent. True, the majority of his most murderous felons fell prey to their own evil machinations (the snake-wrangling stepfather in "The Speckled Band" is a prime example). But if the law itself did catch up with a felon and he was carted off to be judged and then dangled, neither Holmes nor Watson would give the matter a second thought.

Holmes might even have attended the execution—as did Watson, in his capacity as presiding physician—when Lord Blackwood was hanged at the outset of Guy Ritchie's first *Sherlock Holmes* movie. One assumes, however, that even in the capacity of a mere bystander, both men would have behaved with considerably more decorum than many of the onlookers drawn to such events.

No expense was considered too great if it led to a ringside seat at an execution, and spectators would often begin arriving many hours—if not days—in advance, to be sure of an advantageous view. Given the chaos that inevitably ensued, it is miraculous that only once, during a hanging in 1806, did the proceedings end in tragedy, when twenty-eight people were crushed to death in the crowd.

William Thackeray, in his early capacity as a newsman, reported in *Fraser's Magazine* on one hanging, the execution of Courvoisier, a Swiss-born valet who murdered his master and then, when asked why, claimed he was given the idea by a book he read, Ainsworth's *Jack Sheppard*. Thackeray's description of the scene might be applied with equal validity to any hanging of the period:

"As we enter Holborn the town grows more animated . . . it is twenty minutes past four [in the morning] as we pass St Sepulchre's . . . by this time many hundreds of people are in the street and many more are coming up Snow Hill."

There they would wait, playing cards, talking, joking, laughing, until the condemned man was led for the last time out into the daylight, often to add to the crowd's entertainment with jests and speeches.

Thackeray again, this time referring to the gallows. "There it stands, black and ready, jutting out from a little door in the prison. As you see it, you feel a kind of dumb electric shock, which causes one to start a little, and give a sort of gasp of breath."

As the hour approached, "a great murmur arose, more awful, bizarre, and indescribable than any sound [I had ever heard]."

The condemned man appeared. "He turned his head here and there, and looked about him for an instant with a wild, imploring look. His mouth was contracted into a sort of pitiful smile." The executioner pulled the death cap over the convicted man's head, he was given a few moments to beg Heaven's forgiveness, and then the bolt was drawn. And when the deed was done, a mighty roar went up from the crowd. The beast was dead.

The jail itself also attracted its visitors, come to marvel at the myriad species of wretchedness and degradation within those walls. (Bedlam, too, was a noted tourist attraction at this time.) The sightseers walked from cell to cell, block to block, perhaps with a perfumed handkerchief held delicately to their noses, and armed with a stick to beat off—or simply to tease—the felons they encountered.

The conditions within Newgate, even at this late a date, were appalling. Adults and children of both sexes alike were incarcerated, the latter often for crimes almost trivial in their nature.

An 1832 article in *Fraser's Magazine*, titled "A Schoolmaster's Experience in Newgate," spoke of children imprisoned for "stealing a comb almost valueless, for a child's sixpenny storybook, for a man's stock and . . . for pawning his mother's shawl."

Inmates, whether awaiting trial or already proven guilty, were treated with the same disdain, cut off from the outside world by the exclusion of all newspapers, bound to remain silent at all times (a ruling that could never be enforced!), poorly fed apart from when a visitor or warder might smuggle in a loaf or two to give away or sell, abused by guards and fellow prisoners alike, and forced to endure the most revolting squalor.

Sewage flowed down open drains that ran through the cells and corridors, clothes and bedding were ragged and flea-infested, and the only inhabitants not bound by the establishment's draconian regime were the rats that existed side by side with the prisoners.

Waste, human and otherwise, was piled up in every corner, and every conceivable vice was practiced and even condoned by authorities who cared more for their own peace and quiet than for the welfare of their charges. Illness and injury were allowed to run their course, whether their destination be death or disfigurement. The cold and the stench were unbearable. Many of these problems, addressed in 1835 by the Select Committee on Gaols and Houses of Correction, remained unchecked for almost another half century, until finally in

1881 the reform lobby succeeded in having all prisoners, bar those awaiting trial at the Central Criminal Court (the Old Bailey), transferred to other, "modern" establishments.

It didn't help. Writer W. T. Stead (*My First Imprisonment, London 1886*) was one of the men incarcerated here during this period. "There is the chill and silence of the grave. Overhead the tiers of cells, with their iron balustrades and iron stairs, rose story after story. It was as if you were walking at the bottom of the hold of some great petrified ship, looking up at the deserted decks."

Finally, in 1902–3, Newgate was demolished.

Sated as we are by so many subsequent prison memoirs, and by the manifold changes in the prison system in the years since then, it is difficult for the modern reader to understand the precise hold Newgate exerted over the British public of the eighteenth and nineteenth centuries. The aforementioned modern preoccupation with crime and violent death goes only part of the way toward explaining it.

The visibility of Newgate's inmates, and of their final moments on earth—the mock funeral procession which led them to the last drop, the priest's final benediction and the cowled figure of "Jack Ketch" the executioner, the dance of death as the trapdoor yawned beneath them, and the sudden jerk as their neck snapped add something more to the equation. But still, Newgate exercised a fascination that we might dissect endlessly yet never arrive at a more than a mere glimmering of the truth.

The Strangely Readable Case of the Newgate Calendar

Enter any Englishman's home in the years on either side of the dawn of the nineteenth century and there were three books you would almost inevitably find.

The first was the Bible, already an ancient, tattered tome, usually inscribed with the rudiments of the family tree by each of its successive, related owners. The second was a thumbed copy of Bunyan's *Pilgrim's Progress*. And the third was the *Newgate Calendar*. Or, to give it its full title, *The Newgate Calendar, Or The Malefactors' Bloody Register*.

Originally published in 1773, this five-volume work approached encyclopedic proportions in its cataloguing of eighteenth-century crime. Nightmarishly engraved and lurid with detail, it sold prodigiously, and it haunted the land.

The men and women who peopled the calendar were as real to their readers as were their own friends and family. They were the bogeymen with whom parents would frighten their children, the ghosts from whom the lonely servant would cower when the firelight flung its mysterious shadows on the parlor walls, the formless fiends who stalked the country graveyard in the dead of night.

What became the *Newgate Calendar* started life merely as a succession of bulletins detailing the latest executions carried out by the prison. As time passed, however, and the notion arose that there was a very powerful morality to be drawn from these tales of crime distinctly *not* paying, the bulletins were bound into book form and began to elaborate on the crimes that preceded the punishment.

Here we read of "William Cady . . . who shot a Woman before the Eyes of her Husband for the Wedding-Ring she had swallowed." Of Moses Drayne, "ostler, hanged at Brentwood . . . for the Murder (by a Chelmsford Innkeeper and his family some Years before) of . . . a guest." Of Thomas Wilmot, "a Notorious Highwayman who hated and maltreated Women."

Writer George Romilly, who later distinguished himself in the fight for criminal reform, recalled in his memoirs (1840) how the *Calendar* "cost me many sleepless nights. My dreams . . . were disturbed by the hideous images which haunted my imagination by day." Almost sixty years later, in "The Adventure of the Three Garribeds," Sherlock Holmes professes to carry "a portable *Newgate Calendar*" in his head, at the same time as he sympathizes with Watson that "it is not part of your profession" for him to do likewise.

The calendar, and such of its successors as *The Annals of Newgate*, published in 1776 by John Villette, the *Newgate Ordinary*, and *The New Newgate Calendar*, published in 1826 by Andrew Knapp and William Baldwin, prided itself upon its accuracy.

It provided a firm base from which others' flights of fancy could take wing and soar through every walk of life. Like the prison itself, however, its effect upon literature was surely its most lasting.

The late 1820s and early 1830s saw the sudden explosion of popularity in England of a strain of literature that critics, for the most part disdainful, were swift to describe as "Newgate."

With roots that stretched back a century (John Gay's *The Beggar's Opera* was the theatrical sensation of the 1720s), not to mention that which still propagate almost two hundred years on, these books scarcely proffered a new development. Crime and the criminal had exerted a fascination upon all aspects of the arts since time immemorial, and the Newgate novels simply acknowledged that, by amplifying the deeds of sundry criminals to (anti-) heroic proportions. They took from the pages of history, and the calendar itself, a personage of the lowest, basest character, a jailbird, a convicted felon, a hanged man, and portrayed his adventures in a wholly new light, to arouse sympathy, interest, and admiration for him.

Without exception, the Newgate novels were conceived as exercises in sensationalism. They echoed the concerns and interests of the working classes as evinced by the massive popularity of published copies of famous confessions and testimonials, hawked on the streets for a penny a time by enterprising local printers. That they rose above that level was, in many ways, coincidental. The actual authors—Charles Whitehead, William Harrison Ainsworth, Edward Bulwer, and, to a lesser degree, Charles Dickens and William Thackeray—had greater pretensions toward literary credibility, it is true, and several went on to realize them. At the time, however, the merits of their work were very secondary to their themes, the noncriminal subplots irrelevant.

Jeremy Brett and Edward Hardwicke as Holmes and Watson, 1984   *Photofest*

It was a narrow tightrope that they trod. The existence of the criminal, either as an individual (the highwayman Dick Turpin, the murderer Eugene Aram, the housebreaker Jack Sheppard) or a stereotype (Dickens's Artful Dodger and Bill Sykes), was essential. The crime, in the main, needed to be an end in itself, not a means to an end.

Robin Hood, stealing from the rich and giving to the poor, would have been an unsuitable candidate for a Newgate novel. Roxanna, forced into prostitution by circumstance, ditto. Maybe the hero's admirable qualities were best exemplified by the enactment of some heroic feat—Jack Sheppard twice escaping from Newgate, Dick Turpin's midnight ride to York, Eugene Aram's scholarly accomplishments, and so forth. But the Newgate novel demanded no lesson or moral, no great satire, no mighty revelations or profound philosophies. The be-all and end-all of the Newgate novel was the crime and the criminal. All else was superfluous.

The fascination of Newgate, or rather, of its inmates, to these authors is self-evident. Crime sells. One needs only inspect the tabloid and online media of today to realize it still sells today. But more than that, the writers of the time were themselves performing against a backdrop of drama and intrigue no less captivating than any web woven by the criminals whose lives and escapades they now sought to put down in print.

The British Isles were undergoing their final, violent transition from the feudal system of government that had served since the middle ages and before, to the democratic basis that the so-called Three Revolutions (French, American, and Industrial) had inspired the common man to demand.

Reform and revolution were on every tongue, and from nowhere could the ideal scenario, that of man liberated from the conventions or dictates of society, be better drawn than the annals of criminal lore. And what better repository of criminal lore was there than Newgate Prison?

Not every novel that takes for its basic premise either the exploits or the conditions of the common criminal can be referred to as a Newgate novel. The story of criminal literature, be it Conan Doyle or Ellery Queen, Agatha Christie or Jessica Fletcher, is by definition a study unto itself.

Neither can it be stated that the political turmoil of the age was manifest only in the works of the Newgate novelists. Shelley's *Prometheus Unbound* was published very shortly after the Peterloo Massacre; Wordsworth, Keats, Byron, and Coleridge, the direct literary descendants of the first signs of political discontent, all wrote their greatest pieces during, or within very few years of, the Napoleonic Wars and the ensuing Tory reaction to the social problems that it bred.

The discarding of classical traditions and the diction that they represented spilled over, too, into the writings of Sir Walter Scott. His Waverley novels commenced in 1816, the year after the Napoleonic War ended, and—until Scott himself had exhausted the various permutations of the theme a little more than midway through the series—proceeded to revolutionize the popular conception of the historical novel.

Prior to Scott, the historical novel was essentially a study in the manners and rituals of the aristocracy, a blending of royal pomp and feudal grandeur. The working classes, beyond providing a witch, a rustic, or a bandit to the speaking cast, were seldom portrayed in any form greater than a homogenous mass of humble servitude or turbulent mischief.

Scott, in selecting for his heroes and heroines characters from history's humbler streams, and infusing them with characteristics far more exemplary than the stereotypical faults and virtues beloved by authors of previous eras, not only swept away the pompous mannerisms which had hitherto characterized the genre, but also indicated the only direction in which the novel, if it was ever to truly reflect the changing society around it, could go.

The ever-expanding consciousness of the lower orders required heroes in every field, and with general standards of literacy increasing at no less a rate, the novel lay very high on the agenda. It is no coincidence that the work of the aforementioned poets, like that of John Gay before them, and Scott contemporaneously, addressed the common man in language he could understand—a cause of some friction among their peers, it is true, but a friction that by its very existence for almost the first time allied the republic of letters with the world of the working man.

The Newgate school, then, was nothing if not a child of its generation. While Bulwer's Paul Clifford and Eugene Aram, treating of a highwayman in the first instance, a killer in the second, were both conceived and written several years before the Parliamentary revolution of the 1830s, the first stirrings of which (the Catholic Emancipation Act of 1829, the Parliamentary Reform Act of 1832, and the Poor Law Reform of 1834) were already plain, the speed with which the staff of *Fraser's Magazine*, to name but the most vociferous of Bulwer's critics, were to condemn the author's so-called liberal morals is equally indicative of the state of ferment into which England was plunging.

No matter how powerful the rising generation might be, the literary world as a whole remained closeted, traditionalist, "stuffy." Ideas and ideals put across by Bulwer, amplifying those of Scott and Shelley to a deafening pitch, were rejected out of hand by his peers; they reflected the thoughts of the reform lobby, not of the establishment, and the likes of Fraser's were nothing if not establishment.

The nature of the Newgate school, then, was seen as one of rebellion, and at its best it could be construed as a blow against the established (mal)practices within the British judicial system. At its worst, however, and in the light by which it was viewed by its detractors, it was little more than a blood-and-thunder recounting of dastardly deeds of years gone by, spiced liberally with sympathy for the devil and an inevitable dance from Tyburn Tree somewhere toward the conclusion of the final act.

More than that, though, it was governed by parameters at least as strict as those that surround the spy story, the love story, the detective story of today.

Few people truly understood those parameters; fewer still chose to abide by them. The works of George Borrow, Thomas Burke, Catherine Crowe, Thomas Gaspey, William Godwin, Thomas Holcroft, Theodore Hook, T. H. Lister, Mary Sherwood, T. S. Surr, and Frances Trollope, vital to the development of crime as a theme in popular Victorian—and later—literature, owe little to Newgate beyond, perhaps, the provisions it made for the furtherance of such a theme after it itself had been run out of town.

The heroes of their novels, for the most part, were the men who fought against crime, not the criminals themselves. Or they were purely imaginary criminals, drawn from life, perhaps, but nevertheless possessing no more tangible a hold over the public's imagination than could be derived from the pages of the novel.

The Newgate novelists drew their heroes straight from the pages of history. Paul Clifford and Dick Turpin, whose respective adventures fired Bulwer and Ainsworth's imaginations, did exist, the former in theory, if not in actual fact.

So did Jack Sheppard, the housebreaker; Eugene Aram, the murderous scholar; and Richard Savage, the killer poet. And under another name, so did Fagin, the irascible old man who unsuccessfully engineers Oliver Twist's downfall in the greatest of Dickens's earliest novels. They existed and, in so doing, had already become the stuff of legend.

The authors who took those lives and wove them into fiction were embellishing those legends, furnishing them with new attractions. For the first time in over one hundred years, since the days of *The Beggar's Opera*, the public—particularly, it was said, the "lower orders"—was offered literary characters drawn from among their own number, role models who came from dust, were hastened back to dust, but who spent the period intervening living life as they wanted to, bucking the system, thumbing a nose at society, and living free of each and every constraint that governed their own lives.

Imaginary villains could have given a similar impression, but how much more exciting it was to know that these men really had lived and really had done so much of what they were credited with. At a time when men were fighting, sometimes dying, to break out of society's bondage for the common good, few readers caught up in these monthly adventures appreciated that the men of whom they read, who fought those same bonds just as valiantly, did so out of selfish gain. It was enough that they fought. And not even the disdain of those people who had sighted the contradiction could sway them from their judgment.

Conan Doyle would not have been aware, at least at an early age, of the political and social backdrop of the stories he devoured. To his young eyes, they were exciting adventures, ripping yarns, thrilling rides, violent excursions packed with all the ingredients that a young man could desire. Daring, courage, fisticuffs, brilliance. And just a soupçon of the supernatural to twist one's dreams as thrillingly as the stories themselves.

"There was triumph in [Turpin's] eye," Ainsworth wrote as he concluded one especially gripping chapter of his breakthrough novel *Rookwood*. "But the triumph was checked as his glance fell upon a gibbet near him to the right . . .

> [He] approached the spot where it stood. Two scarecrow objects, covered with rags and rusty links of chain, depended from the tree. A night crow [screamed] around the carcasses. Nothing but the living highwaymen and his skeleton brethren were visible upon the lonely spot. Around him was the lonesome waste of the hill, o'erlooking the moonlit valley; beneath his feet a patch of bare and lightning-blasted sod; above, the wan declining moon and skies, flaked with ghostly clouds; before him the bleached bodies of the murderers.
>
> 'Will this be my lot, I marvel', said Dick looking upwards with an involuntary shudder.
>
> 'Ay, marry it will,' rejoined a crouching figure . . .

4

The Adventure, Although It Was Not Titled Thus, of the Study in Scarlet

In which we Investigate the Holmesian Home, are Introduced to its Residents, and Wonder why we have Suddenly been Banished to Utah

For any visitor to London keen to seek out the world of Sherlock Holmes, there is but one place to start: in the shadow of Sherlock himself. The gaunt nine-foot statue was erected on the corner of Baker Street and Marylebone Road in 1999, and cynically we could muse that it is but another by-product of the modern insistence upon raising as many high-profile sculptures as possible in an attempt to take people's minds off the fact that real historical artifacts are being allowed to decay or be swept away everywhere else.

In truth, this particular representation is not a bad example of the modern sculptor's art. At least its subject is recognizable, as opposed to the chicken-liver constructions that lurk outside some of the country's other most notable haunts and venues. The work of John Doubleday (who also created a Holmesian monument for the people of Meiringen, Switzerland, close by the Reichenbach Falls), its commissioning was the culmination of a seventy-year campaign for Holmes to be commemorated in London; author G. K. Chesterton first floated the notion in 1927, and it had sailed in and out of the public eye ever since.

In 1996, however, the Sherlock Holmes Society of London redoubled its efforts and, having obtained funding from the Abbey National building society (whose own headquarters occupied the site where Holmes's home would have stood), the work proceeded.

The statue was not to be realized without opposition, most significantly from those people who pointed out that placing a statue of Holmes on Marylebone

John Doubleday's Holmesian monument in Meiringen, Switzerland   *Michael Yew/Wikimedia*

Road was akin to marking the Boston Tea Party with a commemorative plaque out on Route 128.

Baker Street itself, however, can be considered too narrow and congested to have hosted what all concerned seemed convinced would become a modern magnet for tourists, a meeting place for tour groups, and a prominent landmark for visitors of all persuasions. And so it has proven. Why, that's why we are standing there now. Because Baker Street itself is just a few short steps away.

The Strange Case of the Address That Isn't There

In the realm of fiction, perhaps the greatest achievement that any writer can hope to accomplish is for his character to step outside of the story and to become a living being.

It is one that precious few have truly achieved. Ainsworth accomplished it with Dick Turpin, the highwayman hero of *Rookwood* and, subsequently, a small industry's worth of books, movies and tourist attractions; and Daniel Defoe did it with Robinson Crusoe, in a novel whose original title, *The Life and Strange Surprizing Adventures of Robinson Crusoe, of York, Mariner: Who lived Eight and Twenty Years, all alone in an un-inhabited Island on the Coast of America, near the Mouth of the Great River of Oroonoque; Having been cast on Shore by Shipwreck, wherein all the Men perished but himself. With An Account how he was at last as strangely deliver'd by Pirates,* would surely discourage all but the most patient of modern readers.

Likewise, Ian Fleming's James Bond is generally granted sufficient import to stand as a cipher for any kind of British secret service activities, as a raft of "real-life Bond"–type headlines will testify. In each of these instances, however, there was a living archetype (or, perhaps, stereotype) upon whom the story was based, whose own scant adventures would be clothed and fleshed by the authors' embellishments and inventions.

In a fourth example, Bram Stoker's Dracula, a reality has been created upon the bones of countless legends and superstitions; in a fifth, Charles Dickens's Fagin, an archetype was simply transposed into shorthand.

Rarer, far rarer, is the creation who is birthed with no recognizable flesh-and-blood antecedent whatsoever, who sprang fully formed and functioning from the imagination of one man to grasp that of so many millions more. To a point where today, more than a century and a quarter later, his life and times are more easily recited than those of any living contemporary he might have had. Whose quotations and observations are as widely repeated as any TV comedian's catchphrase, and whose home is better known, and certainly attracts more visitors, than any that his creator resided in.

This particular point was thrust home in early 2013 with a series of news reports surrounding the fate of the Undershaw Hotel in Hindhead, Surrey. A sprawling three-story red brick house of late Victorian conceit, it was built for Arthur Conan Doyle himself in 1897 (it became a hotel in the 1920s), and it was here that he wrote both *The Hound of the Baskervilles* and the stories contained in *The Return of Sherlock Holmes*.

One of the first properties in the vicinity to be lit by electricity, which was manufactured using the estate's own generator, its eleven bedrooms catered for all the guests that its owners could dream of, and its dining room could seat thirty bodies. The billiard room was lined with illustrations of Holmes, and just across from the house's nearest neighbor, the Royal Huts Hotel, was the soccer pitch upon which Undershaw Football Club played their games. The football club that Conan Doyle founded.

Such a grand heritage, however, could not stop the building from being abandoned in 2005, nor from falling into disrepair and decay in the years since then. At the time of writing, its fate remains undecided. It might be returned to life as a hotel; it might simply be demolished and replaced by something shiny and modern. Either way, its legendary status in the world of Conan Doyle is no guarantee of its survival.

Not when there's a statue to go visit . . . .

Undershaw is beautiful, melancholy, and off the beaten track; 221b Baker Street, on the other hand, is sturdy, legendary, and redolent with atmosphere and has been attracting thousands of visitors every year for more than a century. Which is a remarkable achievement for an address that does not exist. That has never existed. Rather, the crowds troop up the road looking for where it might be, pausing when the guide book tells them they have arrived at the right spot, and then going home happy with their souvenirs and photographs, because the street vendors and gift shops make a dizzying trade, as well.

For 221b is where Sherlock Holmes lived and worked, in an outwardly unprepossessing upstairs apartment in a similarly unremarkable building on an equally undistinguished street that links two of London's busiest thoroughfares, the shopper's paradise of Oxford Street and the more utilitarian Marylebone Road.

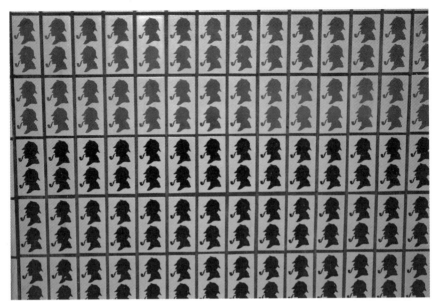

Going underground—a wall of Sherlocks at Baker Street tube. © *Steve and Betsy Mortensen*

Madame Tussaud's and the London Planetarium wait here; so does Baker Street tube station, a key point on the oldest underground railroad in the world. Regents Park, home to the London Zoo, lies to the north; once-plush Mayfair, the costliest property on the London Monopoly board, sits to the south. Named (according to some sources) for the architect who planned it in the eighteenth century, Baker Street itself was a reasonably well-to-do residential neighborhood, and it retained that cachet even after it was subsumed by commercial interests.

The Beatles' Apple Boutique stood on Baker Street during 1967–68; pop singer Dusty Springfield once lived there, and so did the nineteenth-century prime minister William Pitt the Younger. During World War II the Special Operations Executive, heading up Britain's wartime espionage activities, were based there and nicknamed themselves the Baker Street Irregulars, a name lifted wholesale from the pages of Sherlock Holmes.

Arthur Conan Doyle, on the other hand, never lived there. Nor in any of the myriad other London locations with which the astute reader might associate Holmes. No, not even Newgate.

The Protracted Adventure of the First Successful Story

The violence that characterized the Newgate theme of novel writing was far from Conan Doyle's mind as he schemed *A Study in Scarlet*, the novel that would introduce Sherlock Holmes to the world.

At the same time, however, it irrevocably colors the tale. In the years to come, *A Study In Scarlet* would be remembered more for the momentous first meeting of Sherlock Holmes and Doctor John Watson; for their move into the apartment at 221b Baker Street; for the unlikely friendship that swiftly developed between these two unlikely men—one a military veteran, down-to-earth and urbane; the other an arrogant, calculating narcissist with an infuriating habit of guessing at the most personal details of another person's life. The fact that his guesses were usually correct, and were not, therefore, guesses at all, did not pardon his often unforgivable rudeness.

All of these things were a part of the story. But they were simply background coloration, flesh on the characters whose adventure the first-time reader will be following. What did it matter where they lived? Who gave a hoot whether Watson had served in Afghanistan? Such trifles would become vitally important to the story once Conan Doyle began writing *further* stories—and perhaps suggest that he had already at least considered a world in which Holmes and Watson might become recurrent characters in future tales. For now, however, yes; it was just background material, The real meat was the murder.

The story, like almost all of those that will follow, is narrated by Watson.

A visitor arrives at 221b, and we learn that Holmes is already a detective of some renown, schooled in arts that are far beyond any that a conventional policeman, or even an entire police force, was capable of turning its hand to. The sciences of observation, deduction, a forensic analysis of the facts, and so forth.

A body has been discovered in a derelict house in the south London suburb of Brixton. On the wall, in blood, is daubed the word RACHE—German for "revenge." Already, the police are on the scene, Inspectors Gregson and Lestrade, and again, the modern reader feels that thrill of recognition. Two more old friends.

At the time, however, they were just a pair of plods from whose humiliation Holmes seemingly extracted as much pleasure as he would from solving the case. Later, we learn of the Baker Street Irregulars, the gang of urchins and youths whom Holmes has recruited to assist him in his inquiries. Again, today we know them well and warm to their introduction. In 1885, they simply supplied a little more background *bumph*.

Holmes sets to work, and there is a point where it feels as though *A Study in Scarlet* is doomed to become simply a litany of brilliant deductions from Holmes, and astonished responses from Watson and whoever else might be around when the great detective speaks. Parts of this story really are dull, and while the tediousness will be remedied by the discovery of a second body, a close friend of the original victim's, ultimately all that does is set the stage for another round of deductions.

Placing the book to one side for a moment, the reader remembers the old adage that a fictional detective is only as good as the clues he is given, and that the mark of a great detective storyteller is the ability to hide those clues in plain sight.

Here, Conan Doyle falls down completely. The Holmes of *A Study in Scarlet* may be portrayed as a man who has already launched himself into his career as a "consulting detective," but the author of his adventure is clearly a beginner. Too many deductions are drawn from observations to which the reader has not been privy; too many revelations seem to fall out of the blue. A good detective story should keep the reader guessing until the end. But it should also allow the reader the opportunity to solve the puzzle before the sleuth. Which is not an easy task if the best of the clues are known only to the author.

The first we learn of the murderer, for example, is when Holmes arrests him. And the second half of the story, in which the background to the two murders is expounded, detracts even more from Holmes.

Set forty years earlier, in what was then the Utah Territory of the infant United States, the tale essentially devolves into a fictional feud fought out against the real-life development of the Mormon church. It is a story from which Holmes and Watson are singularly absent; a tale that might as easily have been told in isolation; an outline, perhaps, for one of author G. A. Henty's stirring sagas of historic adventure in exotic climes. It certainly bears little resemblance to the shape and nature of any subsequent Sherlock Holmes adventure, although that again is a fact that we glean only with hindsight. At the time, *A Study in Scarlet*, for all its faults, *was* the story of Sherlock Holmes. The first, the only and, quite possibly, the last.

In his mind, prouder though he was of the unfolding mystery than any other novel he had yet attempted, Conan Doyle knew that *A Study in Scarlet* was simply one more attempt to make his mark in the world of long-form storytelling. Had it suffered the same fate as its predecessors, lost in the mails or rejected out of hand, he would have returned to the drawing board and Sherlock Holmes might never have been heard of again.

Indeed, it was only desperation born of bitter disappointment that allowed Holmes to thrive in the first place. Cornhill was the first publisher to reject the novel, the magazine returning it with a polite note explaining that the tale was too long to be run in a single issue of the magazine, but too short to be serialised. Plus, the editor grumbled, it was too similar in style to the "shilling shockers" (successors to the penny dreadfuls of earlier infamy) that overflowed from every bookseller's racks, offering cheap and tawdry thrill-a-minute tales to a reading public that could not tolerate anything more substantial.

This was not, in all honesty, an especially fair summary of the book's contents, but it nevertheless served as a firm indictment of mainstream publishing's attitudes toward detective and crime tales at that time.

The Bristol-based publishers Arrowsmith returned the manuscript unread. Frederick Warne & Co. followed suit. Only one publisher showed any interest in the Study: Ward, Locke & Co., who not only made the derisory offer of just £25 pounds for the story, but also seasoned that disappointment by warning that it would not see print for at least another year.

"Dear Sir," began the letter, dated October 30, 1886. "We have read your story and are pleased with it. We could not publish it this year as the market is flooded at present with cheap fiction, but if you do not object to its being held over till next year . . . . Yours faithfully, Ward, Lock & Co."

Was that, then, the measure of *A Study in Scarlet*? Cheap fiction, a shilling shocker, a novelette that deserved no more payment than he might have expected from a shorter story published within a more prestigious magazine? Cautiously, Conan Doyle ventured to ask whether there would be any royalty attached to the publication. Back came the answer: No.

Conan Doyle was—perhaps "bereft" is too dramatic a word. But he was decidedly unhappy, for reasons that no less a personage than Doctor Joseph Bell, Holmes personified, detailed when he was interviewed by *The Bookman* in 1894. His unwitting role in the creation of Sherlock Holmes was common knowledge by then, and he was therefore ideally placed to pontificate upon the true meaning of cheap fiction and how Conan Doyle had produced nothing of the sort.

"Every bookstall has its shilling shocker, and every magazine which aims at circulation must have its mystery of robbery or murder. Most of these are poor enough stuff; complicated plots, which can be discounted in the first chapter, extraordinary coincidences, preternaturally gifted detectives, who make discoveries more or less useless by flashes of insight which no one else can understand, become wearisome in their sameness and the interest, such as it is, centres only in the results and not in the methods."

Holmes, however, like Conan Doyle, was raised far above this milieu by virtue of the author's "education as a student of medicine [which] taught him how to observe, and his practice, both as a general practitioner and a specialist, has been splendid training for a man such as he is, gifted with eyes, memory, and imagination."

Or, as Conan Doyle had Holmes announce in his second adventure, *The Sign of Four*, "My mind . . . rebels at stagnation. Give me problems, give me work, give me the most obtuse cryptogram or the most intricate analysis, and I am in my own proper atmosphere. I can dispense then with artificial stimulants. But I abhor the dull routine of existence. I crave for mental exaltation. That is why I have chosen my own particular profession, or rather created it, for I am the only one in the world."

Such debates regarding its contemporary literary merit notwithstanding, *A Study in Scarlet* was to appear within *Beeton's Christmas Annual*. This was the latest edition of a now indeed annual magazine-style book launched in 1860 by Samuel Orchart Beeton, the husband of "Mrs Beeton," author of Victorian England's best-selling, and still legendary *Book of Household Management*. There it would be one of several stories, all the work of different authors, and targeted at the casual reader . . . people embarking on long railroad journeys for example, or those requiring some light entertainment that would not especially tax the intellect. Cheap fiction. Shilling shockers.

Conan Doyle sighed and signed the contract. Then he sat back to wait out the annual's publication by beginning work on a new novel, *Micah Clarke*.

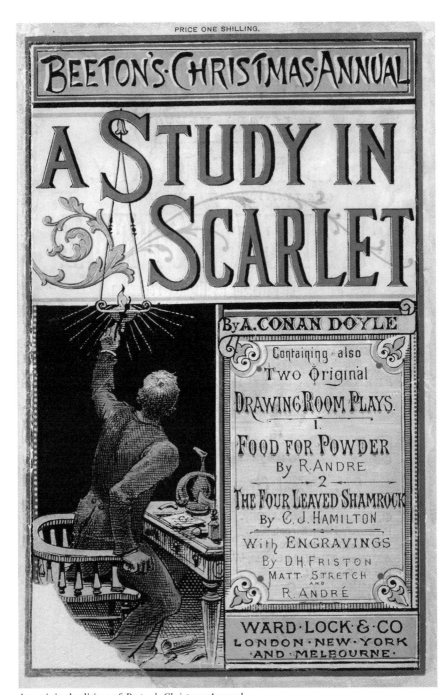

An original edition of *Beeton's Christmas Annual*.

An historical adventure set in and around the Duke of Monmouth's anti-Catholic uprising in 1688, and thus styled firmly in the thrall of Harrison Ainsworth (whose own *James the Second, or, the Revolution of 1688* had visited this same era back in 1848), *Micah Clarke* would not see the light of day until after *A Study in Scarlet* was published; by which time Conan Doyle had finally tasted the success he craved for so long. *Beeton's Christmas Annual* had sold out its entire print run, and of all the stories contained therein, *A Study in Scarlet* was by far the one that excited the most comment.

Perhaps *The Graphic* would sigh wearily, "it is not at all a bad imitation but it would never have been written but for Poe, Gaboriau and [Robert Louis] Stevenson." But the same review also enthused, "Those who like detective stories and have not read the great originals will find the tale full of interest. It hangs together well and finishes ingeniously." This term would be echoed resoundingly elsewhere. "The author shows genius," declared *The Scotsman* newspaper.

To which Conan Doyle might well have responded, "elementary . . . ."

An original edition of *A Study in Scarlet*, as published in *Beeton's*, remains the jewel in any collection of Holmesiana, a sight that very few collectors or fans have been privileged to even see. In 2012, however, a copy from the estate of the Holmes's greatest collector and expert, Richard Lancelyn Green, went on display at Portsmouth City Museum, prompting the City Council's head of culture, Stephen Baily, to remind us, "when Conan Doyle first started writing Sherlock Holmes's adventures 125 years ago, he could never have realized he'd created a global icon."

Comedian and media personality Stephen Fry, a patron of the Arthur Conan Doyle Collection Lancelyn Green Bequest, continued, "Holmes is imperishable." But he also offered a caveat that Conan Doyle himself rarely tired of repeating.

That sometimes, Holmes's "reality, manners, traits, habits, turns of phrase, style of dress, his violin, cocaine, tobacco, deerstalker and magnifying glass obscure the achievements of Sir Arthur Conan Doyle, a man quite as remarkable as his best known creation."

Indeed he was. But even Conan Doyle sometimes wearied of having constantly to remind people of that fact. Celebrated his seventy-first birthday in 1930, the old author remarked for what must have been the thousandth time how tired he was of hearing himself described as the author of the *Sherlock Holmes* stories.

"Why not, for a change, the author of *Rodney Stone* or *The White Company* or *The Lost World*? One would think I had written nothing but detective stories."

5

The Adventure of the Rapidly Coalescing Holmesian Universe

In which Holmes gets High, Watson gets Married, and London becomes a Character in Her own Right

O f all the markets in which *A Study in Scarlet* was published, few were so vociferous in their praise as the United States.

Conan Doyle was initially less than thrilled with the book's appearance on these shores; no copyright agreement whatsoever existed between the UK and America, which meant American publishers could just pick up any British book they chose and publish it without regard for such niceties as permission, royalties, or any payment whatsoever.

Without a care in the world, original works by British authors could be edited, rewritten and retitled willy-nilly. *A Study in Scarlet* was swiftly picked up by sundry American bookleggers, pirate editions flooding onto the shelves as reviewers fell over themselves to celebrate Sherlock Holmes. Conan Doyle was as angry as any author could be.

But the battle that Charles Dickens, to name but the most vociferous opponent of the iniquity, had been fighting ever since (among other things) he discovered his *Oliver Twist* recycled and revised as *Oliver and the Jew Fagin*, would soon be over. In 1891, the two nations finally came to a mutual understanding over authors' right to protect their own works, ensuring that no British author would again need to fear the immoral deprecations of American publishing.

A couple of years before that, however, a handful of gentlemen existed in the trade who likewise believed that copyright should be universal. Among these was Joseph Marshall Stoddart, the publisher of the Philadelphia-based *Lippincott's Magazine.*

In August 1889, Stoddart ventured to London with the express purpose of signing up the cream of English authorship for a proposed UK edition of his magazine. He returned home with Conan Doyle and Oscar Wilde in the bag, the latter promptly offering him *The Picture of Dorian Gray*, his first and only novel. Conan Doyle, on the other hand, ventured *The Sign of Four*, the next installment in the Sherlock Holmes saga.

An admittedly fanciful account of this meeting opens Douglas Preston and Lincoln Child's novel *White Fire*—fanciful because there is no evidence whatsoever that Wilde whiled away the evening by recounting a tale so grisly and ghastly that Conan Doyle was to spend the remainder of his life so haunted by its horror that he revisited it in both *The Hound of the Baskervilles* and a later mystery, too.

Nor can we believe the modern authors' claim that it was Wilde who gave inspirational flesh to Conan Doyle's then apparently murky understanding of who and what Sherlock Holmes really was.

But any reader demanding evidence that Conan Doyle had at least loosely sketched out an entire life for Sherlock Holmes, long before that life became practical, need only read a few pages of *The Sign of Four*.

We return to Baker Street. We return to the comforting womb of Mrs. Hudson, the long-suffering housekeeper who oversees Holmes and Watson's version of domesticity. We return to the bafflement with which Watson, and any other witness, receive Holmes's pronouncements. We even recall a vague reference to the detective's less salubrious leisure activities in the first book, as the opening lines declare them in glowing Technicolor:

> Sherlock Holmes took his bottle from the corner of the mantelpiece, and his hypodermic syringe from its neat morocco case. With his long, white, nervous fingers he adjusted the delicate needle and rolled back his left shirt cuff. For some little time his eyes rested thoughtfully upon the sinewy forearm and wrist, all dotted and scarred with innumerable puncture-marks. Finally, he thrust the sharp point home, pressed down the tiny piston, and sank back into the velvet-lined armchair with a long sigh of satisfaction.

The man was an intravenous drug user, to the shock (vicariously pleasurable or otherwise) of his readers, but to the undisguised horror of Watson:

> Three times a day for many months I had witnessed this performance, but custom had not reconciled my mind to it. On the contrary, from day to day I had become more irritable at the sight, and my conscience swelled nightly within me at the thought that I had lacked the courage to protest.

Cocaine, Holmes's drug of choice, was still legal at the time, a nerve tonic that was common in many households. There was, however, growing disquiet within the medical community, at least, regarding its unregulated use and the consequences thereof, and perhaps Conan Doyle spoke his own thoughts on the subject through Watson's dismay. Holmes's habit, however, had another purpose. It ensured, once and for all, that nobody would ever mistake Holmes

PLAYER'S CIGARETTES

SHERLOCK HOLMES.
"THE ADVENTURES OF SHERLOCK HOLMES."

From the days when cigarettes were cool, a giveaway card from British Players.

for any conventional kind of detective, and it painted a flaw that rendered the superhuman all too human.

Holmes would draw upon both those qualities—his vastly superior intellect, and his instinctive understanding of what made the average man tick—as he strove to unravel this latest mystery.

The adventure opens, in what would become time-honored fashion, with a visitor to 221b. Mary Morstan is at the end of her tether, desperately seeking some clue as to the whereabouts of her father, missing these past ten years, and seeking, too, to learn who is the mysterious benefactor who has been sending her a gift of a beautiful single pearl every year for the past six. (A plot line, if we might digress, that would also inspire one of the greatest mystery novels in recent fictional history, Stieg Larsson's *The Girl with the Dragon Tattoo*.)

As for what brought her to Holmes now, as opposed to at any time in the past six years, she had received a letter with the most recent of the pearls, describing her as having been sorely wronged and asking her to meet with the sender. She understandably fears what might now befall her; and Holmes is intrigued by the mystery surrounding her. He takes the case.

What follows is a rip-roaring adventure, a shilling shocker in all but name, and this time Conan Doyle had no fear of such a term . . . not since *A Study in Scarlet* had been published in that format in July 1888 (with illustrations commissioned by the author from his own father, Charles) and proved an even greater success than before.

Murderous subcontinental Sikhs who recalled the terror of the Thuggees, the professional assassins who once roamed India, slaughtering their victims in the name of the goddess Kali. The ghosts of the Indian Mutiny, fifty years past but still a defining moment in the history of the British Empire. A dwarf with a blowgun, shooting poisonous darts at all who crossed him. A beautiful woman, a mysterious benefactor, a guilty secret, a one-legged man. A thrilling boat chase down the River Thames. These were the ingredients that fueled *The Sign of Four*, and all were so far from the somewhat stilted pastures that mired down so much of *A Study in Scarlet* that any doubt that might have been entertained regarding the potential longevity of Sherlock Holmes was firmly locked away.

Here was a detective for the ages. An adventurer for all time and all tastes. And that despite Conan Doyle's subsequent admission, "I know nothing about detective work, but theoretically it has always had a great charm for me. The great defect in the detective of fiction is that he obtains results without any obvious reason. That is not fair, it is not art."

The Sign of Four was published in *Lippincott's Magazine* in February 1890 edition and won the praise of all who read it. Just one question hung unanswered. What was Holmes going to do without his Watson? The doughty doctor had fallen hard for their client; waxed rhapsodic about her "large blue eyes . . . singularly spiritual and sympathetic"; avowed, with just a suggestion of braggadocio, that "an experience of women which extends over many nations and three separate continents" had never prepared him for the sight of a face "which gave a clearer promise of a refined and sensitive nature."

He had proposed marriage, and Mary Morstan had accepted. Now he was away, any reasonable reader must have assumed, to provide for his wife, to make money to facilitate the making of babies, for a life of domesticity and bliss far removed from the wild ride that Sherlock Holmes had shown him.

Fortunately for all, Holmes was not a reasonable reader. In fact, he was scarcely reasonable at all.

The Adventure of the City That, According to Samuel Johnson, a Man Can Only Tire of When He Is Tired of Life

Of all that Conan Doyle accomplished as he wrote *The Sign of Four*, nothing pleased the author more than his depictions of London, the "vast and accurate knowledge . . . which I display," as he remarked in a letter to *Lippincott*'s Joseph Stoddart. "It might [therefore] amuse you to [learn that] I worked it all out from a Post Office map."

Of course Conan Doyle was no stranger to the city. He had visited it many times, dating back to that trip when he first set eyes upon Baker Street when he was just fifteen. And he had explored it even more thoroughly during that two-month visit to his uncle in Chelsea, when he scoured the docks in search of adventure and came close to taking the Queen's Shilling and signing up to fight in a far-off war, the same war that Doctor Watson had now returned from.

But still his knowledge of the city was less intuitive than he liked to think, and as one reads the earliest cases of the great detective, the city is mapped out as indeed a map. Departing the Lyceum Theatre, where Conan Doyle's teenaged self once saw the great Henry Irving bring Hamlet to life, Watson's narrative admits, "I lost my bearings and knew nothing save that we seemed to be going a very long way. Sherlock Holmes was never at fault, however, and he muttered the names as the cab rattled through squares and in and out by tortuous by-streets. 'Rochester Row,' said he. 'Now Vincent Square. Now we come out on the Vauxhall Bridge Road. We are making for the Surrey side apparently. Yes, I thought so. Now we are on the bridge. You can catch glimpses of the river.'"

No physical descriptions more than an awareness of the "soggy streets" that a wet September evening would produce; nothing to suggest any personal kinship with the names that he rattled off. Yet it was a hallmark of Conan Doyle's writing that one cannot help but find oneself riding alongside Holmes in the carriage, breathing the same cold night air as he, feeling the same cloying damp on one's skin, and witnessing the same familiar vistas as they flash past the window.

London is the uncelebrated third partner in Holmes and Watson's relationship. More than Mrs. Hudson, more than Inspector Lestrade, more even than Moriarty—the one character with whom their names are most frequently, inextricably, linked—London dominates the story of Sherlock Holmes with a presence that is almost human, a quality that the inhabitants and students of the living city itself would scarcely argue with.

Two thousand years of history already hung in the city air when Holmes sallied forth from 221b for the very first time. The Celts had a settlement on the banks of the River Thames long before the Romans arrived to lay the first (and in many places, still visible) foundations of the modern city; over the next four centuries of Roman rule, Londinium would grow into one of the most important political, commercial, and administrative centers in the entire empire.

Neither would it lose that role. Successive invaders built successive cities, or at least made successive marks, until the Normans arrived in 1066 to set in motion the erection of what remain some of London's best-known landmarks, the Tower of London among them.

It was a city of growth, but it was also a city of tragedy. Every schoolchild knows about the great plague of 1664-65 that slaughtered some 70,000 people—one fifth of London's entire contemporary population. Likewise the Great Fire of 1666, which took surprisingly few lives (officially the figure sits at six) but razed much of the city during the nine days before it was extinguished.

But the Celtic Queen Boudicca burned the city 1,600 years before the fire, and lesser plagues ravaged its populace on either side of the pestilence that is regarded as the "great" one. Disease stalked the streets even when the plague was absent; filth slopped the alleyways and poured into the waters long before the Great Stink of 1858 finally convinced the authorities to build London's first-ever sewerage system. (Or, at least, its first since the Romans decided to channel their waste out of sight.)

Terrorism was abroad centuries before Irish nationalists ignited a three-decade bombing campaign in the early 1970s—every year on November 5, the English still remember an attempt, in 1605, to blow up the Houses of Parliament.

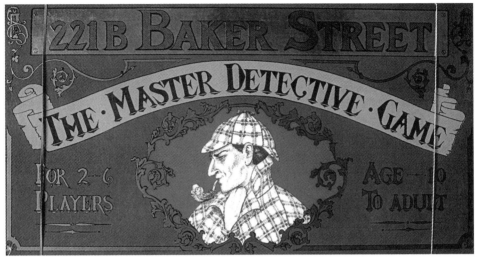

No budding consulting detective should be without this intriguing board game

Famine hit the city as violently as it did the rural countryside. No matter how wealthy the metropolis might appear, poverty was even more rife. It was very easy to starve to death on the streets of Victorian London, and many people did,

Only open warfare, of the four apocalyptic horsemen, had not truly visited modern London in the years before Holmes, although it would make up for lost time in the decades that followed, as the German Zeppelin bombers of the Great War were followed by the Luftwaffe of the second, raining death and flames down upon the historical landscape and, in less than seven years, tearing down more of the old city's history than Londoners themselves had managed in the past three hundred years of progress. Until as recently as the early 1980s, it was safe to say that the look of modern London owed as much to Hitler's bombs as the face of Sherlock's city owed to the wealth of the British Empire.

For his city was one that was in permanent flux. The railroads were coming in, long iron tracks that led to vast brick-and-iron stations that devoured entire neighborhoods. In north London, the need for just three massive terminals, at Euston (built in 1837), St Pancras (1868), and Paddington (1850-54), displaced over 100,000 people.

New streets, wide and bustling, were being planned, sweeping away the old city jumble and again clearing neighborhoods that had stood for hundreds of years. The modern tourist walking down New Oxford Street toward Tottenham Court Road would never guess that back in the time of Charles Dickens, this same location housed one of the most crime-ridden and sinful regions in the entire country, the rookery of St Giles.

In the skies, new buildings were reaching higher and higher; one day, the direst pessimists predicted, mammon would soar even farther into the heavens than the spires of London's many churches, and even the dome of mighty St Paul's Cathedral would lie in the shadow of an office or a bank, a prophesy that today seems impossibly naive. The churches were not simply dwarfed by commerce. Many were demolished to make way for it.

Even the ground underfoot was not sacrosanct. While the engineer Bazalgette was planning and building the miles of sewers that would prevent the city from ever again being lost in a thick fog of effluence, others were carving the pathways of the London Underground, tearing up streets to lay their tracks, then covering them again to keep the trains below the surface (a method called, unsurprisingly, cut and cover).

There were times (dramatically captured in director Guy Ritchie's twenty-first-century takes on Sherlock Holmes) when the entire city must have resembled one vast, never-ending building site.

The city of today, of course, bears little resemblance to that which Sherlock would have known so well, whose shortcuts, alleyways, and darkest corners he committed to memory, never knowing when he might need that particular piece of local knowledge. The Holmes of Conan Doyle's day would be bewildered by all that has befallen his city. But the Holmes of today, the televisual creation of Steven Moffatt and Mark Gatiss, has stepped into his shoes regardless and is as comfortable amid the Shards, Eyes, and Domes of twenty-first-century London as his forefather was among the gentleman's clubs, opium dens, and blacking factories of the late Victorian age. And for the enterprising tourist, there are

John Barrymore *is* Sherlock Holmes.   *Photofest*

well over two hundred locations in and around the city that both men, both Holmeses, could identify in a flash.

London at the turn of the century.

We repeat: It is a vastly different city from that of today, but in many ways, it is even more recognizable than any modern vista.

The skyline is dominated not by office blocks and vast vanity piles—sent soaring to the heavens in the apparent knowledge that if you build a tower tall enough, it will cost way too much to demolish it again—but by churches and cathedrals. Their spires and towers, too, reach toward the clouds, but it is God whom they glorify, not the ego of some fashionable architect who should never have been given that first box of Legos. (Or, more likely, who is compensating now for never having had one in the first place.) Most, besides, are so old that with just a handful of exceptions, nobody even remembers who designed many of them. Given the choice between then and now, only a philistine could argue that the view has been improved.

The streets are as choked with traffic as they are today. But the belching fumes of cars, trucks, buses, and taxis are nowhere to be seen or smelled. The roar of the internal-combustion engine has been supplanted by the trot of horses' hooves, although it has to be acknowledged that the animals' "exhaust fumes" are often just as overpowering as any cloud of diesel, and just as noxious when you take a sudden lungful.

And then there is the fog. Pea-soup thick and moist enough that every breath feels like drowning, London's fog is actually smog, an evil miasma that shifts between ugly yellow, ghastly green, and unforgiving black depending upon which pollutants have the upper hand. Soot from the coal fires that burn in every dwelling, sulphur dioxide, and a frightful foulness of every persuasion swim in the mist, particularly when the natural fogs of the Thames rise up and transform the air into what the Londoners called, indeed, a pea souper. Which, for reasons that our very airways will squirm at the mention of, occasionally became a pea and ham soup.

It was as recently as 1956 that the British government finally acted to rid its capital city of this choking scourge, pushed into action by the soul-scouring winter of 1952, when a smog descended so thick and ugly that, for five windless days that December, more than four thousand people died of respiratory disease and up to eight thousand more may have been fatally sickened.

Prior to that, prior to the Clean Air Act that finally rid the city of its most deadly visitor, the London fog was as much a part of the capital as the churches, the traffic, the world-famous monuments whose names and faces trip off the tongue (St Paul's Cathedral, Big Ben, Buckingham Palace, Piccadilly Circus, you know them all), and everything else with which we associate the metropolis. It was a part of the fabric of London, and today it is part of the city's charm.

Its literary charm, anyway.

Charles Dickens was not the first author to speak of the fog, but he is certainly one of the most famous. Published exactly a century before the Great

Smog of 1952, we are just three chapters inside his *Bleak House* when Esther arrives in London, convinced that she has just missed the excitement of a great fire. "For the streets were so full of dense brown smoke that scarcely anything was to be seen."

"O, dear no, miss," replies the young gentleman who meets her. "This is a London particular." And when it becomes apparent that Esther has never heard such a term, he hastens to explain. "A fog, miss." Forty years later, Frances Hodgson Burnett's *A Little Princess* described an afternoon when "the yellow fog hung so thick and heavy . . . that the lamps were lighted." T. S. Eliot mused on "the brown fog of a winter dawn," and, of course, the fictional industry that has grown up around the deprecations of Jack the Ripper still paints the nocturnal fog as the only accomplice the killer ever needed. As indeed it was for many another villain of the age.

But no character, fictional or otherwise, has ever seemed so much a part of the fog, and all that it contains and conceals, as Sherlock Holmes. Becloaked and earnest, his deer-stalker hat thrust down on his head, his eyes glistening with the anticipation of his latest hunt, Holmes emerging from the smoky tendrils of a London fog is much a component of his visual iconography as any scene, real or imagined, that print, cinema, TV, or radio has ever caused us to conjure.

And no wonder.

In *A Study in Scarlet*, the first Holmes story ever published, "a dun-coloured veil hung over the house-tops." In "The Adventure of the Bruce-Partington Plans," "a dense yellow fog" that has settled over London will soon be transformed into "a greasy, heavy brown swirl . . . [that] condens[es] in oily drops on the windowpane." For four days that week, Doctor Watson hazarded, "from the Monday to the Thursday I doubt whether it was ever possible from our windows in Baker Street to see the loom of the opposite houses."

But Conan Doyle offers the fog its greatest role early on in *The Sign of Four*.

There, "dense [and] drizzly . . . [it] lay low upon the great city. Mud-colored clouds drooped sadly over the muddy streets. Down the Strand the lamps were but misty splotches of diffused light which threw a feeble circular glimmer upon the slimy pavement." And so on and so forth, until the fog is as much our companion as either Holmes or Watson.

The absorbed reader will already be adjusting his or her muffler, unconsciously securing the uppermost buttons, pulling the hat farther down. None of which offers much more than the most superficial protection against the fog, but on a night like this, the tiniest things can make a difference.

To see the city through Conan Doyle's eyes, then, is to peer through a murky gloom that sometimes feels as thick and solid as the walls and sidewalks that it shrouds.

Literature, however, allows us to peel back time, and both the improvements and the damage that it has wrought throughout the intervening century; to brush away the fog, to sweep away (or, at least, replace with new ones) the smells;

to wade through changing tastes and fashions with no more effort than it takes to turn the pages of a book.

The Strange Case(s) of Gideon and the Rivers of London

Written, with becoming serendipity, at approximately half-century intervals in the aftermath of Sherlock, two series of crime novels echo and replicate our earlier observation that London is the third partner in the team of Holmes and Watson: J. J. Marric's "Gideon" novels, written more or less annually between 1955 and 1976, and amounting to a total of twenty-one separate books; and Ben Aaronovitch's "Rivers of London," just four novels published since 2011, but equal to both Marric (a pen name, incidentally, for the prolific crime writer John Creasey) and Conan Doyle in their depictions, their absorption, and, most of all, their love for the city.

Aaronovitch's adventures are pure children of today. They follow the career of Peter Grant, a young constable in the Metropolitan Police who is seconded into a mysterious and seldom-mentioned department dedicated solely to super-natural and magical crimes. This concept naturally throws wide open a door through which reader and critic alike can shout "Harry Potter" in a variety of Snape-like voices, but Aaronovitch has sensibly taken that into account. His own characters are prone to the same observations themselves.

Sherlock Holmes is remarkable, at least in the light of both his reputation and Conan Doyle's own fascination with the supernatural, in that he is staunchly opposed to any mystery having any kind of origin that is not provably manmade. He meets a vampire, but it is a child with a blowpipe. He meets a spectral hound, but it is a down-to-earth trickster. And so forth.

Peter Grant does not have Holmes's faith in the absolute truths of science, and with good reason. Among the characters he encounters in the first of the books, *Rivers of London* (published as *Midnight Riot* in the United States), are indeed the rivers of London—Father Thames, Mama Thames, Beverley Brook, Oxley, Cecilia Tyburn, Fleet, Lea, Brent, Ash . . . each and every one of them named for one of the manifold waterways that, across history (and beneath the modern city) run through the city, without most passers-by even being aware they exist.

Visit Sloane Square underground station and marvel at the vast circular metal pipe that runs above the tracks. It contains the Westbourne River. Walk Fleet Street and ask yourself what lies beneath? The Fleet River. Travel west to Stamford Brook and ponder the derivation of its name. Long ago buried beneath the ever-growing metropolis, the children of the Thames are every-where you walk, and each one, according to *Rivers of London* (and several thou-sand years of mythology, too) has a guardian goddess or god. It is these with whom Peter Grant consorts in a novel that utterly captivates, not only via its unfolding plot, but also by the sheer delight with which Aaronovitch describes and involves the city.

Suburbs that the visitors ignore and which Londoners take for granted are given the same fresh life in Aaronovitch's books as they were in Conan Doyle's, and if a future generation of guides should ever institute walking tours of Peter Grant's London, they will discover the same wealth of incidental detail and debris as the Holmes walkers of today delight in. The brutal braggadocio of modern designs might strike today's viewer as coarse and unnecessary. To the future, however, they will be nostalgia and, of all the myriad novels that have told tales of London in the past fifty years, the "Rivers of London" series feels like the one that best preserves the ever-changing city of today.

In exactly the same fashion, J. J. Marric's "Gideon" novels capture, and freeze, the city during its last major spurt of redevelopment and growth. The 1950s, when the series began, saw the city still in the process of rebuilding from the Second World War. Hitler's bombsites remained a familiar sight (and would continue so into the early 1970s), and for many people displaced by the Blitz of the early 1940s, home remained the same "temporary" maisonettes into which they were originally shepherded once peace broke out.

Now, however, the planners were moving in, ambitiously at first, with visions of a city that might rival New York for height and drama, but scaling back as the realities of finance and planning permission kicked their dreams into play. A city of skyscrapers was replaced by clusters of "tower blocks," high-rise housing that may have been designed with the best intentions but that ultimately served only to take a slum population that once spread horizontally and realign it vertically instead. A harvest that Aaronovitch's Peter Grant would one day be reaping. The 1960s housing estate that is the centrepiece of the fourth book in his series, 2013's *Broken Homes*, has a modern history at least as vile as any overpopulated, underpoliced slum of the previous century.

Gideon, rising up the echelons of Scotland Yard, was no stranger to those dens; he might even, had he been of a literary turn of mind himself, have compared them to the rookeries of nineteenth-century London, into which Holmes occasionally plunged on a case, and from which his gaggle of spies and informants, the Baker Street Irregulars, were undoubtedly drawn.

Parades of stores opened, concrete and laminate, edging out established businesses as the rents soared to match the modernity of the premises. In 1963, incoming British prime minister Harold Wilson pledged the construction of a new world, a "Britain that is going to be forged in the white heat of [a techno-logical] revolution," and the Gideon novels capture this flux with the same photographic precision as Conan Doyle fixed the London of Victoria's building boom.

But the city was changing, and its criminals were changing. It was the age when simple bank jobs were supplanted by heists; when crowbars and knuckle dusters were replaced as the weapons of choice by "shooters"; when the old order of things—of gangs that paid loyal fealty to their leaders, and policed their own manors with military guile—was swept away indeed by the white heat of technology.

Holmes, Watson and some fog.

When we open the first of Marric's wonderful books, 1955's *Gideon's Day*, the London and Londoners over whom presides Detective Superintendent George Gideon of the CID (Criminal Investigation Department) would still be recognizable to Sherlock Holmes—as indeed was the CID itself, founded in 1878 to oversee Scotland Yard's plain-clothes detectives.

Also recognizable were the police headquarters that he knew as Scotland Yard. Originally opened on Great Scotland Yard itself, back in 1829, it had already outgrown its surroundings by 1890, and New Scotland Yard, the lair of Lestrade, was opened on the Victoria Embankment.

But that base, too, would eventually prove inadequate, and in 1967, the year in which Marric published *Gideon's Wrath*, the headquarters were shifted again, to a new office building on Broadway. From whence, it was reported in May 2013 it will soon be moving again, this time to a site developed on what is (at the time of writing) still a largely Victorian-era police station in the same Westminster neighborhood.

Larger, then, and far more formidably equipped than anything Holmes could have witnessed, Scotland Yard remained Scotland Yard, and the problems with which Lestrade battled, Gideon continued to wrestle.

Other things that changed but stayed the same: The poverty of the east end, the roughness of the docks, the cunning of the crooks. And the fog. The pea soupers that Holmes knew (and Gideon remembered from his youth) had now been chased away. But the city was still prone to impenetrable miasma.

"Tall trees . . . seemed to be swallowed by the fog," we read early on in the aptly titled *Gideon's Fog*. "The trees close to the road were solid enough at the base, but even their higher, skeletal branches appeared to be fading away. Office workers . . . some holding torches, the beams pointing downwards, were already wraithlike figures."

But the categories of fear were changing, and by the time we reach the last of Marric's novels, 1976's *Gideon's Drive*, we might have been plunged into a comparative hell on earth, so much has changed, so much has been lost. Now the criminals are a psychological basket case avenging the recent death of his pregnant wife; an on-the-run rapist with an eye for leggy hippie chicks; and a three-strong consortium of investors and bankers, looking to corner the market in supermarket shares by cornering the market in stolen food.

Holmes would have been baffled. What is a supermarket? What is a hippie? And death by childbirth, to him, was just a fact of life.

The process would continue, has continued. Peter Grant takes for granted even the crimes that most horrified Gideon; they are now sufficiently common-place to seem run-of-the-mill. His dilemmas, even if we strip away the super-natural bent of "Rivers of London," are of a nature that Gideon could never have dreamed and that Holmes might never have believed. "When you have eliminated the impossible," the latter was fond of saying, "whatever remains, however improbable, must be the truth." But they are truths that he would never have considered.

London, though . . . London remains London, her spirit proud and indomi-table, as unaffected by the nonsensical monstrosities with which modern-day vanity insists upon adorning her as it was by the carbuncles of the 1980s, the clinkers of the 1960s, the eyesores that every decade, in every century, has overlaid upon her face.

The excitement with which Conan Doyle, wife Louisa, and their two-year-old daughter Mary first moved to London in spring 1891 is the same as the thrill with which countless millions have arrived there in the century-plus years since then; a crowded, stinking, noisy, bustling, thrilling, amazing metropolis in which anything was possible, everything was marvelous, and beauty and beastliness were simply next-door neighbors.

Despite his successes, Conan Doyle himself was nothing remarkable the day he first moved to London and would have attracted few glances even from people who were aware of his name. He had published little over the past year, a consequence of four months spent studying ophthalmology in Vienna, preparatory to opening a new practice in the English capital. He was a doctor who wrote in his spare time, that's all, and no matter where his ambitions might ultimately have lain, that was all he presented himself as. He found a home in Bloomsbury, close by the British Museum, at 23 Montague Place; and a surgery at 2 Upper Wimpole Street, just around the corner from the legendary lair of the city's most well-heeled medical practitioners, Harley Street.

He did not expect his new practice to become instantly successful, and so it proved. No less than in Southsea when he first opened there, business started out slow; so slow that he was able to finish another historical romance, set during the Hundred Years' War, *The White Company*. Its impetus undisguisedly drawn from the tales of chivalry and knightly derring-do with which his mother had entertained him as a child, *The White Company* was published as a monthly serial in *Cornhill* magazine later in the year, and it remains one of Conan Doyle's best-loved novels.

Indeed, had he turned his mind to it, there is little doubt that Conan Doyle could have continued to make a reasonable living firmly in the footprint of Sir Walter Scott and Harrison Ainsworth, turning out historical potboiler after historical potboiler, and the literary world would have prospered as a consequence. Thoroughly researched, revealingly detailed, Conan Doyle was a natural scene-setter, as capable of transporting the reader to the fields of fourteenth-century France (the era of *The White Company*) as he was to any of the more urban landscapes for which he would ultimately become renowned.

His stories combined learning with adventure in a manner that only the most gifted author was able, the knowledge slipping into the reader's mind almost unnoticed, but with permanence regardless; and though his leading characters tended to be fictional, nevertheless they were drawn from archetypes that were as recognizable as any living soul.

But always, nagging at the minds of both his readers and admirers, his critics and publishers, was one question: Where was the next Sherlock Holmes?

6

The Sensationalist Case of the Victorian Periodical

In which we Discover *The Strand*, Marvel at the *Illustrated Police News*, and Investigate a few of London's own Mysteries

The mid- to late nineteenth century was the heyday of the literary magazine. Always a power in the world of fiction, it was the magazines that gave so many of the era's greatest authors their first, invaluable shove into the mainstream: *Fraser's*, *Blackwood's*, the *Edinburgh Magazine*, and so many more.

Both Ainsworth and Dickens repaid their debt to the format by putting their names and talents to new publications—the former's *Ainsworth's Magazine*, in which a number of its namesake's novels made their debut; the latter's *Household Words* and *All the Year Round*; and barely a year went by without a hopeful new title setting sail.

Now a new player had arrived on the scene. In January 1891, just as Conan Doyle was setting out for Vienna, a former furniture salesman named George Newnes launched *The Strand*.

Newnes was not a novice in this ultracompetitive world; he had, in fact, already made a small fortune as the publisher of *Tit-Bits from All the Most Interesting Books, Periodicals and Newspapers in the World*—which was, as its lengthy (and eventually abbreviated) title suggested, composed of stories, news, and features drawn from any publication that caught its editor's eye.

The Strand was to be different. Visiting the United States, Newnes had been impressed by the sheer quality of the leading magazines, a far cry from the sometimes sensational and often gimmick-ridden state of the British market. (A state of affairs that *Tit-Bits* had played its own part in creating.) *The Strand* was to echo the stateside model; it looked in particular toward the *Lippincott's* of early Holmesian renown, by showcasing only the greatest writers, illustrators, and photographers available.

It would be an upmarket publication, then, but it would not demand an upmarket price. Declaring each issue to "cost sixpence but be worth a shilling," Newnes flooded the stores with 300,000 copies of the maiden issue of *The Strand*, and every copy was sold. Soon, even a small collection of the fledgling magazine offered a bulging bag of fascinating features: across *The Strand*'s first half dozen issues, readers were courted with tales that ranged from a translation of Hungarian author Moritz Jokai's "Barak's Wives: A Story for Children" to "A Day with an East End Photographer," featuring the evocative work of J. L. Wimbush; from Voltaire's "The Two Genies" to a study of "Old Stone Signs of London"; and on to a certain A. Conan Doyle's "The Voice of Science."

Authors the caliber of Rudyard Kipling, Rider Haggard and H. G. Wells lined up for inclusion in *The Strand*, while the Queen of England herself, the septuagenarian Victoria, not only allowed Newnes's authors unprecedented access behind the closed doors of royal life, she also contributed a number of etchings with which to illustrate the pieces and even proofread the articles before publication.

Thus *The Strand* was not dedicated solely to fiction. Throughout the magazine's first ten years of publication, editor Herbert Greenhough Smith published eighteen thousand stories and articles, written by some six thousand authors, and culled from a postbag that brought him some forty thousand manuscripts. Among these, and the many thousands more that appeared in the decades to come, we find authors expounding on such topics as "How My Plots Come to Me" and "The Book I Most Enjoyed Writing"; guides to amateur conjuring and playing golf; and op-ed features demanding to know "Is the British Climate Maligned?" and "Should Women Serve as Soldiers?"

Today, almost 125 years after its foundation, *The Strand* appears impossibly stuffy, a reminder (and perhaps even the epitome) of an age in which writing was the pursuit of the privileged—a far cry indeed from the almost self-immolating democratization that the profession has undergone since the arrival of the Internet.

The authors who contributed to *The Strand* did so not only because they had something to say, but because there was an audience that wanted to hear them say it. By comparison, the blogs, the op-eds, and all the other vehicles for expression that exist today are nothing more than graffiti sprayed on walls that nobody has bothered to wipe away. If *The Strand* ran a photograph of a cat, it was because it was an interesting cat. And interesting cats belonged to interesting people.

Not that the magazine's readers were expected to remain silent. The opinions of the common herd would be invited via the magazine's postbag, or through the competitions that were the Victorian-and-beyond equivalent of modern interactivity. In 1916, then, readers were asked "Who Is the Worst Man Who Has Ever Lived?" and were informed, as King George V ascended to the throne in 1911, "How It Feels to Be Crowned."

In an age without radio or television, a world in which publishing was considered the ultimate in mass communication, *The Strand* was the most massive communicator of all, at least within the realm of monthly magazines. By 1914, its circulation was estimated at two million readers, or one out of every twenty-three people living in Britain at that time.

Arthur Conan Doyle was a unique ingredient in this success.

The Strand magazine—Holmes's home from home.

The Astonishing Case of the Author Who Could Name His Own Fee

It was Conan Doyle's newly acquired agent Alexander Pollock Wyatt (founder of the world's first dedicated literary agency) who made the introduction, submitting the author's "The Voice of Science" while *The Strand* was still in the preparatory stages, and being rewarded with its appearance in the third issue, in March 1891.

It's a dry story, wordy and overwrought, a tale of skewed romance among the test tubes and microscopes. But editor Greenhough Smith was sufficiently impressed to request more from Conan Doyle, and the author was swift to respond, not with a story but with a notion.

It was his opinion, he said, drawn from many years of studying the literary market, that while serialized novels remained a vital element within many magazines (and, of course, a vital cog in the publicity machine, as well), both writer and publication would be better served by a series of separate stories featuring the same cast of recurring characters than by a chapter-by-chapter recounting of a book.

From the reader's point of view, it meant that an issue could be missed, or mislaid, without damaging his or her comprehension of an unfolding monthly plot; from the writer's perspective, it meant tales could be told in a natural fashion, without forever having to grasp for the chapter-ending cliffhanger that would bring the reader back for more.

"I believe I was the first to realize this," Conan Doyle later avowed. "A number of monthly magazines were coming out at that time. . . . Considering these various journals with their disconnected stories, it had struck me that a single character running through a series, if it only engaged the attention of the reader, would bind that reader to that particular magazine."

Then, having convinced Greenhough Smith of this necessity, he began casting around for a suitable leading man. He did not look far. "I felt that Sherlock Holmes, who I had already handled in two little books, would easily lend himself to a succession of short stories."

He would be proven correct, too. No sooner had the first Sherlock Holmes tales appeared in *The Strand* than *The Bookman* magazine was exclaiming that "every magazine which aims at a circulation must have its mystery of robbery or murder . . . . Dr Conan Doyle has made well-deserved success for his detective stories and made the name of his hero beloved by the boys of this country by the marvelous cleverness of his method."

Greenhough Smith, too, had no doubts as to the nature of the treasure that had fallen into his lap. No sooner had Conan Doyle submitted his first two Sherlock Holmes stories, "A Scandal in Bohemia" and "The Red-headed League," than the editor "at once realized that here was the greatest short story writer since Edgar Allan Poe."

Greenhough Smith recalled "rushing into Mr Newnes's room and thrusting the stories before his eyes . . . . Here, to an editor jaded with wading through reams of impossible stuff, comes a gift from Heaven, a godsend in the shape of the story that brought a gleam of happiness into the despairing life of this weary editor. Here was a new and gifted story-teller: there was no mistaking the ingenuity of the plot, the limpid clearness of the style, the perfect art of telling a story."

Immediately Greenhough Smith commissioned four further tales, offering Conan Doyle what must have seemed the impossible sum of thirty guineas for each. Impossible because, for the first time in his adult life, Conan Doyle could now imagine settling down to work at the profession he loved more than any other. "As I surveyed my own life . . . I saw how foolish I was to waste my literary earnings in keeping up an oculist's room in Wimpole Street, and I determined with a wild rush of joy to cut the painter, and to trust for ever to my power of writing." It was May 1891 (in his autobiography, he mistakenly claimed it was August), and Conan Doyle was at last "my own master."

The following month, Conan Doyle moved his family out of central London to a new home in what was then the leafy southern suburb of South Norwood, a three-story, sixteen-room red brick villa at 12 Tennison Road. Close, his younger self might have reminded him, to the Crystal Palace in Sydenham where, at age fifteen, Uncle Henry had taken him to view the life size dinosaurs that stood on display.

"There I made my first effort to live entirely by my pen," he wrote later, and he certainly suffered no false modesty as he continued, "it soon became evident that I had been playing the game well within my powers and that I should have no difficulty in providing a sufficient income."

In this, he was greatly aided by his agent, Wyatt. Not only did the man succeed in convincing *The Strand* to increase Conan Doyle's fee from thirty guineas to £150 for the first series of stories, he also manufactured a bidding war for the stories in the United States. By the time *The Strand* was ready for a second string of Holmesian adventures, Conan Doyle's fee had soared to an unbelievable £1,000. Per story!

Doubtless, Conan Doyle believed he merited such extravagant sums. "The difficulty of the Holmes work was that every story needed as clear-cut and original a plot as a longish book would do. One cannot without effort spin plots at such a rate. They are apt to become too thin or to break."

Furthermore, with the specter of financial hardship seemingly exorcised from his life, "I was determined . . . never again to write anything which was not as good as I could make it, and therefore I would not write a Holmes story without a worthy plot and without a problem which interested my own mind, for that is the first requisite before you can interest anyone else."

The Wondrous Adventure of the Scandalous Crime Rag

There is a multitude of reasons why Sherlock Holmes proved such an instant hit, first with readers of *The Strand*, and then with people who would *become* readers of *The Strand*. Literacy rates were soaring as Britain began to reap the rewards of the Elementary Education Act of 1870, by which all children between five and twelve years of age were embraced (and not without considerable controversy and opposition) by the concept of universal education.

A five-year-old in 1870 would be in his or her early twenties when the first Holmes stories appeared in the magazine, and if the sheer wealth of publications that were available at the time is any indication, this group became avid readers. Newspaper circulations soared, publishers' account books prospered, and now a new complaint arose. As early as 1878, Lord Shaftesbury was claiming to have noted that those old literary standbys, the penny dreadful and shilling shocker, were creeping insidiously "not only in the houses of the poor, neglected and untaught, but into the largest mansions, penetrating into religious families and astounding careful parents by [their] frightful issues."

A decade later, the impossibly prudish Edward Salmon's study of modern reading trends, *Juvenile Literature as It Is*, threatened that the existence of this same pernicious rubbish would inevitably lead to the "moral and material ruin of the working class." Salmon built his entire case around the promotion of reading material better suited to young minds—and material such as the novels of Charles Dickens, who, in a poll of some fourteen hundred boys and girls he selected from the (chiefly middle- and upper-middle-class) readership of the *Boy's Own* and *Girl's Own* papers, finished an easy winner.

But pernicious rubbish was what people wanted, and pernicious rubbish was what the publishing industry flourished upon. The most traditionally "serious" titles notwithstanding, no newspaper worth its cover price would dream of going to press without a fresh sensation on its front page; and, if there were no sensations to be had, then they would just invent some.

It was the era of the *Illustrated Police News*, now regarded as one of Britain (and, therefore, the world's) first "modern" tabloid newspapers, a weekly digest of crime, scandal, death, and superstition, all relayed in the most lurid tones imaginable. Graphic line drawings conveyed dramas that photography never could; "eye witness reports" elaborated details that might never have made the official police report. Between 1864, when the title was born, and 1938, when it folded, the *Illustrated Police News* was a one-stop repository for all that was shocking, graphic, and, for the armchair reader, so satisfying. (With glorious period accuracy, a copy of the paper is even seen being avidly consumed during Guy Ritchie's maiden Holmes movie.)

This was the appetite that Conan Doyle was tapping into—the average law-abiding citizen's relentless fascination with his *un*-average, law-breaking counterpart. And just as modern students of current affairs reflect that there seems to be so much more evil in the world today, without necessarily allying that increase to the fact that there are so many more outlets reporting upon it and vying to outdo one another with their latest shock horror headline, so the last decade of the nineteenth century likewise seemed choked by murder, theft, arson, deception, destruction, and death. Not because those incidents were necessarily on the increase. But because it was so much easier to read or hear about them.

The *Illustrated Police News* made certain of that.

But what of the police themselves? How did they view the concept of an all-conquering, all-deducing superhero detective?

Wryly.

The Real Life Adventure of the Contemporary Detective

Fred Wensley joined the Metropolitan Police's uniformed branch in January 1888. He was appointed to the plain-clothed CID in October 1895 and, over the next thirty years, rose to the rank of chief constable—a "long and exceptionally distinguished service," said *Police Orders* when he retired in 1929, to be remembered as one of the most efficient, but more importantly, respected of his era. Respected, that is, from both sides of the law-abiding fence.

His early years in the service speak of the rigors that a policeman faced in the age of Sherlock Holmes. He suffered several beatings at the hands of mobs that rose up to protect one of their number from arrest, and following one, he spent as long on the sick list as his assailants did in prison, a total of four months. "There were no ethical rules in the . . . code for a rough-and-tumble with a policeman," he wrote in his (so-gripping) autobiography, *Forty Years of Scotland Yard*. "I thought every rib in my body was broken."

A gifted detective even during his years on the beat, Wensley's transfer to the CID, and his berth in Whitechapel, in the East End, allowed him a unique and lingering glimpse inside the reality of life for Conan Doyle's literary police officers. "Men and women ripe for any crime from murder to pilfering were to be found in its crowded slums and innumerable common lodging houses." We are afforded some understanding of Conan Doyle's penchant for crooked foreigners by Wensley's observation that "the off-scourings of the criminal population of Europe—Russians, Poles, Germans, Austrians and Frenchmen—found a refuge there. British as well as foreign carried knives and guns which they did not hesitate to use."

We see the shadow of the criminal genius Moriarty pass by: "Organized gangs of desperate men and lads, armed with lethal weapons, infested the streets, terrorizing whole areas, blackmailing tradesmen, holding up wayfarers and carrying out more or less open robbery."

They all needed to be caught.

The more Wensley saw of detective work, he wrote, the more it fascinated him. "Brain and body were constantly on the alert." But while he admitted there were "tricks in every trade," and detection was no exception, he was adamant. "I could not . . . miraculously deduce the author of a crime from a piece of burnt matchstick." What he could do was say, "often with reasonable certainty, who was the probable author of a crime by the circumstances in which it was carried out."

A modern reminder of the terror of the Ripper.   *© Steve and Betsy Mortensen*

Like Lestrade, Gregory, and the rest of Holmes's Scotland Yard allies, Wensley was not perfect. Sometimes he blundered, sometimes he missed the mark altogether. And on one instance that he recounts in his autobiography, a piece of deduction that *would* have made Sherlock proud was undone by a criminal who had obviously read the same books.

A series of burglaries was under way, and all seemed to be the work of one man. And, according to a single specimen discovered at one of the crime scenes, this individual had a fancy for elaborate, foreign-made buttons.

A few days later, Wensley was certain he had his man, a known criminal who was walking up Whitechapel Road wearing a waistcoat adorned with the exact same buttons, *from which one was missing*.

Inquiries were made. The button had been lost on the night of the break-in. The man was arrested, charged, and soon up in court, before the magistrate. At this point he broke the stoic silence that had enveloped him since his arrest, by speaking up in the most public arena possible. The button that the police had in evidence still had its shank attached. But they had not inspected his waistcoat (which, in those days before items were routinely taken into police care to be used as evidence, he was still wearing), and in court it was shown that the shank from his missing button was still in place. Thus, unless the court believed that a button had been made with two shanks, it could not be the one he had lost.

No matter that it was obvious that he had simply had somebody provide him with a shank that he had then attached to the waistcoat. No matter that he was as guilty as the day is long. The court had no alternative but to acquit the man, and Wensley had no choice but to stand silently by as the freed man wallowed in triumph. "Thought yourself clever, didn't you?" he taunted Wensley. "I was too clever for you that time."

One wonders how Holmes would have responded under similar circumstances?

The Strange Case of the Strange Cases That the Police Were Never Able to Solve

Another factor in Holmes's swift preeminence is surely the number of "unsolved mysteries" that seemed to assail society at that time.

Conan Doyle himself had already ventured into the realm of real-life mysteries with his (albeit fictional) inquiries into the disappearance of the crew of the *Marie Celeste*, and what a case that would have made for Holmes to unravel.

Since that time, however, the average British newspaper reader had simply been barraged by further such conundrums.

The Mysterious Case of the Headless Torso of Whitechapel, for instance. In October 1888, while work was under way on what would become the new headquarters for, of all people, the Metropolitan Police, one of the construction workers discovered a black cloth parcel containing a headless, one-armed female torso. A match, the police surgeon swiftly declared, for the right arm and shoulder that had been discovered on the riverbank at Pimlico the previous month. Of the head, however, there was no sign, and of the murderer, no clue. The Whitechapel Mystery remains unsolved to this day.

How about the Chilling Adventure of the Gagged Corpse? On January 1, 1890, having spent Christmas with family in Scotland, a young maid returned to her Chiswick home to discover her mistress dead. Margaret Louise Bryden lay in the generally unused back bedroom, fully clothed, on her back with her head hanging over the edge of the bed. Inside the unfortunate woman's mouth could be seen an amount of cloth—the bag for her dressing gown. In her gullet, the pathologist revealed, lay her false teeth. But there were no signs of struggle or violence, and the original coroner's verdict was death by misadventure. Mrs. Bryden, he decided, had accidentally swallowed her own false teeth, then tried to fish them out with the bag.

As one would.

Hardly surprisingly, other parties disputed his findings, and when a postmortem returned its own verdict of willful murder, the hunt was on for the perpetrator of a most bizarre killing. He or she was never found.

There was the Mouse-Murdering Mystery of Jill the Ripper. Jack, of course, had never been caught, and by 1890, the first amateur Ripperologists were already in full cry, barking up whichever tree they deemed most likely to bear evidential fruit. Conan Doyle was among them, and that October, his theory that the killer might have been a woman received considerably more traction than before when Mary Pearcey was found guilty not only of murdering her lover's

The movie's black and white, but the Woman's in green!

lawful wife, crushing her skull and severing her head, but also of smothering the woman's baby daughter.

Blood was spattered on the walls of Pearcey's home; gore stained a poker and a carving knife. An apron, of the sort that might protect a butcher's clothing from being soaked, hung nearby. But Pearcey proclaimed her innocence to the end. The blood was that of mice that she killed with the aforementioned implements of destruction, she swore, but to no avail. She was hanged two days before Christmas, and if Sherlock Holmes had only cared to venture just a few yards down from 221b, Madame Tussauds not only exhibited Pearcey's likeness, but also purchased the murdered baby's perambulator and the contents of Pearcey's kitchen to add further realism to the gruesome tableau.

But did Pearcey really kill Phoebe Hogg and her child? And, if so, had she killed before? Those questions, though oft-asked in the years since the crime, have never been answered.

So many crimes, so many questions. Who was the woman found dismembered on a canal tow path in Nottingham in 1892, and who was responsible for her grisly demise?

What was the truth behind the Harmondsworth Vampire, a seemingly spectral creature that murdered and then drained a woman of that town?

What was the true fate of the *Marlborough*, a passenger and cargo ship that disappeared without a trace somewhere between New Zealand and England in

1890, but whose marooned crew might have been briefly sighted on an island off Cape Horn, by another vessel, the following year?

Later in life, Conan Doyle would turn detective himself and was instrumental in clearing the names of several high-profile criminal suspects, including Oscar Slater, convicted in 1909 of slaughtering Marion Gilchrist in Glasgow the previous year.

For now, however, he was as baffled as anybody by the endlessly churning mill of murder ground out by the daily papers, and he was no more capable of solving the crimes than the police themselves seemed to be.

But he knew a man who was.

7

The Adventure of the Adventures of Sherlock Holmes

In which we Revisit the Twelve Stories that Constitute Watson's first Book of Memoirs, commencing with the Singular Saga of *A Scandal in Bohemia*

Conan Doyle wrote quickly. The first of his new Sherlock Holmes stories, "A Scandal in Bohemia," was delivered in time to lead off the July 1891 issue of *The Strand*, and this magnificent story arguably ranks not only among the best of all Holmes's adventures, featuring one of the strongest-ever supporting characters, but also served as the inspiration behind one of Holmes's finest-ever television adaptations.

The story begins with not one but two visitors to 221b: the now happily married Doctor Watson, dropping by on a social call, and the masked and mysterious Count Von Kramm, an agent for what he describes as an unnamed but wealthy client. In fact, agent and client are one and the same; the visitor is, Holmes swiftly deduces, Wilhelm Gottsreich Sigismond von Ormstein, the Grand Duke of Cassel-Felstein and the hereditary King of Bohemia, and having been figuratively unmasked, the visitor drops the pretense and tells his tale.

Five years before his recently announced engagement to the Scandinavian princess Clotilde Lothman von Saxe-Meiningen, the Grand Duke enjoyed what we shall discreetly term a liaison with Irene Adler, a radiant American opera singer at that time engaged as prima donna of the Imperial Opera of Warsaw.

As young lovers do, the pair exchanged letters and had their photograph taken—at a time, we remember, when photography was still something of a novelty. It would be bad enough were the princess's family to learn of this relationship, but how much worse were they to read the letters, see the photograph . . .

In vain, the Grand Duke had offered to purchase the incriminating items from Miss Adler, then fruitlessly had his agents try to secure them by force. They stole her luggage—the items were not within. They burgled her house—the letters could not be found. And now Adler was threatening to bundle them up and mail them to the Grand Duke's future in-laws.

Holmes is his last hope.

And Holmes is a failure. He does not secure the photograph or the letters; he is, in fact, led a very merry dance by Miss Adler, who was not for a moment taken in by the disguises Holmes adopted to win entrance to her home or secure the trust of her staff.

Yes, he discovered the whereabouts of the photograph, by watching her reaction when Watson ignited a smoke bomb, then followed up with a lusty cry of "fire." Because, he declares, a person always looks to the safety of their most treasured possession at moments of such calamitous import.

But he is unable to grab it now, and when he returns to the house, it is gone, replaced by an innocuous photo of Adler alone and a short note assuring him that the photograph is still in her possession and will remain there for as long as the grand duke leaves her alone. She retains it for protection, not for blackmail.

At which point the grand duke cannot help but voice his admiration for the woman. "Would she not have made an admirable queen? Is it not a pity she was not on my level?" To which Holmes agrees, although it is unlikely he is speaking of breeding and royal connections. Adler was indeed on a very different level to the king; she was, in fact, on a par with Holmes himself, with a brilliant mind and a cunning disposition. She was the first—and, as it transpires, the only female—person who ever got the better of the great Sherlock Holmes.

So much better, in fact, that when the king asks Holmes how he should be paid for his services, the detective asks for just one thing. The photograph of Irene Adler.

We can, and many authors and commentators have, conjecture Holmes's true feelings for Irene Adler. Love has been suggested; respect is implicit. Admiration. Longing. What, the scholars ask one another, might have transpired had Holmes and Adler met as equals alone, and not as adversaries. Her playfulness in outsmarting him is not a characteristic that Holmes ever shared, but he would certainly have recognized it and perhaps striven to understand it. Imagine that, a humorous Holmes!

Instead, we are left with the distinct impression of a lovelorn Holmes, despite the detective being apparently unable to even acknowledge such an emotion. Watson admits as much in the first lines of the story:

> To Sherlock Holmes she is always *the* woman. I have seldom heard him mention her under any other name. In his eyes she eclipses and predominates the whole of her sex. It was not that he felt any emotion akin to love for Irene Adler. All emotions, and that one particularly, were abhorrent to his cold, precise but admirably balanced mind. He was, I take it, the most perfect reasoning and observing machine that the world has seen, but as a lover he would have placed himself in a

false position. He never spoke of the softer passions, save with a gibe and a sneer. They were admirable things for the observer—excellent for drawing the veil from men's motives and actions. But for the trained reasoner to admit such intrusions into his own delicate and finely adjusted temperament was to introduce a distracting factor which might throw a doubt upon all his mental results. Grit in a sensitive instrument, or a crack in one of his own high-power lenses, would not be more disturbing than a strong emotion in a nature such as his. And yet there was but one woman to him, and that woman was the late Irene Adler, of dubious and questionable memory.

Adler has haunted the Holmes canon in other ways, too. When William Gillette staged the first-ever theatrical presentation of Holmes in 1899, "A Scandal in Bohemia" was among the tales that he at least partially incorporated. Movies in 1916 (with Gillette again cast as the detective) and 1922 (John Barrymore) restaged the story; so did Orson Welles's *Mercury Theatre on the Air* in 1938.

She is mentioned in Peter Cushing's television version of "The Adventure of the Blue Carbuncle," performing in London that Christmas and inspiring Holmes to acquire tickets for the event.

Author William S. Baring-Gould paints the couple in a degree of domestic bliss, working as a theatrical double act during the years that followed Holmes's supposed death; writer Carole Nelson Douglas portrayed Adler alone becoming a detective and following in Holmes's own footsteps. Authors have foisted children onto the couple, and embroiled them in adventures more far-fetched than any that Conan Doyle might have envisioned for them. And television and movies have enlisted some of the most beautiful actresses of their era to portray her, and with good reason.

Conan Doyle never revealed who, if anybody, inspired the creation and character of Irene Adler. But among the contemporary beauties who might have formed a model, the American actress Lillie Langtry, the lover of the future King of England (at this time Prince of Wales), Edward VII is seldom far from view. Neither is the dancer Lola Montez, lover of the King of Bavaria.

The screen has hastened to echo those beauties. Charlotte Rampling, Gayle Hunnicut, Morgan Fairchild and Anna Chancellor have all portrayed Adler in TV and cinema, but the aforementioned finest of all adaptations (and portrayals) was that delivered by Steven Moffat and Mark Gatiss, and actress Lara Pulver, as the opening story in the second series (2012) of the BBC's *Sherlock*.

In common with other adventures in the two series, "A Scandal in Belgravia" (note the slightly amended title) only hinted at existing stories, as opposed to remaking them. In this particular instance, Adler is a dominatrix who possesses compromising photographs of a member of the British royal family, a situation that leads Holmes (so unwillingly that he refuses to dress for this, or any other occasion) and Watson to Buckingham Palace, where they are charged with retrieving the pictures.

The battle of wits that follows, again, only skims the intricacies of the original scandal, preferring to layer on details of its own. But still it emerges as fresh an adaptation of Conan Doyle's original as any modern re-creation can. Indeed, *Sherlock* (as aforementioned) succeeds on many points, but most of all in its ability to both rewrite and reframe the century-plus-old stories. "A Scandal in Belgravia" may be the greatest of all the twenty-first-century Holmes adventures screened so far (an accolade that its casting of Pulver only amplifies), but it is not the only triumph that can be laid at the door of the original Bohemian rhapsody.

Holmes was the headline attraction in that issue of *The Strand*. But Conan Doyle was not alone in contributing to the masterpiece. The illustrator Sidney Paget, too, deserved all the accolades that would soon be showering down, for it was he who took Conan Doyle's original pen portrait of the sleuth and transformed it into an archetype.

So much about this commission and its successful execution was happenstance. To begin with, *The Strand*'s art editor W. H. J. Boot had not even considered Sidney Paget as a likely candidate for the commission and might not, in fact, even have heard of him. His first and only choice was Paget's brother Walter, a well-known artist whose past creations included excellent illustrated editions of *Robinson Crusoe* and *Treasure Island*.

According to legend, however, Boot could not recall Walter's first name, so he simply addressed the commission to "Mr. Paget, the Illustrator"—and Sidney opened it. As well he might. Well respected as a magazine artist in his own right, albeit of less renown than his brother, Sidney Paget accepted the commission as his own and quickly turned out the required pen-and-ink illustrations.

The familiar image of Holmes would develop only gradually. Not until the 1893 publication of "Silver Blaze" would the detective be granted his deerstalker hat and Inverness cape, the costume in which he is most frequently portrayed and recognized.

But even before then, Paget's Holmes became the definitive article, and of all the artists and actors who have attempted to create a Sherlock in the years since then, not one has truly successfully extracted him from the beaky-nosed, pointy-chinned, superciliously detached beanpole that stepped out of the pages of that first story in *The Strand*.

The Adventure of the Red-Headed League (first published in August 1891)

Conan Doyle was commissioned to produce one new Holmes adventure a month for an initial run of six months, and so August 1891 brought "The Adventure of the Red-Headed League," perhaps the most comical of all the Holmes stories. And, for explorers of period London, it is one of the most atmospheric.

There is something about the London Underground that is intrinsically Holmesian, despite the detective rarely setting foot within it, at least so far as the writings of Doctor Watson are concerned.

Perhaps it is because the two grew up together. Baker Street, the nearest tube station to Holmes's home, was among the first stops ever opened on the system, on January 10, 1863, and by 1892 the tracks that led from Baker Street had expanded their reach not only far across the city, but outward, punching into the countryside of Aylesbury, Buckinghamshire, some fifty miles distant.

Paget investigates the Red-Headed League.

It never forgot its most famous denizen, however, and by the 1980s, Baker Street greeted tourists and commuters alike with platform walls paneled with the distinctive silhouette of the locale's most famous resident.

As Holmes's closest station, it stands to reason that both he and his many visitors would have used Baker Street regularly, although only once does the station take a named place in a story, when Alexander Holder, the banker entrusted with the beryl coronet (in the adventure of that name), catches the tube to Baker Street on his way to visit Holmes.

Other locales served by the underground naturally feature in the stories, again without the stations themselves necessarily receiving an actual visit. But Holmes was a frugal man, and the underground was cheaper than taxis and faster than buses. He was a curious man, too, who could never have resisted the opportunity to observe so many different castes of Londoner at such intimately close quarters as the bustle of the underground permitted. And he was an intensely driven man who had already mapped out the streets of the surface in his mind. Of course he would be compelled to consign their underside to memory, too.

The tube of today is surprisingly similar to that of a century ago. Just as crowded, just as malodorous, just as noisy. True, modern architecture may have stepped over that of earlier years, with featureless steel and glass where warm brick and tile once stood, and the posters pasted to the wall across the tracks have changed, as well. In 1900, signage featured Old Gold cigarettes, Nestlé's Swiss Milk ("richest in cream"), property for sale and rent; today . . . well, today's commercial concerns are as gaudy and unconvincing below ground as they are above.

But the trains are quieter and cleaner, and though a map of the tube still resembles a bowl of multicolored strands flung against a wall, the London Transport Museum in Covent Garden is alive with books and pamphlets that detail the network's growth and history, from a single yellow line in the 1860s, to the spaghetti spectrum of today.

Aldersgate Underground station was one of the stops on that original single line, and one of the heartbeats of "The Adventure of the Red-headed League," the final stop on Holmes and Watson's investigation into the mysterious titular society. A straight ride on the Circle Line from Baker Street, Aldersgate took its name from one of the ancient gates into the city of London, living on in the name of the street that ran out from the gate itself. Indeed, at the time the story was written, despite Watson referring to it only as "Aldersgate," the underground station's full name was indeed Aldersgate Street and had been since it was opened in 1865.

It was 1910 before the name was shortened to what most travelers, like Watson, had long since abbreviated it, although one will search in vain for it on any tube map today. In 1924, the station became Aldersgate & Barbican and, in 1968, Barbican alone. Today, the streets that Holmes and Watson investigated during the course of this tale are buried beneath the prepossessing prison-like mass of the Barbican Centre, opened by Queen Elizabeth II in 1982 and, as recently as 2003, voted "London's ugliest building."

At the same time, it was scarcely a picturesque neighborhood even when Holmes visited, a warren of once reasonably grand houses and shops that had long since fallen into disrepair. The General Post Office had its headquarters there, a proud building though one that was already approaching the end of its usefulness (it was vacated in 1910), but the neighborhood itself was poor. It was the ideal location, then, for the dastardly deeds about to play out.

The story begins with the arrival at Baker Street of a struggling pawnbroker, Jabez Wilson. Business is down, debts are mounting. When his newly hired assistant, Vincent Spaulding, spots an advertisement in the newspaper offering well-paid work to redheaded applicants, the gloriously flame-haired Wilson applies and is the only man out of a lengthy line of hopeful carrot tops to be employed.

He is asked when his store is at its quietest. Afternoons, replies Wilson, and he is promptly hired, for the princely sum of four pounds a week, to visit the league's headquarters ever afternoon to copy out the *Encyclopedia Britannica*. This pointless commission goes along happily (and well remunerated) for a number of weeks, until the day Wilson turns up at the office as usual, to be greeted by a sign announcing that the league had been dissolved.

The Underground grew up with Sherlock, and he stalks its stations to this day.

© Steve and Betsy Mortensen

Understandably perplexed, and seriously regretting that lost four pounds a week, Wilson visits Holmes in the hope of discovering an explanation for this entire queer affair. Answers which Holmes is able to provide almost immediately after visiting Wilson's shop and discovering that it is next door to a bank. Whose vault, unbeknownst even to the bank manager, is firmly in the sights of the Red-Headed League, taking advantage of Wilson's absence from the shop to tunnel through the connecting wall. One look at the state of Vincent Spaulding's trousers, with their scuffed and filthy knees, is enough for Holmes. He unmasks Spaulding as the mastermind behind the heist, and the case is solved.

A Case of Identity (September 1891)

Mary Sutherland, a wealthy woman of independent means, is at her wit's end. Her fiancé, a shy and retiring chap named Hosmer Angel, has gone missing, and in his absence, Ms. Sutherland realizes how little about him she really knows.

He works in an office in Leadenhall Street, but which office? She has no clue.

What does he do there? She is uncertain.

Where does he live? He has never said—if she needs to write to him, she uses his post office box.

What does his handwriting look like? Who can say—all of his letters, including his signature, are typewritten.

All around, he is a veritable man of mystery, and yet only when he left her standing at the altar on their wedding day was her curiosity seemingly aroused.

Holmes, on the other hand, is barely stretched by her dilemma. Studying Ms. Sutherland's demeanor, he realizes she is both nearsighted and a little stupid. Investigating her background, he discovers a stepfather, Mr. Windibank, who is just five years her senior, and a rapacious mother who would love to get her hands on Ms. Sutherland's fortune. Delving deeper, he realizes that the mysterious Hosmer Angel only ever met with his fiancée while Windibank was allegedly out of the country on business. And that the two men use the same typewriter.

Given Ms. Sutherland's nearsightedness (and stupidity), Holmes deduces, it would be a moment's work for Windibank to disguise himself sufficiently to fool his stepdaughter. That he also appeared able to seduce her, of course, raises questions in the reader's mind that firmly plant this tale among the less savory echelons of Holmes's many cases; but that is what he has done, and the only question now on Holmes's mind is, how to proceed?

He knows Ms. Sutherland will not believe him, and he is aware that Windibank has, as yet, not broken any laws. But he does threaten to beat the man within an inch of his life unless the charade is brought to an end, and that appears to satisfy him. Well, that and the knowledge that one day, Windibank's iniquities will catch up with him and he will doubtless end his life with a rope around his neck. But that is a fate that must await some future turn of events, and a future detective. For now, Holmes declares, there is nothing more to be done.

The Boscombe Valley Mystery (October 1891)

For once, a stranger does *not* call at 221b to enlist Holmes and Watson in some mysterious personal quest. It is Inspector G. Lestrade of Scotland Yard who makes contact, the "little sallow rat-faced, dark-eyed fellow" whom Holmes first encountered in *A Study in Scarlet* and who, before this latest adventure is over, will have further been termed "a lean, ferret-like man, furtive and sly-looking."

These qualities may or may not have been valued in the London constabulary of the early 1890s, but they would have garnered a knowing nod from many a reader—who him- or herself might well have been on the receiving end of the kind of justice meted out by Lestrade's real-life contemporaries. Police corruption, according to a variety of period sources, was as rife in the 1890s as at any other time in criminal history. So, as evidenced by the force's continued failure to solve so many aforementioned criminal mysteries, was police incompetence.

Not since *A Study in Scarlet* had Holmes been called upon to investigate an actual murder. But the Boscombe Valley Mystery thrust him into the heart of a real doozy. The case with which Inspector Lestrade was requesting the detective's assistance took place out in the Herefordshire countryside, where a local man named Charles McCarthy had apparently been shot by his estranged son, James. A suggestion of doubt, however, clung to what lesser minds might have considered an open-and-shut case, and Holmes was employed to tug on the resultant threads.

Lestrade was correct to be cautious, and there was a signal lesson to all those critics of the police force, who believed they should simply weigh in with truncheons at the ready and set about anyone who looked even vaguely guilty. The law needs to be cautious, it needs to be sure, and Lestrade wasn't sure.

Rightfully so. Holmes quickly realizes that a third player has been on the scene. True, James was seen walking toward the lonely pool where his father's battered body was discovered; true, James had been carrying a gun. Perhaps, as an eyewitness reported, they had even argued and come to blows. But when James rushed to the lodge keeper's house, calling for help, it was not because he had killed the older man. It was because someone else, hidden away in the woods, had done so.

This someone, Holmes soon observes, was taller than James; was left-handed; walked with a limp. And then the backstory comes pouring out. McCarthy, during a youth spent living in Australia, had been a wagon driver on a gold convoy that was held up by bandits. One of those bandits, John Turner, had spent his share of the booty on moving to England and buying land. There, by some circuitously coincidental route, he met again with McCarthy, who threatened to expose the now respectable landowner's past unless he was kept provided with money and a home.

Enter McCarthy's son James, who fell in love with Turner's daughter. McCarthy conceived a fresh plot. If the pair married, then he could assume control of the entire estate and the ill-gotten fortune that lay behind it. Turner was backed into a corner and struck out in the only way left open to him.

So yes, Turner murdered McCarthy. But that, the solution of the crime, was not Holmes's concern. He was hired to prove James McCarthy's guiltlessness, and that he accomplished. Either the police would do the rest of the job, or they wouldn't. Either way, an innocent man remained free.

Case solved.

The Five Orange Pips (November 1891)

It is surprising—or, given the attitudes prevalent in late Victorian Britain, perhaps not—just how many of Sherlock Holmes's most dastardly adversaries turn out to be foreign: Subcontinental Indians, Utah Mormons, Australians.

England had its share of criminals, of course. Bank robbers and confidence tricksters, murderers and arsonists, burglars and footpads. But even the lovely Irene Adler had been an American, and here came another band of exotic miscreants, in the form of a band of fiendish American southerners.

The story, as it was relayed to Holmes and Watson by a young man named John Openshaw, began in 1869. In that year, Openshaw's uncle Elias returned to England after years spent living in Florida. Fighting on the Confederate side in the American Civil War, the elder Openshaw had risen to the rank of colonel, and the souvenirs of his time across the ocean were packed into trunks that he kept locked away in a room that John was prohibited from ever entering.

His curiosity was piqued, of course, but he obeyed his uncle's injunction. But then a second mystery presented itself, a letter postmarked in Pondicherry, India, that contained five orange pips and the inscription K.K.K. Soon after, the old colonel was found dead in a pool in the garden.

That was in 1883. Two years later, the mysterious K.K.K. sent another communiqué, postmarked Dundee and this time addressed to Elias's brother Joseph. "The papers," it demanded without any other word of explanation, were to be left on the sundial. Three days later, Joseph, too, was dead.

Holmes thought quickly. Given Uncle Elias's Stateside sojourn, K.K.K. unquestionably stood for the Ku Klux Klan, those hooded terrorists who rode out of the chaos at the end of the Civil War with a dream of a nation that was as white as the sheets they wore. Holmes asked whether John had any idea what the papers could be—the young man said no but recalled that Elias had burned a quantity of documents shortly before his death. Could they, Holmes wondered, have somehow related to the Klan and, more specifically, to that organization's sudden collapse in March 1869? Around the same time as Elias returned to England?

The following day, John Openshaw is found dead, his body floating in the River Thames.

Holmes has already guessed that whoever was mailing the letters was probably aboard a sailing ship. The delay between communications, and the world-spanning reach of the sender, dictated that. Checking the recent shipping records, he discovered just one vessel, a sloop out of Savannah, Georgia, *The Lone Star*, which had docked in Pondicherry in early 1883; in Dundee in early 1885; and in London just a week ago, connecting it to all three slayings.

Holmes notified the police, but he also mailed five orange pips to the captain of *The Lone Star*, which promptly upped anchor and departed. The murderous fiend would not escape, however, and we hope that his crew were just as ill-mannered as he. Running into a violent storm in the mid-Atlantic, *The Lone Star* vanished and was lost with all hands.

The Man with the Twisted Lip (December 1891)

The last of the six stories Conan Doyle was commissioned to write in his original contract with *The Strand*, "The Man with the Twisted Lip" opens with Watson making his way into one of the east end's most dangerous opium dens, to bring home the husband of one of his wife's closest friends.

The man, an addict, has been missing several days, and his despairing wife is in no doubt that he is crashed out in those unsavory surroundings. Thus are we introduced to a slice of Victorian London that history most mercifully swept away long ago.

Located on the (fictional) Upper Swandam Lane, the Bar of Gold offers such a reasonable facsimile of so many period vice holes that one could almost be glad *not* to have to cross its threshold. "Upper Swandam Lane," according to Watson, "is a vile alley lurking behind the high wharves which line the north side of the river to the east of London Bridge. Between a slop-shop and a gin-shop, approached by a steep flight of steps leading down to a black gap like the mouth of a cave, I found the den of which I was in search."

A hell hole of the blackest repute!

"Through the gloom one could dimly catch a glimpse of bodies lying in strange fantastic poses, bowed shoulders, bent knees, heads thrown back, and chins pointing upward, with here and there a dark, lack-lustre eye turned upon the newcomer. Out of the black shadows there glimmered little red circles of light, now bright, now faint, as the burning poison waxed or waned in the bowls of the metal pipes."

Thus spool out the opening breaths of "The Man with the Twisted Lip," a tale that puts one in mind of another story, by another author, in which the evils of another opium den are laid bare to the attentions of another great detective. *The Moonstone*, by Wilkie Collins, is generally regarded as the first detective novel ever published in the English language. Certainly it beat Conan Doyle to the punch by a full two decades; originally published in 1868, a serial in Charles Dickens's *All the Year Round* magazine, sundry episodes within *The Moonstone* arguably offered up the bare bones around which Conan Doyle would place any amount of Sherlockian flesh. Collins's den, by the way, is called the Wheel of Fortune, but so black is the air, so foul is its reputation, that it is difficult to tell the two apart.

Arriving at the Bar of Gold, Watson is astonished to find Holmes has got there before him, albeit on a very different mission. Disguised as an old man, he is seeking information about a missing man, a respectable country businessman named Neville St Clair. He, too, has gone missing, with just one clue as to his whereabouts. In London on a mission of her own, his wife is certain that she espied him in an upstairs window of this same den.

But she was forbidden entry by the den's Indian owner, a Lascar, and when she returned with the police, they initially found nothing. A search of the room in which she thought she saw her husband revealed it to merely be the home of a filthy beggar named Hugh Boone.

A more thorough search, however, turned up clothes that she recognized as her missing husband's, and when the missing man's coat was discovered in the river just outside the opium den, its pockets weighted down with coins, the police arrested Boone for St Clair's murder.

It was, they decide, a closed case, and Holmes was initially inclined to agree with them. But then the bereaved Mrs. St Clair received a letter from her husband, dated after his disappearance, and showed it to Holmes. He hastened to the police station where the still-filthy Boone was being held, washed the man's face—and revealed the missing St Clair.

The man, Holmes learned, had been living a double life, a country gentleman by day, a professional beggar by night, earning enough to both finance his family's lifestyle and pay off a serious debt. Needless to say, his wife had no idea of any of this, and Holmes agreed to keep the wretched man's secret, so long as he sought out a more respectable profession in the future. St Clair acceded, and perhaps it is the reader alone who is left with a vague sense of unease as Conan Doyle resorted again to the notion of a mere, if masterful, "case of identity" being the solution to what had hitherto felt like a gripping mystery.

As we have already mentioned, *"The Man with the Twisted Lip"* was the sixth and final Sherlock Holmes story of Conan Doyle's initial commission. But of course the story, and the success, could never be allowed to rest there. Greenhough Smith promptly demanded a further half dozen, at the same generous rates of pay, and Conan Doyle naturally agreed.

Yet he was not altogether content with the manner in which his career was panning out. No matter that Sherlock Holmes was firmly established as the literary sensation of the age. No matter that his name was invoked even in "serious" news reportage, as journalists and other observers looked on at cases that had apparently perplexed the regular authorities and wished that a real-life Sherlock Holmes could descend and solve the crime in minutes.

Conan Doyle continued to regard his creation as a mere trifle, at least when compared with all of the other ideas that were also buzzing around in his head—the novels that he could have been writing, the stories he could have been dreaming. Almost all were placed to one side, barreled out of the way by the behemoth that was Sherlock Holmes. He did complete one novel, a somewhat turgid tale of the Huguenot persecutions in seventeenth-century France, *The Refugees: A Tale of Two Continents*, and began work on another, set during the era of the Napoleonic Wars, *The Great Shadow*. But there was so much more he could have been writing.

Even the ease with which he reduced his Holmes stories to formula did not lessen his despair. He estimated each tale took a week to complete, from first conception to final polish. First he would come up with a problem and a solution. Then he would design the characters and sketch the tale. Then, with all these ingredients in place, he would settle down at the desk in his study, and if he could turn out three thousand words a day, he considered himself doing well.

The money was too good to spurn. He set to work on the next six tales.

The Adventure of the Blue Carbuncle (January 1892)

"The Adventure of the Blue Carbuncle" is another of the tales that allows the Holmesian scholar to set forth on a voyage of discovery around London, this time with the emphasis on the city's pubs.

Many public houses appear in the adventures, and some will elude even the most redoubtable modern-day detective. These include the Alpha Inn in "The Adventure of the Blue Carbuncle." No gazetteer will ever unerringly guide you to its location. But if you cross the road from the British Museum and make your way to "the corner of one of the streets which run down into Holborn," the Museum Tavern is likely enough the hostelry in which we can reenact the revelries enjoyed by Henry Baker and the Goose Club.

There has been a pub on this site since at least the early eighteenth-century. Originally called the Dog and Duck, so named from a hunting cry, its lease was issued by the Duke of Bedford in September 1854 and permitted one Richard John Maddren to open the Museum Tavern, opposite the equally newly opened British Museum.

"A solid, plain pub," wrote Louis T. Stanley a century later, in his indispensable *The Old Inns of London*, "with an excellent snack-bar patronised by students and intellectuals."

And goose enthusiasts.

Other Holmesian hostelries await. The Anerley Arms in Norwood, not far from another of Conan Doyle's own residences, is a bit player in "The Adventure of the Norwood Builder," for example. But for now, make your way down to Northumberland Street, and there, one of modern London's best-known Sherlockian attractions awaits.

The Sherlock Holmes public house has been here since 1957, when what was then called the Northumberland Arms was selected as the final resting place for a Sherlockian exhibition that was originally created for the Festival of Britain in 1951 and had been seeking a permanent home ever since.

Of course the pub was renamed in honor of its new theme, and with Conan Doyle's family providing their own support, the life and times of Holmes were placed upon permanent public display.

Stuffed and mounted, but no less fearsome for that, the head of the Hound of the Baskervilles is here. So are Watson's old service revolver and Holmes's pipe, displayed within a re-creation of the detective's private study.

Holmes might balk at some of the prices charged, though. In 1914, a pint of beer cost 3d (around 25 cents at the contemporary exchange rate), at a time when the average weekly wage was around one pound, fourteen shillings, and fourpence—eight dollars, give or take. Roughly a century later, that same pint costs three pounds—or the equivalent of more than two weeks' wages in Sherlock's day.

It's enough to make you turn to drink.

Published in *The Strand*'s Christmas edition, "The Adventure of the Blue Carbuncle" opens with Watson dropping by 221b to wish season's greetings upon his friend, only to find Holmes deep in contemplation of a rather battered old hat.

A man named Peterson had delivered it; this hat and a Christmas goose had been dropped by a man during an encounter with some ruffians on the street, and Peterson simply sought Holmes's assistance in returning the hat to its rightful owner—a Mr. Henry Baker, who then makes himself known after an advertisement is published in a newspaper.

The goose, needless to say, is destined for the Petersons' Christmas table. But Peterson soon returns to see Holmes after his wife discovers some most unexpected stuffing within the bird. A blue carbuncle, a jewel that Holmes recognizes as having been stolen from the Countess of Morcar during her recent visit to London.

But how did it wind up in a goose's crop?

Baker, the bird's original owner, has no idea. But he sets Holmes on the trail of the salesman he purchased it from, a man named Breckinridge, who, it transpires, has had just about enough of people coming to him with stupid questions about geese. It seems that someone else wants to track down the carbuncle. This individual fortuitously turns up just as Holmes is about to take his leave, and he spills the entire story—a tale of a panicked sneak thief who, convinced he is about to be apprehended for the crime, feeds the jewel to what he thought was the most recognizable of the geese that his sister is fattening up for sale. The goose has a distinctive black bar on its tail. His sister agrees to make him a gift of the bird—without mentioning that she has two that fit that description. Inevitably, the thief, James Ryder, is presented with the wrong one and has been seeking the other ever since.

Further details of the crime emerge. The countess's own maid was Ryder's accomplice. Another man, Horner, had been framed for the crime. At any other time of the year, Holmes would simply have sent for Lestrade immediately. But it is Christmas, and Holmes was hired merely to return the hat to Henry Baker. The decision to involve himself in the rest of the mystery was his own. If the police want to find the true thief (Holmes is certain the case against Horner will be dropped), then let them do the legwork.

Extracting only Ryder's pledge to leave the country immediately, Holmes allows the man to go free.

Happy Christmas.

The Adventure of the Speckled Band (February 1892)

A tangled web of bedraggled family finance lies behind one of the most imaginative of all the Sherlock Holmes adventures, a once prosperous family brought to near ruin by a succession of wastrel heirs and now struggling to provide even a modest annuity for the two daughters in the event of their marriages. There is but one solution. The girls must die.

This much Holmes swiftly deduces from the story he hears from the distraught Helen Stoner—distraught because her sister, Julia, newly engaged to be wed, had passed away on the eve of her marriage in the most mysterious circumstances, with a scream and the final words, "It was the band, the speckled band!" Now Helen has announced her own wedding plans, and she fears she might be about to meet a similar ghastly end.

Doctor Roylott, the girls' stepfather and sole guardian following their mother's death sometime earlier, *is* the obvious culprit, because it is he who will have to fork out for the annuity. Neither does he seem overly concerned about raising anybody's suspicions. He is a violent man, short-tempered and abusive. His prized collection of exotic pets has the run of the house, and so does a band of gypsies to whom Roylott has rented some rooms. The girls obviously lived in fear of both his moods and his peculiar household, and Helen continues to do so.

When Roylott informs her that she is to move her possessions into her late sister's bedroom, she does so, and her nights are beset by misgivings: strange noises that sound through the room at night; a mysterious bell cord that disappears into a ventilator above her bed; a bed that is bolted to the ground.

Neither is his stepdaughter the only person he seeks to intimidate. Holmes, too, comes face to face with this most disagreeable man, when Roylott visits 221b to demand to know why Helen was there. When Holmes refuses to answer his questions, the rogue takes a fire iron from the grate and bends it. He is, his actions seem to say, an uncommonly strong man.

Holmes is not scared (and returns the poker to its original shape with his bare hands once his visitor has departed). Traveling to the family home, he and Watson arrange with Helen that she will spend the night in her old bedroom, while her visitors take up their station in Julia's room. And there, they solve the riddle.

Roylott had spent time in India. He owned a menagerie of exotic beasts, some of which he had trained to answer simple commands. That low whistling that Helen heard, for instance? It was the sound of Roylott directing the deadliest of all his pets, an Indian swamp adder, to descend the bell rope over the bed and await the slightest movement from the sleeping girl below. It had put paid to Julia already. Now it merely waits for Helen to have a restless night. The speckled band.

But Holmes is ready for it, attacking the snake before it can attack him, and sending it hurtling back up the bell rope, through the ventilator, and into Roylott's room. There, infuriated and frightened, the beast sinks its deadly fangs into the first person it sees. Roylott is dead, and Holmes vaguely muses that the responsibility for the man's death in many ways rests with him.

But, he shrugs, "I cannot say that it is likely to weigh very heavily upon my conscience," and there we have the answer to a question that is often asked about Holmes's sense of morality and humanity. He is not quite an advocate of "an eye for an eye." But he would have made a good dentist.

The Adventure of the Engineer's Thumb (March 1892)

In this tale, slight and seldom cited among Sherlock Holmes's most exacting or engrossing adventures, a young consultant hydraulic engineer, Victor Hatherley, is visiting Doctor Watson to have a rather nasty wound dressed. His thumb has been severed in an industrial accident, and only as he tells his tale does Watson find himself wondering whether it might be a case for Holmes. It is, the doctor's narration points out, one of just two cases that he brought personally to the great

Sidney Paget's art played a major part in confirming the Holmesian imagery.

detective's notice, and the bored reader might well decide there is a reason for that.

Hatherley, it transpires, had received a commission from a Colonel Lysander Stark. He was to journey to a country house where the colonel had recently installed a hydraulic press, for the purpose of compressing fuller's earth into bricks. He would be paid generously for his time—fifty guineas—and the only condition he was required to abide by was to keep the entire enterprise secret.

Incidental details allow Holmes to shine. Hatherley reports that it was a long carriage ride from the railroad station to the house. Holmes, once he has ascertained that the house is just a short distance from the station, points out that the cunning colonel disguised its location by driving six miles past the house and then turning around to drive six miles back.

Ill omens, too, flash. Upon arriving at the house, Hatherley is warned by a woman to make his escape while he still can. He ignores her, but he has a growing sense of unease concerning this entire operation. These misgivings are borne out when he examines the press and realizes, far from compressing fuller's earth, it is being used to manufacture small metallic discs. He has stumbled upon a counterfeiting operation, and when the colonel realizes that Hatherley knows the secret, he attacks.

Only narrowly does Hatherley escape from the machine, which the colonel has switched on in the hope of crushing the hapless engineer. But leaping from a window, he is less fortunate, as the man brings a cleaver down on his hand and hacks off the thumb that led him to Watson in the first place.

There will be no comeuppance for the colonel and his accomplices. No matter that Holmes, Watson, and a deputation of police make straight for the house. They arrive to discover that, in the scuffle, Hatherley's lamp had set fire to the press, a blaze that spread in turn to the rest of the house.

The counterfeiters have fled with whatever treasures they could salvage. The case, such as it is (and it really isn't much—Holmes's greatest deduction was figuring out where the house was), is solved. It is up to Scotland Yard to bring the counterfeiters to justice.

The Adventure of the Noble Bachelor (April 1892)

It is surprising, when one actually sits with the original Sherlock Holmes stories and pushes all awareness of his brilliance and renown from one's head, just how mundane so many of these "adventures" are.

How even the word "adventure" often seems somehow misplaced. For, brilliant as Holmes's deductions appear, the mysteries themselves seem scarcely worth his attention, and one smiles wryly while watching the twenty-first-century Sherlock, as Holmes airily dismisses any number of would-be clients because their problems are so beneath his contempt.

His nineteenth-century predecessor, though he would occasionally protest that the world was too dull, apparently had few such qualms.

Hatty, the American-born bride (yes, another perfidious foreigner) of Lord Robert St. Simon, has disappeared, vanishing from the reception at her father's home immediately after their wedding service.

Nothing had prepared His Lordship for such a turn of events, not even the fact that Hatty was uncharacteristically snappy toward him once the ring was on her finger, and when pressed to recall any unusual or even mundane event at the ceremony itself, the baffled lord draws a total blank—well, apart from that moment when Hatty dropped her wedding bouquet and a gent seated in the front pew picked it up and returned it to her. Oh, and a minor scene involving one of St. Simon's former paramours, a dancer named Flora Miller.

There was nothing, however, that could have caused his radiant bride to abruptly announce "a sudden indisposition" and vanish.

Holmes looks deeper and discovers Hatty has since been sighted entering Hyde Park with a strange man. Her wedding dress and ring have been found on the banks of the Serpentine, the so picturesquely named lake that sits in the heart of the park. And Holmes immediately sees through the mystery; he has, in fact, encountered similar cases in the past. He simply needs to locate Hatty to fill in the details. Which she does.

Hatty was already married but had assumed her husband dead and gone after he disappeared while prospecting for gold, back before she left her American homeland. In fact, he had survived the Apache Indian raid in which he was said to have perished and, having traced Hatty to London, took up position in the front row of the church. He passed her a note when she dropped her bouquet—in shock, one assumes, at seeing him—and she fled to rejoin him at the first opportunity she found.

The Adventure of the Beryl Coronet (May 1892)

Ah, this is a good case, albeit a very simple one.

A leading banker, Alexander Holder, has recently taken temporary possession (as collateral for a loan) of the Beryl Coronet, a fabulous jewel so valuable that he dare not leave it in a bank vault. Instead he takes it home, where, to his horror, he awakens to find his own son (a habitual gambler and incipient wastrel) apparently in the act of prizing three of the beryls from the coronet.

The beryls have now disappeared.

Desperate to avoid scandal, Holder instead invites Holmes to try to trace the missing jewels. Immediately, a range of suspects far more believable than son Arthur presents itself: the servants; Holder's niece Mary; the maid's peg-legged boyfriend; or even a Knight of the Realm, Arthur's longtime friend and professional rake Sir George Burnwell. Or maybe two of them acting in concert?

Holmes studies footprints in the snow outside the house. He speaks with each of his suspects. And he retrieves the jewels. The felons, Mary and Burnwell, escape, but Holmes is not perturbed. Mary was foolish, not only to involve herself with a man such as Burnwell, but also to depart with him. "I think that we may safely say," Holmes muses, " . . . that whatever her sins are, they will soon receive a more than sufficient punishment."

The Adventure of the Copper Beeches (June 1892)

The twelfth and, for the time being, the final Sherlock Holmes adventure, "The Adventure of the Copper Beeches," hinges around the misadventures of Violet Hunter, a young lady who has just received an offer to work as a governess at almost three times her previous salary.

Her employer Jephro Rucastle, however, has a veritable shopping list of bizarre stipulations, all of which he blames upon his wife's fancies. Violet must wear the clothes they ask her to wear; she must sit wherever they ask her to sit; she must accede to Rucastle's hobby of amateur photography; and, most important of all, her long hair must be cut short.

Holmes is intrigued, but of course there is no mystery to be solved until one presents itself. Violet announces she will take the job; Holmes reminds her that he is just a telegram away; and two weeks later he receives one, begging him to meet her in Winchester, a city close by Rucastle's estate at Copper Beeches.

There Violet describes further peculiarities. Rucastle was a born comedian, but his wife never even smiles at his jokes. The child she was hired to look after is an absolute brute, who takes particular delight in torturing small animals. One entire wing of the house has been shut off and darkened. The servants, a married couple named

Sidney Paget on the trail of the beryl coronet.

Toller, seem both disagreeable and, in Mr. Toller's case, permanently drunk. And the grounds are patrolled by a great mastiff dog that is forever kept so hungry that Violet has been warned never to leave the house after dark.

More mysteries: She found a collection of clothes, and locks of hair, in a locked drawer that were identical to her own. And one of those dresses in particular, an electric blue one, seemed to have so bewitched Rucastle that he regularly requests her to wear it, then sit in a certain chair in the front room, reading. She is also ordered never to turn around to the window behind her, but with her curiosity aroused, a small mirror allows her to steal a glance, and she sees a man standing in the garden, watching her.

It is the darkened wing that most intrigues Holmes—with good reason, as it swiftly transpires. For somebody is being held prisoner there: Rucastle's daughter Alice, who has fallen in love with a neighborhood man and who, in a blatant reiteration of the speckled-band adventure, stands to receive upon her marriage a handsome annuity from her late mother's estate that Rucastle cannot afford.

His attempts to force Alice to renounce her fiancé are in vain; rather, they succeed only in driving the girl to sickness and, ultimately, brain fever. So he locks her away in the mystery wing, while hiring Violet—whose short hair and taste in clothes echo Alice to a T—to go about her day-to-day business without any care for the man who stares lovelorn into the house.

The plot unravels, the mystery is solved. Rucastle is savaged by his own mastiff while trying to prevent Alice's escape, and he ends his life an invalid. Alice and her fiancé depart and marry. And Watson, briefly, entertains hopes that Holmes might have finally fallen in love with a woman, for his attentions to and interest in Violet certainly exceeded any he had previously exhibited.

But no, it was the mystery that entranced Holmes, not the woman at its heart, and while she goes off to work as the principal at a girls' school (a post that Holmes arranged for her), he returns to 221b, a bachelor still.

8

The Adventure of the Memoirs of Sherlock Holmes

In which Conan Doyle composes his Second Series of Short Stories, we Reveal the Truth about Holmes's Most Beloved Catch-Phrase, and the Author arrives at a Most Singular Determination

The series was over.

Twelve stories that posterity would recall as (and an imminent best-selling collected edition would title) *The Adventures of Sherlock Holmes* had been published, and Conan Doyle was now among the most successful, most admired authors in the land.

So successful, so admired, that when Greenhough Smith approached him about writing a dozen more stories, Conan Doyle seriously considered refusing.

Perhaps the tales, once he started writing them, were easy enough. But the plotting, the designing, the time spent on Holmes that could have been better devoted to weightier projects, all of these things added up to an onerous and perhaps even repetitive routine.

He sought an escape route. The thousand pounds per story that his agent demanded of *The Strand* was one. No publisher, Conan Doyle believed, would be foolhardy enough to pay such an exorbitant rate for a mere short story.

But George Newnes, presiding over the greatest circulation rise he could ever have dreamed of, barely batted an eyelid. And so, Conan Doyle gritted his teeth and settled down to create the next twelve adventures of Sherlock Holmes.

The Adventure of Silver Blaze (December 1892)

This is the story that, upon release as a movie in 1941, lured American viewers in with the title *Murder at the Baskervilles* (its UK title was simply *Silver Blaze*), an attempt to draw upon the success of the hound, of course, derived solely from the story's setting. And what a setting it is.

Dartmoor is one of the seven wonders of Britain, a vast expanse of wilderness that is simultaneously among the most beautiful and the most desolate landscapes in the country. Covering some 368 square miles on the southwestern peninsula, it is pocked by great granite sculptures known as *tors* but is littered, too, by bogs and swamp.

Britain's largest concentration of Neolithic and Bronze Age remains are here, ranging from ancient field systems to standing stones and the remains of settlements—relics of a time when the moors' climate (and therefore landscape) was considerably drier than it is today. Of more recent vintage, ruined farmhouses and the remains of a once prosperous tin-mining industry rise out of nowhere, while parts of the moor have also been used by the armed forces for training purposes since the Napoleonic Wars two centuries ago.

Perhaps Dartmoor's best-known features, and certainly its most notorious inhabitants, however, are its supernatural ones. Pixies live here, and so does "the beast of Dartmoor," a large black cat. A headless horseman rides the moor's narrow lanes; a bridge is haunted by a pair of disembodied hairy hands that will seize the steering wheel of any unsuspecting motorist and force him into the river. There are ghosts aplenty, and of course, the Devil dropped by once, to seize the soul of a gambler named Jan, and damaged a village church tower in the process.

The Wish Hounds are a pack of hellish curs that ride in search of the souls of unbaptized babies; and of course there is a great spectral black dog whose legend inspired Conan Doyle to write *The Hound of the Baskervilles*.

Sherlock Holmes's first visit to Dartmoor, however, had a considerably more mundane purpose. For days, the newspapers of the land had been transfixed by the disappearance of one of the most successful race horses of the age, Silver Blaze, and the murder of the horse's trainer, John Straker. A massive blow to the head had killed him instantly.

The police, headed up by Inspector Gregory, had already taken a man into custody, a London bookmaker named Fitzroy Simpson. Holmes, however, was convinced that there was more to the story than meets the eye, including the most vexatious question of all: Where was the horse?

There was, after all, no reason for Simpson to kill the animal. Neither was there any real point in him having stolen it. What was he going to do with it once he got it home? The answer, Holmes is convinced, is closer to hand than any outlandish conjecture might allow, and so it proves.

Recalling the case of "The Man with the Twisted Lip," and the wonders that can be accomplished with a pot of paint, Holmes approaches an altogether different-looking nag and announces, "You have only to wash his face and his leg in spirits of wine, and you will find that he is the same old Silver Blaze as ever." The animal has been disguised.

Other mysteries arise and are unraveled: A guard dog that did not bark at the sight of an intruder in the stable. A normally vigilant stable boy who is discovered to have been drugged with opium, despite eating only a meal provided at Straker's own table. A small blade that was found with the body, matching that which caused a sudden outbreak of laming among another farmer's sheep. And a milliner's bill in the dead man's pocket made out to one William Derbyshire. This, Holmes quickly discovers, was a pseudonym that Straker himself used.

The clues pile up. Straker was in need of fast cash to satisfy an unexpectedly expensive mistress. First he drugged the stable boy, and then he crossed the stable without alerting the dog . . . because the dog knew him and would not, therefore, sound the alarm.

He led Silver Blaze out onto the moor, intending to fix an upcoming race by injuring the horse with the knife—he had practiced on the sheep, so knew what he was doing. But so, it seems, did Silver Blaze. The horse lashed out, delivering Straker a fatal blow with one of its hooves.

There are a few inconsistencies in the story, which the alert reader may or may not stew upon once it has been read. But "The Adventure of Silver Blaze" remains one of Holmes's best-loved adventures, and one of Conan Doyle's, too. Making a list of what he considered to be the best Holmes stories, the author ranked it in thirteenth place.

The Adventure of the Cardboard Box (January 1893)

One of the most controversial of all the Sherlock Holmes stories, "The Adventure of the Cardboard Box" endured a checkered history even at its own author's hands. It was excluded from the first edition of *The Memoirs of Sherlock Holmes*, the bound volume that collected the second series of Holmes stories from *The Strand*, and while the first American edition did include it, it was swiftly excised from there, too.

Conan Doyle also removed a short passage regarding Holmes's ability to read Watson's mind and placed it in another story (*The Resident Patient*); and finally, the adventure's very subject matter seems to have alarmed and repulsed readers of the age. How many other stories, after all, begin with a woman opening a package that has just been delivered to her home and discovering three human ears within?

Despite the gory nature of the discovery, Lestrade was not, initially, impressed. The woman, Susan Cushing, had recently let rooms to three medical students, only to evict them because of their boisterous behavior—a scenario with which Conan Doyle, remembering his own high-spirited youth, might well have felt some sympathy.

A scene from Sidney Paget's vision of the Cardboard Box adventure.

Another scene from the Cardboard Box.

Clearly, the police inspector decides, the package was a prank by those same students. Ears could not be that hard to come by in an environment such as theirs, and besides, the package was postmarked Belfast, the hometown of one of the students.

Holmes is less certain. The ears were preserved in common salt. No medical student would have resorted to that. The ears had clearly been hacked off the heads where they once resided. Even the dullest student would have been tidier. The handwriting on the package showed the sender to be ill-educated, and the knot used to tie the package suggested he was a sailor.

"HE LIFTED THE LITTLE CHILD."

Rarely did Holmes get things as wrong as he would when confronted with the yellow-faced child.

No, the ears belonged to people who had met a far grislier end. Susan Cushing's sister Mary, for instance, who has not been seen for some time. Her lover, too, has vanished. But not her husband, an ill-educated sailor named Jim Browner, who Holmes swiftly reveals had murdered them both, then hacked off the ears as an (admittedly ill-conceived) warning to the third of the Cushing sisters, Sarah—who once shared an address with Susan, and whom he blames for the breakdown of his marriage in the first place.

An ugly tale, then, and a brutal one. But, paradoxically, one of the most suspenseful of them all.

The Adventure of the Yellow Face (February 1893)

Holmes is bored. Bored, bored, bored. Visitors bring him cases and he solves them before the story has even been told. So bored that when he returns home from a walk to discover he has missed a potential client, he amuses himself by examining the pipe that the visitor inadvertently left behind and delivering a full physical description of the man. When he returns shortly after, he proves every one of Holmes's assertions true.

Grant Munro is distraught. His wife Effie, the widow of an American (shall we even effect surprise at that?) who died in one of the century's yellow-fever outbreaks, has been deceiving him. She has been paying secret visits to a cottage not far from the family home in Norbury (close by the Conan Doyle family's own residence). There, Munro is outraged to discover when he follows her one day, a yellow-faced man lives in considerable luxury, with a picture of Effie on the mantelpiece.

Clearly, decides Holmes, her first husband did not die. Rather, like that other presumed-dead American of his recent acquaintance ("The Adventure of the Noble Bachelor"), reports of his demise were premature, and he has now set up house close by his inadvertently bigamous spouse, perhaps for reasons of blackmail, perhaps out of undying love.

Either way, Holmes is going to unmask the man, marching to the cottage while Effie is visiting, and tearing the mask (for Holmes had already deduced that he wore one) from the husband—and then stepping back in amazement as he, Watson, and Munro instead find a young girl staring back at them.

Effie explains. Her first husband was an Afro-American, and their daughter Lucy, therefore, was of mixed race. This was major stigma in the Victorian world, and one that she was convinced no decent man would want to entertain under his own roof. She claimed, therefore, that both husband and daughter had been killed by the fever; in fact, Lucy survived and had been brought to England by Effie, and installed in the cottage.

All eyes turn to Munro. How would he react? With love, of course! "He lifted the little child, kissed her, and then, still carrying her in his arms, he held his other hand out to his wife and turned towards the door."

Now Watson is left to bear the brunt of a thwarted Holmes's injured pride. How could he have got the circumstances so wrong? How had his natural fallibility failed him so publicly? How could this least humble of men ever recover from such a blow?

But the detective, too, surprises him. "Watson," he says. "If it should ever strike you that I am getting a little overconfident in my powers, or giving less pains to a case than it deserves, kindly whisper 'Norbury' in my ear, and I shall be infinitely obliged to you."

The Adventure of the Stock-Broker's Clerk (March 1893)

Of all the peculiarities that pock the world of Sherlock Holmes, most refreshing is the preponderance of people who believe a recent job offer is too good to be true. In a world (then as now) overrun by those who would get something for nothing, then defend their culpability in any subsequent ill-doing by declaring that they never look a gift horse in the face, the fact that there should be so many folk who wish only to do the right thing is surely gratifying in the extreme.

Either that, or it makes you realize just how damnably suspicious people are.

Thankfully, in the instances raised by Conan Doyle, they are right to be suspicious. Because there are a lot of hoaxers and confidence tricksters out there. Think of that the next time you drop a line to that nice Nigerian banker you met online.

Hall Pycroft has been offered a new job. A trained stockbroker's clerk about to take up a new position with a London-based firm, he has instead been tempted by the offer of a managership with a hardware distribution company being set up in France.

Simply for accepting the post, he will be paid £100, and the only caveat is he should not yet resign his post in stockbroking.

Holmes, who one assumes must be very bored again, agrees with the lad. This is very peculiar indeed. So he, Watson, and Pycroft set off to Birmingham, where the latter is to meet his new employers, the twin brothers Harry and Arthur Pinner. The brothers—and this also arouses suspicions—are so identical that they even have a gold tooth in the same place.

The trio arrive to discover Harry Pinner staring aghast at a newspaper article and preparing to commit suicide. The story is of an attempted break-in at the very stockbrokers office where Pycroft was expected to start work. Pinner, who is indeed an only child, had arranged for the break-in to be committed by an accomplice who would have started work at the company masquerading as young Pycroft.

Something went awry, however. The accomplice did undertake the break-in, but he was not alone. He was joined by his brother, who claimed to be Pinner. And in the course of the burglary, a nightwatchman was murdered. Even worse, the police had captured both miscreants, swiftly unraveled their true identities, and uncovered the brains behind the operation, too. All three could now expect to be hanged

None of this reflects especially brightly on Holmes, whose sole role in the adventure was as an observer, charged with delivering a few sharp (but ultimately irrelevant) deductions, and a nice bon mot to wrap up the tale.

"Human nature is a strange mixture, Watson. You see that even a villain and murderer can inspire such affection that his brother turns to suicide when he learns that his neck is forfeited."

The Adventure of the "Gloria Scott" (April 1893)

There have been many attempts to document and detail the life of the young Sherlock Holmes—that is, the detective in the years before he met Doctor Watson and submitted to having his adventures chronicled.

Few, however, sprang from the imagination of Conan Doyle, but when they did, it was presumably the consequence of the same public demand that inspired all those later stories, movies, and imaginings. People cared.

"The Adventure of the 'Gloria Scott'" is not one of Holmes's most gripping sagas. Indeed, the juvenile who emerges from its pages strikes the modern reader as a quite insufferable know-it-all, not yet mature enough to at least couch his abilities in the veneer of respectability that is conveyed by adulthood (and a good image—the cape and deerstalker were firmly established now). He's simply a precocious brat whose relentless quest to show how smart he is would surely grate on any older person's sensibilities were they to be exposed to it for any period of time.

Pity, then, old Mr. Trevor, a justice of the peace in the tranquil English countryside of Norfolk, whose own peace is about to be roundly shattered by the arrival on vacation of his son Victor and the boy's college friend Sherlock Holmes. Holmes could not even look around the room without delivering a succession of deductions . . . some brilliant, some mundane, some impertinent, and one so personal that no sooner were the words were out of his mouth than the old man had passed out.

It was the suggestion that Mr. Trevor had once been close to a person whose initials were J. A. that did it. Close enough that the old man wanted to forget this person altogether. It was a former lover, the justice explained once he had recovered, but the young Holmes, as unaware as he would ever be of when a matter should be allowed to drop, did not accept that as an answer.

For now, however, he had no alternative. He returned to college and the chemistry experiments that entertained him there, and he put the mysterious J. A. out of his head. Forgot, too, about Hudson, the old shipmate of the elder Mr. T's who came to call one evening, a visit that seemed to send the justice reaching for the bottle before he had even said hello. But it all came rushing back to him when he received a telegram from Victor, begging him to return to Norfolk, where the old man was dying. He was, in fact, dead by the time Holmes reached the house. And the cause of death? Nobody knew, but it was certainly precipitated by the receipt of a certain letter . . .

Victor detailed events at the house during the seven weeks since Holmes took his leave. How the old shipmate Hudson had proven a most disagreeable type of chap, forever complaining, forever demanding. He broke every rule of civilized behavior. He drove the servants to distraction. He provoked Victor to the point where the younger man would have taken him outside and knocked seven bells out of him, had Hudson not seemed so old and frail.

Yet Victor's father brushed all complaints aside. Hudson was his guest and could do as he please.

Finally, Hudson announced he was leaving. Norfolk bored him; he was bound for Fordingbridge, a small town in the notoriously more exciting county of Hampshire, where he intended visiting another old naval pal, Beddoes. And it was from Fordingbridge that Mr. Trevor received the letter that all believed had prompted his demise.

Unfortunately, it made no sense to anyone. Anyone, that is, aside from Holmes.

"The supply of game for London is going steadily up. Head-keeper Hudson, we believe, has been now told to receive all orders for fly-paper and for preservation of your hen pheasant's life."

He sensed a cipher and worked to crack it. Which, of course, he did. Reading only every third word, Holmes was able to discern a far more sinister note. "The game is up. Hudson has told all. Fly for your life."

Blackmail!

A conversation with the doctor who had attended Trevor's final moments on earth provided the next clue, directing Holmes to a locked Japanese cabinet. Inside was found the old man's confession.

He himself was the mysterious J. A. ! Once, a lifetime before, he had been known under the name of James Armitage, a bank clerk who was found guilty of embezzlement and sentenced to transportation to the prison colonies of Australia. Aboard the ship *Gloria Scott*, sailing for that benighted shore, Armitage/Trevor uncovered a plot to hijack the ship, financed by a fellow prisoner and involving not only much of the crew, but the ship's chaplain.

The mutineers arose, the ship was taken, and the only outstanding question at the end of the battle was, what should become of the handful of loyal crewmen who had fought so hard against the criminals?

Armitage, and some others, argued that they should be kept alive, perhaps as prisoners. Others, the majority of the mutineers, voted for their immediate execution.

Horrified, Armitage and his friends—one of whom was the man Beddoes—declared that if the men were to be murdered, then they would not be party to the atrocity. Rather, they would take their chances on the open sea, in one of the ship's lifeboats. And so they were cast adrift—and just in time. The battle aboard the *Gloria Scott* had ignited

Preparing for the Musgrave Ritual, Alan Cox was the *Young Sherlock Holmes.*   *Photofest*

a small fire. As Armitage and the others pulled away, the flames spread to the gunpowder store and the boat exploded. There was just one survivor: Hudson.

There was no international database of criminals in those days. No means by which a man could be identified as anyone apart from who he said he was, except by an eye witness. So when the tiny boat was picked up the following day, and its ragged crew declared themselves to be survivors of a shipwreck, nobody had cause, or evidence, to disbelieve them. They continued on as free men to Australia, where they found employment in the goldfields, and Armitage—or Trevor as he now called himself—and Beddoes struck it rich.

They returned to England and established themselves as reputable citizens, influential men. Until Hudson reappeared.

What happened next? We don't know. The young Holmes was smart, but he wasn't smart enough to follow the mystery through to its true conclusion. What became of Beddoes? What became of Hudson? The police had one theory, Holmes had another. And the reader, no doubt, has another. It's a fabulous story, though, rife with adventure and excitement, and if Holmes were not so insufferable, it could be one of the best.

The Adventure of the Musgrave Ritual (May 1893)

This is another tale torn from Holmes's youth, told to Watson to while away the hours in between more exacting cases. Another job that is too good to be true, perhaps? Another duplicitous American spouse? More severed ears?

The two friends are pawing through a trunk of Holmes's souvenirs. "Here," the sleuth declares, "[is] the record of the Tarleton murders, and the case of Vamberry, the wine merchant, and the adventure of the old Russian woman, and the singular affair of the aluminum crutch, as well as a full account of Ricoletti of the club-foot, and his abominable wife."

Perhaps he intended documenting one of those admittedly gripping-sounding tales. But then something else catches his attention. Something he describes as "something a little *recherche.*"

"You may remember," Holmes begins,

> how the affair of the *Gloria Scott,* and my conversation with the unhappy man whose fate I told you of, first turned my attention in the direction of the profession which has become my life's work. You see me now when my name has become known far and wide, and when I am generally recognized both by the public and by the official force as being a final court of appeal in doubtful cases. Even when you knew me first, at the time of the affair which you have commemorated in *A Study in Scarlet,* I had already established a considerable, though not a very lucrative, connection. You can hardly realize, then, how difficult I found it at first, and how long I had to wait before I succeeded in making any headway.

When I first came up to London I had rooms in Montague Street, just round the corner from the British Museum, and there I waited, filling in my too abundant leisure time by studying all those branches of science which might make me more efficient. Now and again cases came in my way, principally through the introduction of old fellow-students, for during my last years at the university there was a good deal of talk there about myself and my methods.

It is to his cracking of one of these cases, he explains, "the interest which was aroused by that singular chain of events, and the large issues which proved to be at stake, that I trace my first stride towards the position which I now hold."

The adventure of the Musgrave Ritual begins with a riddle, held so sacred to Reginald Musgrave's family that the butler, Richard Brunton, was actually dismissed after he was found to have secretly read it. With him went the maid, Rachel Howells, and Musgrave—a University friend of Holmes—now wants to know where they are. The only clue they have left is a trail of women's footprints leading to the lake, and a bag of rusty metal and colored glass that the searchers dredged from the water.

The riddle, or the Musgrave Ritual as it has been known for the past two centuries, is scarcely the most obtuse example of its art form ever conceived.

"Whose was it?"

"His who is gone."

"Who shall have it?"

"He who will come."

"(What was the month?

"The sixth from the first.)"

"Where was the sun?"

"Over the oak."

"Where was the shadow?"

"Under the elm."

"How was it stepped?"

"North by ten and by ten, east by five and by five, south by two and by two, west by one and by one, and so under."

"What shall we give for it?"

"All that is ours."

"Why should we give it?"

"For the sake of the trust."

Clearly, the ritual is intended to guide the reader to something. Holmes sees that immediately, and one suspects that most of his readers figured that out, as well. The Musgrave family, though not historically renowned for their denseness, had somehow missed this, however, and young Rupert is utterly enraptured as he follows Holmes as he deciphers the thing.

Measuring an oak tree, mapping the site of a now-vanished elm, up to a doorway, into a cellar, over to an empty wooden chest—and there lies Brunton, dead from suffocation. As for Rachel, clearly she was Brunton's accomplice up to this point, and should she ever be found, no doubt she will explain whether she purposefully left Brunton to die in that small, airtight cellar, or whether he suffered an accident and she panicked?

Certainly she did not profit from his death. The junk that she threw into the lake, the rusty metal and colored stones, were of course gold and jewels, all a part—Holmes declares—of the crown of King Charles I, the English monarch who was executed by the Parliamentarians during the Civil War.

The Adventure of the Reigate Squires (June 1893)

Following on from all the retrospection that had so recently beset Holmes, this tale offered Watson the opportunity to recall his own pre-Holmesian past. Exhausted after solving a case in France, Holmes is in need of rest, which Watson declares would be best attained at the estate of a friend of his, Colonel Hayter.

The colonel, explains the faithful doctor, was one of his patients during his time in Afghanistan, and a grateful one, too. He offers the two men the run of his home, down in the country greenery of Reigate, Surrey, but it swiftly transpires that there will be no rest for Holmes.

First he learns of a burglary at a nearby estate, where the thieves made off with the most mundane items they could find, including a ball of string. Then there comes news of a murder at another estate, a coachman whose gunned-down corpse holds just one possible clue, a torn piece of paper with a few words written on it.

Holmes introduces himself to the investigating officer, learns that his reputation (of course) has preceded him, and promptly spots something that the police had missed. The words on the paper are in two different hands, as though two people took turns writing one word each. An expert in handwriting, of course, Holmes is further able to deduce the sex and age of the two writers, and even that they are related to each other. These insights lead him to interview the Cunninghams, the elderly father and youthful son who currently reside at the estate.

The son, Alec, immediately explains how the coachman had disturbed a burglar, pursued him, and been shot dead for his troubles. The father merely says he was in his room smoking at the time and missed the entire commotion. But Holmes knows they are lying. No footprints lead to the site of the killing. No burglar would enter a house where the inhabitants are clearly awake. And the body showed no sign of having been shot at close range. And what of the mysterious scrap of paper?

He ascertains that the handwriting on the note was that of the two Cunningham men, and he sets about searching their rooms. At this point the pair ambush him, intent on preventing him from fulfilling his plan. But they are too late. As Watson and the police rush to the sound of the melee, Holmes declares that both men are the murderers and produces his evidence: the remainder of the torn sheet of paper. Furthermore, examination of Alec's gun proves it to be the murder weapon.

But why? Because it was the Cunninghams who had committed that earlier burglary, hoping to unearth legal papers that might assist them in a property dispute in which they were engaged with the owner of that estate. They did not find it, but the coachman knew of their activities and set about blackmailing them into silence. Instead, it was he who was silenced.

The Adventure of the Crooked Man (July 1893)

"Elementary, my dear Watson." It is one of the most frequently repeated quotations in the English language, and naturally it is attributed to Sherlock Holmes, responding to one of his faithful sidekick's wide-eyed "but . . . how could you possibly have known that?"–style questions.

It is also utterly erroneous. Not once in any of the Holmes stories does the great man, or anybody else for that matter, speak those words. But there is one single occasion when he came close. And it is here, in this tale, as the two friends discuss Holmes's suggestion that the doctor had enjoyed a very busy day.

How does he know? asks Watson.

"'I have the advantage of knowing your habits, my dear Watson,'" replies Holmes.

> 'When your round is a short one you walk, and when it is a long one you use a hansom. As I perceive that your boots, although used, are by no means dirty, I cannot doubt that you are at present busy enough to justify the hansom.'
> 'Excellent!' I cried.
> 'Elementary,' said he.

And that is it. Over 120 years of faithful quotation dismissed by a simple perusal of the printed page. Holmes himself would be proud.

He was proud, too, of "The Adventure of the Crooked Man." That is why he was visiting Watson at the end of, as we have seen, a busy day—to invite the doctor to observe the final stages of an investigation that has kept him enthralled for some time.

It is a murder mystery. Colonel James Barclay, a military man stationed at the army camp in Aldershot, is dead, apparently at the hand of his wife, Nancy. Holmes, however, is somewhat less convinced than other investigators, and much

Jeremy Brett—follow that hansom!   *Photofest*

of the story is taken up with him explaining how he has already blown holes through most of the evidence ranged against the hapless Nancy, including the fact that they alone were in the morning room, embroiled in a ferocious argument, at the time of the colonel's demise.

A third person was in the room, Holmes believes—a person who, somewhat mysteriously, appears to have been accompanied by an oversized weasel. This supposition is borne out when Holmes interviews the couple's next-door neighbor, Miss Morrison.

Out walking with the deceased on the day of the murder, the pair encountered a little crooked man carrying a wooden box. They might have passed him by, had the man not suddenly looked at Nancy and recognized her—he was, she explained, someone she had known some thirty years previous, and while they talked, the neighbor walked on. She did not overhear a word they said, but Nancy was furious when she caught up with her, and she furthermore insisted Miss Morrison swear to remain silent on the entire matter.

How many little crooked men with wooden boxes were in the neighborhood? Not many. Swiftly, Holmes tracked down a certain Henry Wood, a corporal in the same regiment as Barclay, out in India during the Mutiny. And out poured a most terrible tale of reprehensible doings.

Both men were courting Nancy at the time; both believed they were in with a shout. But one day Wood volunteered to undertake a dangerous mission, and taking directions from Barclay, he ran straight into an ambush. He was captured, tortured, left broken and deformed. He was sold into slavery; he lived as a vagabond, and lived for many years as a street entertainer, a self-taught conjurer.

Just two things drove him on. The knowledge, revealed by his captors, that he had been betrayed. By Barclay. And the dream of going home.

And so he did, but it took him many years. He returned to England, knowing his death was near. His injuries were compounded by sickness—hepatitis B, perhaps, and/or malaria. Then he ran into Nancy, followed her home, and flew at Barclay, only for Barclay, upon seeing this terrible ghost from a forgotten past, to suffer an apoplectic fit and keel over dead before Wood could even touch him.

The coroner bore out Wood's story, exonerating both man and woman of the colonel's death. Which left just one riddle. What was an oversized ferret doing at the scene?

Wood readily explained. It was Teddy, of course.

> 'Who's Teddy?' asked Holmes.
>
> 'The man leaned over and pulled up the front of a kind of hutch in the corner. In an instant out there slipped a beautiful reddish-brown creature, thin and lithe, with the legs of a stoat, a long, thin nose, and a pair of the finest red eyes that ever I saw in an animal's head.
>
> 'It's a mongoose,' I cried.
>
> And so it was.

The Adventure of the Resident Patient (August 1893)

It was another of those unconventional business offers that seemed so to intrigue Holmes that drew the brilliant but financially desperate Doctor Percy Trevelyan to 221b. He has recently been set up in a most prestigious medical practice by a man named Blessington, a wealthy investor who is suffering from health problems and claims to enjoy feeling that he has a doctor living close by. He is also enjoying the proceeds of Trevelyan's labors, extracting for himself a full 75 percent of the doctor's earnings in return for his (admittedly valuable) patronage.

So far, the arrangement has gone smoothly. But just recently, Trevelyan has become concerned about his benefactor. The man seems skittish, nervous, agitated, but whenever Trevelyan tried to determine a cause, he was brushed off with a vague story about something Blessington heard about a burglary somewhere in the city.

The situation worsened, however, after a new patient began attending the practice, a Russian nobleman whose son dutifully delivered him to the surgery, then waited patiently in the waiting room for his father to emerge. During this time, it seems, the son took it upon himself to visit Blessington's rooms.

Nothing had been stolen, but Holmes is intrigued—even more so when he and Watson arrive at the address, with Trevelyan in tow, to find Blessington waiting with a loaded firearm. Clearly, the man has slipped beyond mere agitation into absolute fear.

But when Holmes attempts to get some answers, the old man clams up. He simply mentions that he has a large amount of money hidden in his room, while refusing to answer any questions about the mysterious Russians.

> Holmes looked at Blessington in his questioning way and shook his head.
> 'I cannot possibly advise you if you try to deceive me,' said he.
> 'But I have told you everything.'
> Holmes turned on his heel with a gesture of disgust. 'Good-night, Dr. Trevelyan,' said he.
> 'And no advice for me?' cried Blessington in a breaking voice.
> 'My advice to you, sir, is to speak the truth.'

Of course, Holmes has no intention of allowing the mystery to end there. He is already convinced that Blessington knows exactly who the two Russians are, and he also believes that they mean the old man harm. Which is how it transpires. The following morning, Blessington is found dead, hanged from a hook in his bedroom ceiling.

It was suicide, assumes Trevelyan. No, it was murder, responds Holmes. Three other men were in the room when the deed was done, and Holmes has a strong suspicion whom they might be—the two Russians, and a page whom Blessington had recently employed.

A visit to the archive at Scotland Yard fills in the rest of the story: all four men, Blessington (or Sutton, as he was then known) included, were once part of a notorious gang of bank robbers, captured only after Blessington turned informer following a raid in which a bank caretaker was murdered.

One of the gang, Cartwright, had been executed for the murder; the others had received fifteen years jail time apiece. Released at last, they immediately came after the man who squealed on them.

The Russians were not Russian at all, merely common English criminals with a flair for exotic accents and a gift, too, for disappearing. Although the page was arrested, there was little evidence with which to convict him; the other pair simply vanished. Scotland Yard had reason to believe that they were among the victims in the wreck of the steamship *Norah Creina*, off the Portuguese coast some time later. But nobody knows for sure. Not even Holmes.

The Adventure of the Greek Interpreter (September 1893)

Among the cast of characters whom the average Holmes fan considers to be regulars, Holmes's brother Mycroft is among the best known. Which means it is probably surprising to discover that it is only now, more than two years after the detective first stepped into the pages of *The Strand* (and more than five after his literary debut), that either we or Watson meet an elder brother whose deductive skills, Holmes admits, outstrip even his own.

Or would, if he only felt like employing them.

Bruce McRae and William Gillette onstage as Holmes and Watson, 1899   *Photofest*

"If the art of the detective began and ended in reasoning from an arm-chair, my brother would be the greatest criminal agent that ever lived. But he has no ambition and no energy. He will not even go out of his way to verify his own solution, and would rather be considered wrong than take the trouble to prove himself right."

The pair meet Mycroft Holmes at the Diogenes Club, one of the gentleman's clubs with which London once abounded and that the upper echelons of society regarded among the very finest things in life.

Most, however, prided themselves in being, at least to some degree, social. The Diogenes was quite the opposite. As Holmes explained,

There are many men in London, you know, who, some from shyness, some from misanthropy, have no wish for the company of their fellows. Yet they are not averse to comfortable chairs and the latest periodicals. It is for the convenience of these that the Diogenes Club was started, and it now contains the most unsociable and unclubable men in town. No member is permitted to take the least notice of any other one. Save in the Stranger's Room, no talking is, under any circumstances, allowed, and three offenses, if brought to the notice of the committee, render the talker liable to expulsion. My brother was one of the founders, and I have myself found it a very soothing atmosphere.

The visit on this occasion is not entirely informal. Mycroft has been approached by one of his neighbors, a Greek interpreter named Melas, who (and we are no longer even vaguely surprised by this) has become embroiled within a most peculiar business arrangement. One that began somewhat sinisterly, with the arrival of a mysterious visitor, a Harold Latimer, who insisted on Melas accompanying him to Kensington, to undertake some translation work, and then effectively kidnapping him. Locked in a carriage with darkened windows, threatened by a man armed with a cudgel, Melas is reassured only with the promise that he will be compensated for his present hardships. Provided he remains silent about all that should occur. If he should talk of it, however, the consequences will not be too pleasant.

The carriage ride ended at a poorly lit but well-furnished house some two hours later, and Melas was introduced to a man who was clearly being held against his will; he looks starved, and sticking plaster covers his mouth. He was also Greek, and so Melas was able to question him in the man's native language, without the kidnappers—for that is what the wretched man, Paul Kratides, assures him they are—being aware. He is being held in the hope that he will sign some property over to Latimer.

Melas is returned to the carriage and deposited some way away from his home. Rather than return directly there, however, he went to the Diogenes Club to seek out Mycroft; Mycroft in turn recruited Holmes, who immediately pinpoints a clue. A woman had entered the room while Melas was talking to Latimer, whose name appeared to be Sophy. Holmes places an advertisement in a newspaper inquiring whether anybody has any information about her and is swiftly rewarded with an address in Beckenham, on the outskirts of southeast London.

Arriving at the house with Watson and Inspector Gregory, he notes that it is a perfect match for that which Melas described. Less satisfying is the news that Melas has disappeared, collected from his residence earlier in the day by a nervous-sounding gentleman armed with a bludgeon. Clearly, the kidnappers are aware that he betrayed them, and the reader cannot help but wonder if perhaps the advertisement in the newspaper tipped them off . . .

Melas is soon discovered. He and Kratides are inside the house, bound to chairs, while a charcoal fire blazes close by. Both men have been choked by the fumes; Kratides is dead, Melas is close to it. He recovers, however, and Holmes soon unearths the reasons behind this entire affair—as Melas explained, an attempt by Latimer to obtain possession of some property that rightfully belonged to Kratides' sister, the woman Sophy.

The dead man never did sign, however, and knowing they were thwarted, the thugs fled the country. They moved, for who knows what reason, to Hungary, where, it appears, the pair were murdered by person or persons unknown. Holmes cannot help but suspect Sophy may have had a hand in their much-deserved demise..

The Adventure of the Naval Treaty (October/November 1893)

The longest of all the Sherlock Holmes stories published in *The Strand*, "The Adventure of the Naval Treaty" was spread over two consecutive issues of the magazine and is very much a child of its geopolitical time.

Britain, in the early 1890s, frequently considered herself to be surrounded if not by enemies, then at least by rivals, countries that strove to emulate Britain's military and technological power, and would stop at nothing to achieve it. It is a spy story, then, an epic of espionage and double dealing that draws two of the country's most implacable foes, Imperial Russia and Republican France, into play. And would, in many ways, kick-start the entire genre of spy fiction into being.

It is a friend of Watson's, Percy Phelps, who first alerts the detective to the ensuing mystery. An employee at the Foreign Office, Phelps was alarmed to discover, while working late and alone one night, that a crucial naval treaty has been stolen from his office.

How the theft was undertaken, he has no clue. The building was more or less deserted, and he had stepped out of his office for only a few minutes. Two entrances to his office could have been used, but one was within sight of both the building's commissionaire and of Phelps himself, as he hunted down the coffee he had requested sometime before.

The side entrance it was, then, but how? It was a nasty night, pouring rain. Anybody stepping into the building from outside could not have helped but drip water everywhere and leave wet footprints behind, as well. There was no sign of either.

The commissionaire's wife was brought in and searched. She had been in the building for a time that evening, leaving around the same time as Phelps embarked on his coffee hunt. But there was no sign of the treaty about her person. It had completely disappeared, and Phelps, returning home, essentially suffered a nervous breakdown—or a brain fever, as it was known in those days. For two months he remained incapacitated, and when he recovered, it was to discover that his career, like his reputation, had been shattered by the theft.

Holmes was fascinated by the entire affair. The obvious riddles, such as the absence of wet footprints, he easily dismissed. What baffled him was, if the treaty was as important, and its revelation as damaging, as the government seemed to believe, why had nothing more been heard of it?

Eight weeks had passed since its theft, and none of Britain's enemies would have failed to act upon its contents long before that. Perhaps the thief is holding out to see which foreign power might offer him the most money for it? That was a possibility, but the contents of the treaty were set for publication very soon, at which point no foreign power on earth would be in a position to do anything about it.

There is only one possible answer, and Holmes leaps upon it.

The thief is a near-relative of Phelps himself, his fiancée Annie's brother Joseph Harrison. A market speculator who was fast sinking in debt, he had visited Phelps at the office that evening and snatched the treaty on the spur of the moment, knowing it held the answer to all his financial woes. Furthermore, he normally slept in the bedroom where the prostrate Phelps was now resting, and it was there that he hid the document.

But he was unable to retrieve it while Phelps occupied the room, so Holmes decided to make it easy for him. He loudly invited Phelps to spend the night at 221b and then doubled back to the house. Sure enough, Joseph entered the room, retrieved the stolen treaty, and then delivered both himself and that precious paper straight into the arms of Holmes.

Phelps, meanwhile, would make a complete recovery, helped in no small way by the surprise that Holmes arranged for him over breakfast the following morning, hidden away on a serving tray.

At first Phelps insists he is not hungry. He uncovers the tray purely to humor his host, "and as he did so he uttered a scream and sat there staring with a face as white as the plate upon which he looked. Across the centre of it was lying a little cylinder of blue-gray paper. He caught it up, devoured it with his eyes, and then danced madly about the room, pressing it to his bosom and shrieking out in his delight. Then he fell back into an armchair, so limp and exhausted with his own emotions that we had to pour brandy down his throat to keep him from fainting."

Conan Doyle continued writing other tales around his Holmesian duties, and his own private writings insist that he gained a great deal more satisfaction from these stories than he did for Holmes. Incredible as it seems, he had little faith in Holmes as a means of advancing his literary reputation; rather, the detective was a way of paying the bills, and a none too welcome one at that.

His growing dissatisfaction was generally well camouflaged. Explaining the gap in the sequence that separated what we now think of as the first series of stories (*The Adventures of Sherlock Holmes*) from the second (*The Memoirs of Sherlock Holmes*), *The Strand* declared "[Conan Doyle's] reason from refraining from writing any more stories for a while is a candid one. He is fearful of spoiling a character of which he is particularly fond, but he declares that he already has enough material to carry him through another series, and merrily assures me that he thought the opening story of the next series . . . was of such unsolvable character, that he had positively bet his wife a shilling that she would not guess the true solution of it until she got to the end of the chapter!"

That, of course, was "The Adventure of Silver Blaze," and he was correct. It was an ingenious tale. But events at home were certainly destined to rein in his creativity as the series progressed, with none more distracting and damaging than discovering that his beloved wife, Touie, was suffering from consumption. One specialist—indeed, the disease's leading expert, Sir Douglas Powell—sadly pronounced she had just months to live.

It seems strange, and is perhaps an indication of just how self-centeredly Conan Doyle concentrated on his writing, that he had not spotted the disease long before it truly took hold. He had, after all, spent time in Berlin studying consumption just three years earlier, and he was not the kind of man who would ever admit that perhaps his knowledge of a given subject was less than universal. In that regard, he was very much like Sherlock Holmes.

But he missed the earliest signs of his wife's disease, swamped by Sherlock and all those other duties that attended his rise to literary prominence. He was hard at work, too, when he learned of the death of his father, in the asylum in faraway Scotland. Holmes had not simply become Conan Doyle's livelihood. The character had taken over his life.

Even the author's fame seemed determined to ridicule him. Again and again he would accept invitations to address literary societies, and every time he felt confident that he would be asked to discuss the writing that he considered to be literature: his novels, his poetry, even the other short stories that he continued to write.

But every single time, he returned home with his dreams defeated. From first to last, the only questions he was asked revolved around the beast of Baker Street.

There was just one solution. Holmes must die.

9

The Exaggerated Adventure of the Death of Sherlock Holmes

In which we meet Moriarty, Tumble off a Waterfall and Investigate the Adventure of the Final Problem

Conan Doyle was serious. Some might even say he was *too* serious.

"I must save my mind for better things," he rather loftily informed his mother in a letter written around the same time as he made this momentous decision. "Even if it means I must bury my pocketbook with him." He was well aware, whether he liked it or not, that all the fame and fortune that had come his way over the past three years was down to one character and one character alone. Excise Holmes from his creative equation and who knew what might befall him in the future.

He had faith in his own abilities, however—a faith that possibly bordered upon arrogance but that nevertheless was as sincere, and firmly held, as his belief that Holmes was holding him back.

The question was, how should the deed be done?

Looking back over the stories that he had written in the past, one fact stood out like a beacon. Holmes had met many clever men (and one extraordinarily clever woman) in the course of his adventures. Some might even have been termed geniuses. Flawed geniuses, of course, or at least inferior to Holmes's particular brand of that quality. But geniuses nevertheless.

What he had never encountered (that one woman notwithstanding, of course) was an equal. An adversary who was Holmes's match in every way. A master criminal in the same way as Holmes was a master detective. Only his brother Mycroft, he appeared adamant, could be said to rival Holmes in terms of intellect, cunning, and—let us not hide his light beneath a bushel—unparalleled brilliance.

Basil Rathbone never let a single clue pass unnoticed.   *Photofest*

So, to discover (as did readers of *The Strand*'s December 1893 edition) that he had spent the last few months in hot pursuit of just such a man came as a surprise to both Holmes's audience, and to his faithful partner, Doctor Watson.

Nevertheless he had, and patiently, Holmes sketches this most fearful adversary:

> He is a man of good birth and excellent education, endowed by nature with a phenomenal mathematical faculty. At the age of twenty-one he

wrote a treatise upon the binomial theorem which has had a European vogue. On the strength of it, he won the mathematical chair at one of our smaller universities, and had, to all appearances, a most brilliant career before him. But the man had hereditary tendencies of the most diabolical kind. A criminal strain ran in his blood, which, instead of being modified, was increased and rendered infinitely more dangerous by his extraordinary mental powers. Dark rumours gathered round him in the University town, and eventually he was compelled to resign his chair and come down to London. He is the Napoleon of crime, Watson. He is the organiser of half that is evil and of nearly all that is undetected in this great city . . .

We learn more about Moriarty in *The Valley of Fear*, a Holmes novel published after the detective's onrushing demise but (obviously) set sometime previous to it.

In calling Moriarty a criminal you are uttering libel in the eyes of the law—and there lie the glory and the wonder of it! The greatest schemer of all time, the organizer of every deviltry, the controlling brain of the underworld, a brain which might have made or marred the destiny of nations—that's the man! But so aloof is he from general suspicion, so immune from criticism, so admirable in his management and self-effacement, that for those very words that you have uttered he could hale you to a court and emerge with your year's pension as a solatium for his wounded character.

Is he not the celebrated author of *The Dynamics of an Asteroid*, a book which ascends to such rarefied heights of pure mathematics that it is said that there was no man in the scientific press capable of criticizing it? Is this a man to traduce? Foulmouthed doctor and slandered professor—such would be your respective roles! That's genius, Watson.

A genius who, as we join a bloodied and battered Holmes at Dr Watson's house one evening, has just spent the past day attempting to kill the detective.

Three times, Holmes has escaped death at the hands of a man who, in just a few lines of introduction, we now believe to be his arch-nemesis, and all because the sleuth failed to heed a warning delivered to him by Moriarty in person. Stop sniffing around where you are not wanted.

Admittedly, the attempts were clumsy: a cab that tried to run him down as he crossed the street. A brick dropped from the top of a tall building as Holmes walked beneath it. A would-be mugger, armed with a vicious cosh. Coincidences, in the eyes of the police. Nothing that any court of law would even dream of attempting to pin upon the criminal mastermind that Holmes insists is now on his trail.

Moriarty does appear to have reasons for fearing Holmes's involvement. A months-long investigation, says the detective, is about to reach its conclusion.

Holmes—armed and very dangerous.   *Photofest*

Holmes has the evidence he requires to ensure Moriarty and his gang are locked up for a very long time. It would be, he says, the pinnacle of his career as a consulting detective if he were able to bring Moriarty to be booked. And it would be the peak of Moriarty's career as the ultimate underworld kingpin if he were able to halt Holmes in his tracks.

Holmes decides to leave the country and asks Watson to accompany him. Their destination is not clear, and neither are the reasons for even doing this. If Holmes has a plan, he is keeping it to himself. Indeed, this entire mission is shrouded in secrecy. Nobody beyond Watson is aware that they intend to go away, and he is well versed already in disguising his tracks when there is a chance that he might be followed.

So, of course, is Holmes, who additionally disguises himself as an Italian cleric.

So how did Moriarty happen to be on the very same platform, waiting for the very same train, when the pair, arriving separately, reached Victoria Station? And why was he attempting to have the train delayed?

Clearly, Watson was followed, after all, and so the pair change their plans. They alight from the train at Canterbury and await another that will take them to the port of Newhaven.

Hot on their original trail, Moriarty rushes past them on a specially commissioned train of his own. The pair have shaken him off.

From Newhaven to Brussels, from there to Strasbourg. A message arrives for Holmes: Moriarty's gang is now in custody. Only their leader remains at large. The question is, is Holmes now tracking Moriarty? Or is Moriarty tracking Holmes?

The pair continue their journey, on to Meiringen, Switzerland, a town whose touristic allure is dominated by the Reichenbach Falls, a spectacular series of waterfalls whose ultimate height of 820 feet establishes them among the most impressive such features in the whole of Europe.

Conan Doyle and his wife had visited the falls themselves, shortly before Touie fell ill; indeed, the author Silas Hocking, who accompanied them on the trip, later took credit for planting the fatal possibilities of the falls in Conan Doyle's mind in the first place. Apparently, the two men had been discussing Conan Doyle's already germinating notion of killing off Holmes, with the only question being—where should the deed be done?

"Why not bring him out here?" Hocking asked.

"Not a bad idea," replied a laughing Conan Doyle.

None of which was apparent as the two friends, Holmes and Watson, stepped out one day to visit the falls, a twenty-minute walk from Meiringen railroad station. But when a young lad raced up to them and handed Watson a note, explaining that a sick Englishwoman back at their hotel needed his assistance, Holmes certainly knew that something was afoot.

He said nothing; Watson rushed away on what was indeed a fool's errand, and Holmes continued on.

It was the last anybody would see of him. Watson returned from his fruitless journey to find the falls deserted. But two sets of footprints led to a precipitous drop, where signs of a violent scuffle scarred the muddy earth, and a note in Holmes's handwriting explained that he and Moriarty were about to fight to the death. Both men's death.

Holmes's death at the end of the story was not intended to shock the reader. Rather, Watson laid out the sad news at the very beginning of the tale, while publisher George Newnes chose to break the news even earlier, with an announcement in *The Strand*'s downmarket sister, *Tit-Bits*. Before you even read the adventure itself, you knew what was coming. The only question was, how . . . and why?

"It is with a heavy heart," Watson wrote,

> that I take up my pen to write these the last words in which I shall ever record the singular gifts by which my friend Mr. Sherlock Holmes was distinguished. In an incoherent and, as I deeply feel, an entirely inadequate fashion, I have endeavored to give some account of my strange experiences in his company from the chance which first brought us together at the period of the *Study in Scarlet*, up to the time of his interference in the matter of the 'Naval Treaty'—an interference which had the unquestionable effect of preventing a serious international complication."

There, the faithful doctor admitted, he had originally intended to halt his recounting of the adventures of this most remarkable man.

But the world continued to revolve, and the recent publication, he said, of a series of letters written by Moriarty's brother James had forced his hand. Now it was his sad duty to detail

> that event which has created a void in my life which the lapse of two years has done little to fill . . . . I have no choice but to lay the facts before the public exactly as they occurred. I alone know the absolute truth of the matter, and I am satisfied that the time has come when on good purpose is to be served by its suppression. It lies with me to tell for the first time what really took place between Professor Moriarty and Mr. Sherlock Holmes.

It is difficult, in today's world of mass entertainment, of Internet leaks and "coming soon" previews, to perceive of a time when an entire nation, it seemed, was glued to just one set of adventures in any media whatsoever.

Perhaps, in the days before cable and satellite TV, a particular show might scoop up sufficient viewers and arouse sufficient comment that it *felt* as though everyone was watching it: *Dallas. Twin Peaks. Friends.* Sundry long-running soap operas.

Before television, radio was capable of a similar effect. But prior to that, it was books that held the populace in their thrall; and in particular (as we have already seen), those books throughout the nineteenth century were published in serial or episodic format, so that every new issue brought a new twist and turn.

Even so, whatever media we choose, it is a rare tale indeed that becomes so real to so many people that the death of a single fictional character could affect so dramatically the lives of so many real people.

Sherlock Holmes faces death . . . but not for the first time.

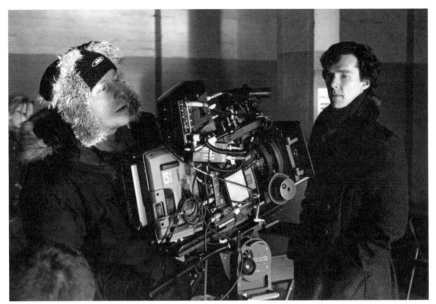

Benedict Cumberbatch preparing to film his own fatal fall, 2010.   *Photofest*

Charles Dickens accomplished it with the serialized tale of *The Old Curiosity Shop* between April 1840 and November 1841 (no less than eighty-eight weekly installments). There, the death of Little Nell provoked widespread grief throughout Dickens's readership, and beyond, as well. People who had never even opened the story seemed to know of the girl, and the tribulations that life had meted out to her, and her demise was so painfully painted, and so dramatically enacted, that English sailors arriving in America in the days after her fate was first published in Britain were greeted by crowds of onlookers, all with just one question on their lips: "Does Nell live?"

Even Harry Potter, perhaps the only twenty-first-century character who could be said to have excited similar attention, could not match that.

Holmes could.

Stories are told of readers flinging their copies of the latest edition of *The Strand* onto the fire, or out of the window, as they read the final words of the final story—the Victorian equivalent of kicking in their television screen, or penning an especially inchoate blog posting. Conan Doyle was accosted on the street; one lady reader, he recalled, hit him with her handbag. Another called him "a brute." A letter from a third began with the words "you beast."

"I never thought they would take it so much to heart," the executioner mewled plaintively.

At the headquarters of *The Strand*, the mailman was bent double as he dragged sack after sack of angry mail into the office, with no less than twenty thousand once loyal followers demanding that their monthly subscription be canceled forthwith.

Others heaped abuse and complaint upon whosoever the reader felt bore the most responsibility for the killing. Some demanded Newnes reason with Conan Doyle, or admit that the whole thing was a hoax. Others cursed Conan Doyle and demanded he recant. Still others theorized that Holmes himself was behind the mystery, a living, breathing Holmes who had gone underground in pursuit of an even bigger fish than Moriarty and would resurrect himself in a month or two, once the felon had been apprehended.

Apocrypha steps in where reality loses its grip. In far-off New York, it was said, dismayed readers announced the formation of societies dedicated to "Keep Holmes Alive." Reports circulated (without a shred of historical documentation, sadly) that distraught fans wore black armbands and other signs of mourning. Dated December 1893, that issue of *The Strand* hit the streets a full month before Christmas. But there would doubtless be many unhappy holidays being spent that year—because the next issue, the first without Holmes, would have just been published, reopening a wound so raw that Conan Doyle would never succeed in stitching it back up.

Two years later, addressing the Author's Club, the author was still defending himself. "I have been much blamed for doing that gentleman to death. But I hold that it was not murder, but justifiable homicide in self defense."

If he had not killed Sherlock Holmes, he avowed, "he would certainly have killed me."

The Adventure of Life after Sherlock

The Conan Doyles themselves journeyed far from London for the Christmas holidays; Touie's health dictated clean, clear, cold air, and so, with an irony that was doubtless not lost upon the family, they returned to Switzerland, to the resort of Davos. There Conan Doyle completed work on his latest novel, *The Stark Munro Letters*—or, as the contemporary fashion for long-winded titles more volubly put it, *The Stark Munro Letters, Being a Series of Twelve Letters, Written by J. Stark Munro, M. B., to His Friend and Former Fellow-Student, Herbert Swanborou, of Lowell, Massachusetts, During the Years 1881–1884, Edited and Arranged by A Conan Doyle.*

A medical drama based in no small part upon Conan Doyle's own days in practice, and in particular upon his relationship with the mercurial George Budd (who appears as James Cullingworth), the book was published in 1895 and naturally provoked another volley of gnashing and wailing from those who felt Holmes had been put to rest too soon.

What interest did they have in the ramblings of so many country doctors, or in the "progressive" religious views that one of said medical men was so tiresomely disposed to deliver? Conan Doyle's disillusion with Catholicism, and any other religion for that matter, was writ large through the pages of a book that few

The final, fatal fall.

people read today, even among those who consider him one of our language's most gifted storytellers.

Like the later writings of H. G. Wells, another great writer whose success in one area (namely the birth of science fiction) bred the self-important assumption that anything else he wrote must be of equal import and entertainment, or those modern rock stars who think a couple of hit records and a pair of expensive sunglasses are qualification enough for a career filled with sociopolitical pontification, Conan Doyle had reached a place, at least in his own mind, where he believed his name alone was sufficient to grant his writings a hearing.

To test the veracity of that assumption, and without venturing any further into this book, the reader is invited to name five subsequent Conan Doyle novels that do not have the name of Sherlock Holmes attached to them.

Okay, then.

He remained, however, one of his profession's leading lights, while his biography teems with adventures that ensured he remained as busy away from Holmes as he ever was while he labored in the detective's thrall.

With poor Touie's treatment still paramount in his mind, the Conan Doyles traveled extensively, wintering in Egypt during 1895–96 and remaining there as the first shots of the Sudan War were fired. Soon Conan Doyle was working as "honourary war correspondent" for the *Westminster Gazette* back home in London, and while it was just a short engagement before the family—now swollen by two children, Mary and Kingsley—needed to return to England, it was an invigorating one for his imagination.

A new novel, *Rodney Stone*, was published, flushing the Conan Doyle coffers not only with an initial £4,000 advance, but with a further £1,500 for serialization rights from *The Strand*, whose initial loss of subscribers back when Holmes was killed off had come slowly crawling back as Conan Doyle at least continued writing for the magazine.

The money allowed Conan Doyle to purchase property—a house in Portsmouth, which he intended to rent out, and a new family home in Hindhead, which he named Undershaw.

He also seems to have shown that the familial apple did not fall far from the tree when he took a lover, Jean Leckie, although memories of his mother's relationship with Bryan Waller (or, rather, his response to it) do not appear to have troubled him. There were differences, after all, most potent being the fact that Ms. Leckie did not move into the family home.

Nevertheless, she was surely the muse behind one of Conan Doyle's most unexpected and controversial novels. *A Duet with an Occasional Chorus* was a romance in which the protagonist, Frank Crosse, continues an old love affair into the years after he is married to another woman.

It was a scandalous tale, and Conan Doyle was swiftly disavowed of his belief that he had penned a novel that would live on long after his earlier writings had been forgotten. Reviews were scathing, readers were horrified, and the author could take solace only in unmasking a slew of especially uncomplimentary reviews as the work of one man, William Robertson Nicoll (the current editor of *The Bookman*), writing for different publications beneath a barrage of pseudonyms.

It was a hollow victory; apparently unbeknownst to Conan Doyle, Nicoll was far from the only writer who supplemented his income in this way, and barely a voice was raised to support Conan Doyle's contention that this "pernicious system" was a "growing scandal."

After all, as one observer pointed out, not every writer was earning £1,000 per month per story, and even fewer could afford to turn *down* that amount simply because they were no longer interested in writing those stories.

It is also possible that they all agreed with Nicoll's demolition of *A Duet*.

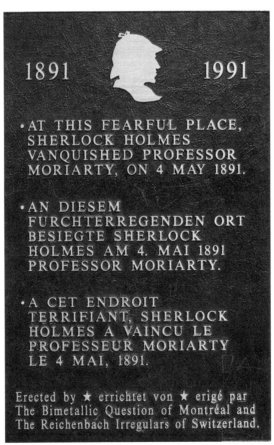

At this fearful place . . . the marker at the Reichenbach Falls. *Juhanson/Wikimedia*

10

The Adventure of the Hitherto Unpublished Episode in the Career of the Great Detective

In which the Sleuth goes to the Theater, the Author goes to War, and Sherlock Holmes . . . Well, maybe he wasn't Quite as Dead as he Claimed to Be

Holmes was dead, but he would not lie down. Conan Doyle may have been proven at least partially correct in his assumption that his name held currency enough to make money whatever he chose to write, but still he would have been foolish (which he most certainly was not) to absolutely distance himself from his greatest creation. Publicity is publicity, after all.

In those distant days when movies were still a flickering experiment, and television and radio were utterly unimaginable, the modern concept of a successful novel being transported into another medium had just one direction in which to move. To the stage.

Conan Doyle, his own thespian ambitions bubbling gently beneath the surface, first conceived a Sherlock Holmes play in 1897. He drafted a tale that (despite its eventual subtitle of "An Hitherto Unpublished Episode in the Career of the Great Detective") actually drew from several already published stories, and he offered it to Herbert Beerbohm Tree, actor-manager of Her Majesty's Theatre in London.

Of course Tree traveled down to Hindhead to meet with the author, and initially he seemed enthusiastic. There were, however, a few small points that he felt should be rewritten—small points that ultimately expanded into a virtual redrafting of Holmes's entire role in the play. At this point Conan Doyle remembered all of the reasons why he had tired of Holmes in the first place and withdrew the play from consideration.

"My weaker work which has unduly obscured my better," he declared, should not be given a new lease of life.

Or maybe he just couldn't face the prospect of rewriting the play. In his own mind, the Holmes he painted on those pages was perfect, and Beerbohm Tree's demands for rewrites were surely drawn from the actor's own ego alone.

Because when the next great actor came knocking, the American William Gillette, Conan Doyle not only allowed the thespian to consider the script, he also acceded to Gillette's request that he, the actor (who was also a proven playwright), be allowed to make some amendments, *not* so much to the story or the character, but so that the play might more easily be staged. Conan Doyle's original, apparently, presented problems with which even the most skilled production team might have fruitlessly wrestled.

Emboldened by Conan Doyle's agreement, Gillette suggested the mystery be tinged with melodrama. Fine, responded Conan Doyle. Romance? Fine. Marriage? Conan Doyle considered this, and then famously sent a telegram back, "you may marry him, murder him, or do anything you like to him."

But when he finally sat back and listened to Gillette read through the entire four-act play, replete with deer-stalker and cape, his delight was unrestrained. "It's good to see the old chap again."

Sherlock Holmes opened on November 6, 1899, at the Garrick Theater in New York City, with Gillette taking the title role for over thirteen hundred well-received performances. Less successful, at least in critical terms, was the play's transfer to London, where it opened at the Lyceum, the theater of Conan Doyle's impressionable youth, in September 1901. British critics, already so protective of Holmes as a British hero, a homegrown

William Gillette as a thoroughly modern Holmes, 1900s style.

institution, bristled at the "burlesque" of Gillette's performance. And while Conan Doyle proudly informed Gillette that "the poor hero of the anaemic printed page [seemed] a very limp object as compared with the glamour of your own personality [onstage]," homegrown criticisms included such terms as "commonplace," "crude" and "predictable."

Still, by the time the play's London run was over, no fewer than four separate touring companies were transporting *Sherlock Holmes* elsewhere around the country, proving that even in death, the detective remained a guaranteed money spinner.

Meanwhile, Conan Doyle had other business to attend to, renewing his admittedly fleeting acquaintance with the horrors of war when he traveled to South Africa to work as a doctor. Ghastly conflict had broken out, a war between the Imperial British and the Dutch settlers, the Boers, and the five months that Conan Doyle remained in the country (until July 1900, less than one-sixth of the war's total duration) not only saw him file regular dispatches back to Britain, but also provided him with sufficient material for a new book, a history of the Great Boer War.

The Unrewarding Adventure of the Political Candidate

Regaled for the quality of his South African reportage, Conan Doyle returned home in triumph and promptly set his sights on a position in government, standing as a Liberal Unionist candidate in that year's General Election, far away in his Edinburgh birthplace.

He was ultimately defeated in a campaign as dirty as any fought today—among the assaults that were directed at Conan Doyle was a leafleting campaign that dismissed him as "a Papist conspirator, a Jesuit emissary and a Subverter of the Protestant Faith," bent on assaulting "everything [that] the Scottish heart [holds dear]."

Conan Doyle responded, prior to the election, by reminding the press that he had not practiced Catholicism since his school days and, afterward, by threatening legal action against the leader of the group that so ruthlessly opposed his candidacy. Later in life, however, he would appear grateful that fate had not, ultimately, destined him for a place in political life; he realized that his existing career as an author had marked him out for far greater things.

The new king, Edward VII, came to the throne in 1901 and promptly revealed himself to be as great a fan of Sherlock Holmes as his mother had been of *The Strand*. When Gillette's play arrived in London that fall, it was Edward who caused the second half of the opening performance to be delayed while he chatted with the lead actor in the Royal Box. And on October 24, 1902, barely two months after the king's coronation, Conan Doyle was summonsed to Buckingham Palace to be knighted for services to the crown, primarily his newspaper work in South Africa. (Conan Doyle's history of the Boer War went on to sell over 300,000 copies in seventeen editions.)

But perhaps more important than any of that, at least in the eyes of the general public, he had commenced the publication of a new novel in *The Strand*, one that he assured Greenhough Smith was a "real creeper . . . full of surprises, breaking naturally into good lengths for serial purposes." For "my usual £50 per thousand words," he declared, the story could be *The Strand*'s.

Greenhough Smith accepted the offer, at which point the canny Conan Doyle dropped his bombshell. For *double* his fee, *The Strand* could double its readership.

The hero of the tale would be Sherlock Holmes.

The Exceedingly Strange, If Somewhat Dubious, Adventure of the Cruelly (Allegedly) Murdered (Allegedly) Co-Author (Allegedly)

We return to Dartmoor, that benighted wilderness in England's bottom left-hand corner. We return, too, to the wealth of myths and legends that flourish there, haunting the locals and terrifying the tourists.

Traveling back to Britain from his South African adventures, Conan Doyle had fallen in with a young *Daily Express* journalist named Bertram Fletcher Robinson, a native of that very part of the world. On board ship and later, as friends who frequently visited one another and even vacationed together, "Bobbles" entranced Conan Doyle with the folklore he had grown up with. A story formed in his mind, an adventure that drew deep from within Bobbles's repository of local lore, and to prove the great man's gratitude, Conan Doyle intended rewarding him with co-authorship of this new adventure.

Petri Wine—the perfect companion for a night by the radio.

Or so he told Greenhough Smith. By the time the first part of the story appeared in print, however, Bobbles's role had been relegated to a mere line of acknowledgment on the first page: "this story owes its inception to my friend, Mr Fletcher Robinson, who has helped me both in the general plot and in the local details."

Conan Doyle was no more or less generous in the dedication that opened the story's first bound edition, the following year. But time saw even these acknowledgments slowly dissipate and, while Fletcher Robinson only occasionally permitted himself to be described (by others) as the joint author of *The Hound of the Baskervilles*, one can only imagine the betrayal this—from all accounts—likable and amenable young writer must have felt.

A betrayal that, a century later, would become the centerpiece of a mystery as perplexing as that of the Hound itself.

Fletcher Robinson died in 1907, a victim of typhoid fever and peritonitis. Rumor, however, was never content to let his death lie as the official record insisted, instead weaving a web of conspiracy that began with the writer making overtures to Conan Doyle for a greater share of the credit for *The Hound of the Baskervilles* and ended with his murder by laudanum poisoning.

On July 26, 2005, ninety-eight years after Fletcher Robinson's death, the London *Telegraph* newspaper published an interview with scientist Paul Spiring, working alongside author Rodger Garrick-Steele in a team dedicated to discovering the truth about the young man's demise.

"We believe there is evidence that what was put on the death certificate was not true and that the cause of death was much more likely to have been laudanum poisoning.

"That raises the question about why he should have been poisoned. We have got what we believe is irrefutable evidence that Fletcher Robinson was cheated out of a considerable sum of royalties because he was much more actively engaged in *The Hound of the Baskervilles* than was acknowledged by Conan Doyle."

Heather Owen of the Sherlock Holmes Society struck back, describing the theory as "highly unlikely and far-fetched. It would be entirely out of character.

"[Conan Doyle] wasn't a poisoning kind of person. [He] wanted the book to be published in joint names but the publishers didn't like that idea because Conan Doyle was the selling point."

Nevertheless, the investigators—whose team also included Dr. Susan Paterson, head toxicologist at the Imperial College in London, and Simon Bray, a consultant archaeological engineer—were determined to ferret out the truth.

While Garrick Steele published his theories in the book *The House of the Baskervilles*, outlining his eleven-year investigation into the mystery, the team approached the parochial church committee for St. Andrew's Church, in Ipplepen, Devon, where Fletcher Robinson was buried, to discuss the body's exhumation and examination.

If the man was poisoned, traces would remain.

Doctor Fernando, forensic pathologist for the Devon and Cornwall Constabulary, explained in another interview, "although there is a long period of time involved . . . it is possible to prove poisoning because you still have the bones which will give very good results when analyzed for toxins. We hope we will find fingernails and possibly hair. If you have bone, hair or fingernails, you can look for arsenic and other heavy metal poisons."

It was not to be. No fewer than sixty different people contacted the diocese to protest any possible exhumation, among them the Rector of Ipplepen and the chairman of the Arthur Conan Doyle Study Group, Squadron Leader Philip Weller. Three years later, in September 2008, the *This Is Devon* online newspaper reported, "Sir Andrew McFarlane, the chancellor of the ecclesiastical court, has ridiculed Mr Garrick-Steele's research and branded the historian 'totally unreliable. This court has been driven to the conclusion that it cannot place any reliance on as assertion made by [Garrick Steele] which is not backed up by an independent piece of evidence or source. On the basis of the material that he has placed before this court he appears to be a totally unreliable historian."

Even Spiring distanced himself from the cause. "This all blew up three-and-a-half years ago and it's been apparent since then that Mr Garrick-Steele did not have much evidence to back up his claim. I had a team of experts ready to test the body, but that doesn't matter. The theory is discredited and it would have been a pointless exercise."

Well, it was pointless apart from the fact that the notion is still out there, unproved and seemingly unprov*able*; and, like every other conspiracy theory, it still has its own nest of subscribers out there on the Internet.

As does the story of the hound itself.

The Hound of the Baskervilles (August 1901–April 1902)

The root of Conan Doyle (and Fletcher Robinson)'s tale lies in the legend of Squire Richard Cabell, of the town of Buckfastleigh. He was, the story goes, a monstrous man, cruel and greedy, violent and evil—a reputation that sprang from the belief that he had murdered his own wife and then sold his soul to the Devil, in exchange for immortality. A deal that the Devil, naturally, is seldom disposed to execute as the seller expects.

The squire passed away on the night of July 5, 1677, and was duly buried in the family sepulcher. But that night, more than one person saw a monstrous pack of spectral hounds descend upon the town from all corners of the moor, to howl and bay at the entrance to his tomb. In life, the squire had been a vociferous hunter, and in death he intended continuing that pursuit.

Every July 5 from then on, the squire would ride again, leading his pack noisily across the moor; and even when he lay silent in his grave, still the hounds were there, howling into the night.

"Good dog. Here, boy!" Rathbone hunts the hound.   *Photofest*

Finally the townspeople tired of the noise and disturbance, and what amounted to a small house was built around the original tomb, sealing the squire inside.

That was the original tale that Fletcher Robinson told Conan Doyle. But then the younger man spun another yarn, the story of the giant black hound with blazing eyes that also haunted the moor. To conflate the two was the work of a moment's imagination for Conan Doyle. To unravel them, on the other hand, was a task worthy of just one person.

Why did Conan Doyle choose to resurrect Sherlock Holmes?

Originally, he didn't. When *The Hound of the Baskervilles* was first conceived, Holmes was nowhere in sight. Neither, however, was any other central character upon whose personality and presence the entire story could be hinged. And the deeper into the story's own mystery that Conan Doyle delved, the more it became clear that he required a detective to make sense of it all. And even he admitted that to have invented a whole new sleuth would have seemed foolish.

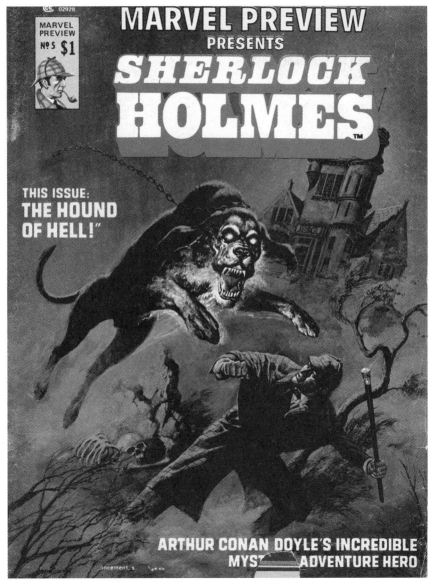

Marvel Comics re-envision Baskerville.

There were commercial, or at least financial, considerations, too. Touie remained seriously ill. True, she had absolutely bamboozled the medics who had once sounded so confident about her life expectancy. But she still required constant medical attention, and that cost money. So did his continued affair with Jean Leckie, a relationship that was now an open secret among his friends and even family, although Conan Doyle would never have sacrificed Touie for his own happiness.

He remained well paid, probably better paid than any other writer of his generation. But he was one of those people who believed, possibly correctly, that you can never have too much money. *The Strand* had already agreed to pay him £50 per thousand words. In terms of future sales and royalties, however, there were two words that could be worth many times that amount.

"I gave [*The Strand*] the alternative that [the story] should be without Holmes at my old figure or with Holmes at £100 per thou[sand words]," Conan Doyle wrote. George Newnes did not even blink as he accepted the latter.

Returning to Dartmoor, returning to the scene of "The Adventure of Silver Blaze," and set some time before Holmes's death at the Reichenbach Falls, the tale of *The Hound of the Baskervilles* begins with the fatal heart attack suffered by Sir Charles Baskerville, owner of the country house Baskerville Hall.

His nephew and sole living heir Sir Henry Baskerville, is now en route from Toronto, Canada, to claim his inheritance, but there are fears for his safety. A curse afflicts the family, a two-century-old blight that began when an ancestor, Hugo Baskerville, sought the assistance of the Devil. He had recently fallen in love with a farmer's daughter, and when she rebuffed him, he kidnapped her and held her prisoner in a bedroom of the house. She escaped, and Hugo was consumed by the need to recapture her. The Devil agreed, and Hugo sallied out onto the darkened moor, confident that he would soon be reunited with his victim. And so he was—but only in death. The following morning, the two bodies were discovered on the moor. The girl had died of fright. Hugo had had his throat torn out by the giant dog that still stood sentinel over his body.

A dog whose gargantuan footprints had most recently been sighted alongside the body of the dead Sir Charles.

The family doctor, James Mortimer, brings the story to Holmes, whose interest is only increased once Sir Henry arrives in London and promptly receives an anonymous letter. Composed from individual letters cut from that morning's edition of *The Times* (probably by a woman, to judge from the nail scissors employed, and the perfume that still hangs to the note, decides Holmes), the note cautions Sir Henry to stay away from Dartmoor. It may or may not also be linked with another mystery—the theft of one of his new boots, followed, shortly thereafter, by the loss of another, older boot. It is almost, Holmes thinks, as though somebody wants to get a good example of his personal scent, in order that a dog might be set on his trail.

Sir Henry will not be deterred. Visiting 221b, he announces his intention of traveling down to Baskerville Hall, then returns to his hotel to make arrangements—with Holmes and Watson not only following him, but also noticing in the process that another gentleman, distinctly bearded, is on the baronet's trail, as well.

Watson alone accompanies Sir Henry and Mortimer down to Devon; Holmes, apparently, has business to attend to in London. They arrive at Baskerville Hall, however, to discover the entire area on alert.

Another of Dartmoor's most infamous institutions is the eponymous prison, built between 1806 and 1809 to house prisoners of war rounded up during Britain's various conflicts of the age—the Napoleonic War with France, the War of 1812 with the Americans, and so on. The vast granite edifice was closed when peace returned, but it reopened in 1851 as a civilian jail, since when it had housed some of the most notorious felons of the age. It wasn't quite Newgate, but in terms of its fearsome reputation, it ran the old pile a close second. Practically escape-proof, both because of its size and its desolate location, the name of Dartmoor struck fear into both the criminal classes and the law-abiding souls who lived around it. For if somebody escaped from Dartmoor, then nobody could feel safe.

Selden, the killer who is now on the loose, is no exception to this rule. Baskerville Hall is a gloomy place at the best of times, but with a murderer on the prowl, even the natural shadows and creaks take on a whole new sinister import. Nobody wishes to stay there any longer than they must, while Watson's visit to the village the following day unearths even more disquieting information. Howling has been heard on the moor by the locals, and when one of them mistakes Watson for the newly arrived Sir Henry, she can barely wait to warn him away from the moor.

With Holmes still absent, Watson takes it upon himself to pursue the mystery. His suspicion, and that of Doctor Mortimer, has fallen upon Barrymore, one of the servants at the hall (and one who bears a close resemblance to the mysteriously bearded gent whom Watson and Holmes saw following Sir Henry in London).

Barrymore has been behaving very oddly lately, skulking around the castle, carrying unexplained bundles, and lighting unnecessary candles in his bedroom window . . . but when Sir Henry and Watson surprise him in his room late one night, he has a plausible, if none too happy, explanation for his actions. The escaped murderer Selden is his brother-in-law, and the candle is a signal to let the wretch know that food has been left out for him.

Watson takes matters into his own hands. Instinctively realizing that Barrymore might still be the key to the mystery of the hound, the doctor makes arrangements for Selden to be smuggled out of the country to freedom. In return, Barrymore is to tell all he knows about any other odd events around the hall. Which he does, by shedding light upon one of the strangest aspects of Sir Charles's death, the fact that he appeared to be waiting to meet somebody at the time he was struck down.

Barrymore speaks of an almost completely burned letter he discovered in the fireplace the morning after the murder, initialed LL and asking Sir Charles to meet somebody at the time and place of his demise. LL presumably is Laura Lyons, the daughter of a local lawyer named Frankland; she was recently separated from her brutish husband.

The Curse of the Hell Hound!

Watson goes to meet Ms. Lyons and hears what appears to be a reasonable explanation; in an age when divorce was almost impossible for a woman to attain, and cripplingly expensive if she was even willing to try, Lyons had intended to ask Sir Charles, a family friend, if he could possibly help her finance the attempt. But he never turned up.

Holmes, however, has turned up; he had, in fact, been there for a while, hiding out in a prehistoric hut and simply observing all that went on. He is just telling Watson his own thoughts on the variety of subplots taking place around Baskerville Hall when he is interrupted by a livid scream. Selden, dressed for his escape in some clothes that belonged to Sir Henry, is dead. Murdered.

Holmes's suspicions appear to be confirmed, but he keeps them to himself. Instead he announces that the whole case has left him baffled and he is returning to London. In fact, he has called for reinforcements in the form of Inspector Lestrade. Then all they need to do is lie in wait on a damp and foggy night, outside a neighboring house where Sir Henry has been invited to dine.

There the killer shows his hand. A gunshot rings out, the hound falls dead, and Holmes and Watson set off in pursuit of its handler. Jack Stapleton, a local naturalist, is in fact a minor heir to the Baskerville fortune, the nephew of Sir Henry's younger brother Rodger and, by all accounts, a thief, a swindler, and now a murderer.

Taking hold of the old legend about the dog, he had painted a hound with phosphorous to ensure a ghostly glow, then set it loose upon the moors. The missing boots, as Holmes had deduced back in London, were intended to provide the hound with Sir Henry's scent.

Stapleton does not escape. Pursued toward his hideout in the nearby Great Grimpen Mire, he loses his footing and is swallowed up in the swamp. Sir Henry can claim his inheritance with no fear of the old legend ever coming back to haunt him.

The Hound of the Baskervilles is the best-known, best-loved, and most successful of all the Sherlock Holmes stories. In the past century, since the first movie version in Germany in 1914, close to two dozen adaptations of the story have been made for radio, TV, and movie, and included among them are some of the greatest visualizations of Holmes ever made.

Neither was Conan Doyle immune to the celebrations that tore through his readership once Holmes was returned to his rightful place on the bookshelves. Nor to the extravagant offers that the world of publishing was prepared to make for more of the same.

The Strand immediately offered to keep Conan Doyle on at a rate of £100 per thousand words if he would contract to six further stories; the American *Collier's Weekly* went even further: $25,000 for six stories, $30,000 for eight, or $45,000 for thirteen. Figures that even Conan Doyle could not believe. But he accepted them. The eternal rest of Sherlock Holmes, undisturbed for almost a decade, was about to be shattered.

The Surprisingly Plausible Adventure of the Return of Sherlock Holmes

In which we learn that Rumors of Holmes's Demise were Somewhat Exaggerated, and are Invited to Thrill once more to the Old Curmudgeon's Feats of Intellectual Gymnastics

The first puzzle to confront Conan Doyle was, how did Sherlock Holmes survive what had surely been a fatal tumble at Reichenbach Falls?

He had already determined that, for the new series to work most successfully, he needed to advance Holmes's career, far easier though it would have been to simply allow Doctor Watson to range nostalgically through a dozen older cases, solved before Holmes's death. But that would also have required no small amount of fact checking, ensuring that the continuity of the original tales remained unblemished.

Dipping back earlier into Holmes's life to unearth further adventures that predated his meeting with Watson was thrown aside for the same reason. As so many authors have discovered in the years of radio, movies, and television, the best heroes all need a sidekick, whether it's the Lone Ranger and Tonto, Batman and Robin, or Robin Hood and his Merry Men. It gives them somebody to talk to; somebody to show off to; and somebody they rely upon if things go awry. Holmes without the familiar shadow of Watson was like eels without jelly. Pie without mash. A jail without birds.

There were other difficulties. A decade had passed since Holmes's death, a period during which the world had galloped on without him. How, for instance, would Holmes cope with the invention of the telephone? The growing preponderance of motor cars? The death of the queen and the accession of the king?

All of these events and discoveries would have had a major effect upon the life of Holmes. But Conan Doyle did not want to involve them. So he didn't. Just as the first two series of stories were set in the early 1890s, several years before they were published, so the new series would essentially pick up where the old one ended, with just three years having elapsed since the momentous events on a Swiss mountainside.

Watson has got on with his life. His practice flourishes, his days are busy, and though he is now a widower, his wife's final days were at least gratified by the knowledge that he was no longer disappearing for days on end, pursuing another of Holmes's hare-brained notions. So, when we rejoin him, walking down the street, it is just another day in the uneventful life of Doctor John Watson.

The Adventure of the Empty House (September 1903)

The doctor's mind is busy, of course. It is the spring of 1894, and all of London is agog at what the newspapers have dubbed the Park Lane Mystery, the apparently motive-free slaying of the Honorable Ronald Adair, son of a top colonial officer in Australia, the Earl of Maynooth.

Watson, whose interest in crime remains as keen as it was during his years with Holmes, is as perplexed as any other reader. The dead man had, by all accounts, led a blameless life, without an enemy in the world. But he had been murdered, shot in the head, in his own sitting room, some twenty feet above the ground. His door was locked, and though the window was open, the ground beneath it was undisturbed.

All of this Watson takes in when he visits the crime scene, in a purely amateur capacity, of course, and it is on his mind as he makes his way home, turning over all that he has deduced and musing over what Holmes would have made of it. A locked room, a steep fall, a much-loved corpse. Such a case could not have failed to entertain the late, great detective.

He walks on, so involved his own thoughts that he scarcely notices the man standing behind him, "an elderly, deformed man" with an armful of books. Watson blunders into the poor soul, and the books tumble to the ground.

"I remember that as I picked them up, I observed the title of one of them, *The Origin of Tree Worship*, and it struck me that the fellow must be some poor bibliophile, who, either as a trade or as a hobby, was a collector of obscure volumes. I endeavored to apologize for the accident, but it was evident that these books which I had so unfortunately maltreated were very precious objects in the eyes of their owner. With a snarl of contempt he turned upon his heel, and I saw his curved back and white side-whiskers disappear among the throng."

Watson returns home and is astonished when the same old man visits him later in the evening, ostensibly to apologize for his rudeness when they first met.

The bookseller gazes at Watson's own bookcases and remarks upon some empty space on one of the shelves. He has some books in his possession, he is certain, that would fit the gap perfectly. Watson turns to inspect the shelves in question, then turns back. And collapses to the floor in a dead faint.

> Sherlock Holmes was standing smiling at me across my study table. I rose to my feet, stared at him for some seconds in utter amazement, and then it appears that I must have fainted for the first and the last time in my life. Certainly a gray mist swirled before my eyes, and when it cleared I found my collar-ends undone and the tingling after-taste of brandy upon my lips. Holmes was bending over my chair, his flask in his hand.
> 'My dear Watson,' said the well-remembered voice, 'I owe you a thousand apologies. I had no idea that you would be so affected.'

Explanations are due, and explanations are given. When Watson asks how Holmes climbed out of "that awful abyss," Holmes responds simply, "I had no serious difficulty in getting out of it, for the very simple reason that I never was in it."

The note he left for Watson had been accurate:

> I had little doubt that I had come to the end of my career when I perceived the somewhat sinister figure of the late Professor Moriarty standing upon the narrow pathway which led to safety. I read an inexorable purpose in his gray eyes . . . .
> I walked along the pathway, Moriarty still at my heels. When I reached the end I stood at bay. He drew no weapon, but he rushed at me and threw his long arms around me. He knew that his own game was up, and was only anxious to revenge himself upon me. We tottered together upon the brink of the fall. I have some knowledge, however, of baritsu, or the Japanese system of wrestling, which has more than once been very useful to me. I slipped through his grip, and he with a horrible scream kicked madly for a few seconds, and clawed the air with both his hands. But for all his efforts he could not get his balance, and over he went. With my face over the brink, I saw him fall for a long way. Then he struck a rock, bounded off, and splashed into the water.

Why did not tracks return from the edge of the ledge, asks Watson. Because, replies Holmes, he arranged it that way. Moriarty, after all, was not the only man who wished Holmes dead. At least three of his henchmen, still at liberty despite the police's confidence, shared their leader's implacable hatred of the detective.

"One or other would certainly get me."

But if they believed Holmes to be dead, they would relax their guard—and Holmes could get them instead. So he scrambled up the cliff face and vanished off the face of the earth. Only his brother Mycroft knew that he still lived, and together they relied upon Watson's skill with the pen to ensure that the rest of the world was convinced of his death.

Since that time, he had traveled. He visited Italy and Tibet. He played the part of a Norwegian explorer named Sigerson, and adopted the mannerisms of a Moslem so that he might enter Mecca. He lived in France as a scientist, and returned to London only recently, lured—of course—by the Park Lane Mystery.

Which very much becomes a case of killing two birds with one stone. Just one other person might possibly have suspected that Holmes was not dead, a member of Moriarty's gang who had also been present at the falls that day and had seen Holmes make his escape.

The detective believed he had thrown the man off his scent by appearing to plunge anew from the rock he had climbed up, but clearly he was wrong. No sooner had Holmes returned to London than he realized his life was still in danger. So he set up a trap.

A waxwork effigy of himself is framed against the draped window of 221b. Holmes and Watson cross the street and enter an empty building directly opposite. The police are stationed elsewhere.

From a series of British cigarette cards depicting characters from Conan Doyle's novels, this was the one that everybody wanted.

The would-be assassin arrives, takes aim at the effigy, and shoots it. Holmes and Watson pounce, and the police burst in to join them, led by the indefatigable Inspector Lestrade. The gunman is unmasked—it is the deceased Adair's whist partner and supposed friend, Colonel Moran. As for his motive, Holmes speculates that Adair had discovered his partner cheating at cards and, being a decent chap, threatened to expose him. But a far more likely solution would be that Moran had simply tired of waiting for Holmes to reemerge and had decided to flush him out of hiding once and for all. By presenting him with a case that seemed impossible to crack.

With Sherlock Holmes, however, very little is as it seems.

The Adventure of the Norwood Builder (October 1903)

Watson was back living at 221b, a widower now, overjoyed to be reunited with his old partner. He had missed the cut and thrust of their adventuring and missed, too, the daily unpredictability of life with Holmes, a man whose moods swung with the weather, to ensure there was never a dull moment.

"The unhappy John Hector McFarlane," on the other hand, is a young south London lawyer who does indeed have great reason to be unhappy. He is under suspicion for the murder of one of his clients, a builder named Jonas Oldacre, whose will, drawn up just the day before the man's death, had named McFarlane as his sole beneficiary, the heir to a small fortune.

For Lestrade, it is another open-and-shut case. The motive is there for all to see, and the evidence mounts up. McFarlane acknowledged he had visited Oldacre on the day of his death. His stick was found in the house, and a fire in the garden showed evidence of human flesh having been burned on it. Lestrade cannot comprehend for a moment why Holmes should involve himself in such a mundane matter.

But Holmes, of course, knows that all is not as it seems. He discovers some dark secrets about the late Mr. Oldacre's past, and a piece of obscure ancient history from McFarlane's, too. Decades earlier, before the lawyer's birth, the builder had been engaged to marry McFarlane's mother. She broke off the engagement when she discovered that her future husband was a cruel and wicked man. It appears he had not changed much during the intervening years.

Holmes continues to dig. He unearths some unusual financial dealings involving Oldacre and another man, named Cornelius. He determines that the builder's will was scribbled haphazardly, possibly on a moving train. And he is reasonably certain that the housekeeper knows a lot more than she is letting on.

Lestrade ups the ante when he discovers a bloody thumbprint, identified as McFarlane's, at Oldacre's house. Holmes counters by pointing out that the print was not there the previous day and could not possibly have been left by McFarlane in the meantime, because he has been in police custody since his arrest.

Lestrade remains unconvinced, so Holmes resorts to his final trick. He lights a small and smoky fire in one of the rooms and then shouts out a warning.

At this point a secret door at the end of one hallway opens, and out stumbles a very much alive Oldacre. He was not murdered, after all. Rather, he was biding his time before reemerging into daylight as the same Mr. Cornelius to whom he had recently written so many checks. As for McFarlane's involvement, Oldacre confesses he was finally taking his revenge on the young man's mother for rejecting him so many years ago. All in all, then, a scheme that is as devilishly convoluted and complex as the deductive process that unraveled it!

The Adventure of the Dancing Men (December 1903)

In this modern age of emoticons and the like, receiving a message comprising nothing but fifteen stick figures executing a peculiar dance would probably not strike anybody as being especially sinister. They'd just assume that the sender had downloaded a new alphabet for their phone and forgotten to change keyboards before texting a picture of their cat.

The inhabitants of late Victorian England did not possess this particular boon to their communicative powers. If they wanted to deluge someone with apparently meaningless hieroglyphs, they needed to create them by hand. And, unless they also attached a key to the code, they ran the risk of the recipient taking the message to Sherlock Holmes.

At least, that is how Mr. Hilton Cubitt of Ridling Thorpe Manor responds when he receives such a message; all the more so since his wife, Elise, has

Holmes and Watson in Zurich—if you can bear it.   *Flyout/Wikimedia*

behaved with the utmost distraction since its arrival. Perhaps Holmes can solve the mystery?

Perhaps he can, but first he needs to know a little more about Elsie. Ah, she is an American. And she has a past—so much of one, in fact, that one of the first promises she ever extracted from Cubitt, even before they wed, was that he would never ask about her past. Apparently, there were some "very disagreeable associations" bound up therein.

Cubitt, displaying that very singular lack of curiosity that seems to afflict so many young men of period literature, agreed. But his silence did not calm his wife's fears.

First, there was the mystery of the letter that arrived from America, which she promptly burned. Then there were the dancing men, peculiar little drawings sometimes found on pieces of paper left out on the sundial and that other times materialized in chalk on walls and doors.

Holmes asks to see every example of the figures that can be found, then painstakingly decodes them—for they are, indeed, a code. A very worrying one! "Elsie," warns the final one. "Prepare to meet thy God."

Holmes makes his way immediately to the Cubitt family home in Norfolk, but he is too late. Hilton is dead, from a bullet wound to the heart; his wife is gravely wounded with a bullet to the head. And the local police have already written the entire affair off as a botched murder-suicide.

Holmes disagrees. Only two bullets have been fired from Cubitt's gun, but there is a third bullet hole in the windowsill and an empty shell casing in the flowerbed outside the room where the victims lie. And besides, he has cracked the code. Is there anybody in the vicinity named Elrige, he asks, and a stable boy answers in the affirmative. Mr. Elrige is a local farmer. And Slaney? asks Holmes. Yes, he is Mr. Elrige's lodger. An American gentleman.

Holmes quickly writes a message, employing the same code of dancing men, and sends the boy to deliver it, then sits back to wait—taking advantage of the lull, of course, to explain what is happening to Watson and the police.

Slaney arrives and is shattered to discover that Elsie is barely clinging to life in a hospital. He believed the message he had received was from her, for he is one of the "very disagreeable associations" that she had been so reluctant to speak of to her husband, a former fiancé who had Chicago gangland connections.

He had followed Elsie to England, determined to win her back no matter what the cost. The dancing men were a code that he knew she would understand, and their increasing belligerence and rage, he explained, was his response to Elsie's refusal to leave her husband and return to Chicago with Slaney.

Finally, Slaney went to the house, intending to plead his case in person, only to encounter Elsie's enraged husband.

Cubitt, he assures Holmes, fired the first shot when their meeting turned ugly; Slaney fired back out of self-defense, killed Cubitt, and then ran. The third shot, Holmes explains, was fired by Elsie herself, attempting suicide. This unexpected blow leaves the latest wicked foreigner in no mood to do anything more than quietly accompany the police to the station and trust in a jury's sympathy to deliver him from the hangman's gallows.

The Adventure of the Solitary Cyclist (December 1903)

Rejection was a rare thing in Conan Doyle's life. He wrote and he was published. That was the natural order of things—had been since *The Strand* first adopted Sherlock Holmes and sent both creator and creation soaring into the stratosphere.

How enraged he must have been, then, when he received the letter from Greenhough Smith asking him to take another look at "The Adventure of the Solitary Cyclist" and weave a little more Sherlock Holmes into the tale. Because, as it stood, it simply wasn't good enough.

Conan Doyle did not disagree. Though he swore to himself that every story in this latest batch of Holmesian adventures should be as good as he could possibly make it, ideas did not come as quickly as he wished they would, and at one point he even suggested to Greenhough Smith that the series be brought to a close after just eight stories. There was, Conan Doyle wrote, a "certain sameness and want of freshness" at large.

But *The Strand* stood firm by its original contract, and with good reason. Advertising and subscriptions would have been sold on the strength of thirteen tales, and any attempt to curtail the adventures early would doubtless have repercussions that *The Strand* did not want to imagine. So Conan Doyle plodded on, but occasionally his flagging enthusiasm could not be disguised.

Even once "The Adventure of the Solitary Cyclist" had been amended, approved, and published, he continued to regard it as one of the lesser tales in the canon, and so it is, a none-too-complicated saga of distant relatives rendered absurdly convoluted and scarcely credible by a curious inheritance and another variation on the overpaid employment opportunities that had become one of Conan Doyle's most tiresome default settings.

Although in this case, there appears to be good reason why Mr. Carruthers, claiming to represent a recently deceased uncle in South Africa, should have hired Miss Violet Smith as music teacher for his daughter, at around double the usual rate for such a position. His business partner, Mr. Woodley, was after her body.

Woodley has now disappeared from the scene, apparently taking Violet's most recent rebuff to heart. She is, after all, already engaged to be married to an electrical engineer from Coventry named Cyril. Later, she will turn down Carruthers's proposal of marriage for the same noble reason.

But now a new suitor appears to have emerged, a bizarrely bearded and sunglasses-clad stranger who follows her on his bicycle whenever she rides out to visit her mother.

Watson alone travels down to Surrey to investigate but returns only with the news that the mysterious cyclist comes and goes from a nearby house, Charlington Hall. Holmes hurrumphs, then makes the journey himself; there, he falls into a fight with Woodley, who has apparently returned to the village, but he, too, uncovers no pertinent new information.

Back in London, however, he is greeted by a letter from Violet, complaining that not only has Carruthers refused to take "no" as an answer to his proposal, but Woodley is bothering her again, as well. She announces she is terminating her employment and will be leaving immediately.

Suddenly seized by fear for the girl, Holmes and Watson return to Surrey to make sure she catches her train safely. They arrive to discover she has gone missing. Setting out in search of her, they encounter the mysterious cyclist, who, having first pulled a gun on them, then turns out to be similarly concerned for Violet's welfare.

The three team up—in search, the cyclist tells them, of Woodley and a former clergyman named Williamson, who also lives at Charlington Hall.

They arrive at the hall in time to find the two men conducting a wedding ceremony, a struggling and protesting Violet being forcibly wed to Woodley, while Williamson officiates. At this point the mysterious cyclist reveals himself as Mr. Carruthers and shoots Woodley.

Then he explains. The mysterious deceased uncle in South Africa had died intestate, meaning his fortune would automatically settle upon his next of kin, Violet. Carruthers and Woodley, hearing of this, resolved to snare Violet into marriage (Woodley won the right to ask first, in a card game on board ship) and, having lured the disgraced clergyman into their plot, proceeded as planned.

But then things went awry. Woodley could not conceal his natural brutish character from the girl and was refused; and then Carruthers fell genuinely in love with her and renounced the entire plot.

His time since then had been spent protecting Violet from Woodley's further deprecations, although why he didn't just tell her at least some of what was happening and offer to walk her to the station instead of adopting that preposterous disguise is just one of the plot flops that scar this tale.

Either way, his machinations appeared to have been wrought for naught. He had seen her married to Woodley with his own eyes. The girl's future was sealed . . . or was it?

No, of course not. As any fool knows, she had been wed against her will; and a defrocked clergyman was no more able to legally marry a couple than Holmes or Watson, or any other man. Violet was free to marry whomsoever she chose, and she had a fortune coming her way, as well.

Carruthers, meanwhile, would receive a light sentence for his part in the plot; Woodley and Williamson would suffer more grievously. It was a very satisfactory outcome. But it was still not an especially good story.

The Adventure of the Priory School (January 1904)

Lord Saltire, the ten-year-old son of the Duke of Holdernesse, has been kidnapped from the preparatory school where he is a pupil. The duke has already posted a reward of £5,000 for the boy's safe return; and the headmaster, Doctor Thorneycroft Huxtable, has asked Holmes to investigate.

The boy's home life is not happy. His parents have separated, his mother moving to the south of France while her husband and son remain in England. The boy clearly misses his ma; everybody seems to know that, and logic (or at least Holmes) would seem to suggest that the boy simply ran away to be with her. There was a clear escape route from his bedroom window and down the thick ivy to the ground. Furthermore, the boy had just that day received a letter from his father, although he did not say, and the duke cannot recall, if anything in there might have upset the lad.

Ah, but the school's German master, Heidegger, has also vanished, together with his bicycle. Very strange . . . .

A few mysterious leads emerge. The boy's cap is discovered in the possession of some gypsies camped near the school. They claim that they simply found it, but any student of British literature will know that gypsies are always the first to be blamed in any story they are luckless enough to blunder into, and this one is no exception.

Bicycle tracks are found. One set, identified as belonging to the missing German, end with the discovery of the teacher's corpse, his head bashed in. The other leads nowhere and is in any case obliterated by the hoof prints of passing cattle. Which is strange, Holmes later declares, because he has not seen a solitary cow the whole time he has been in the area, much less cows that canter, gallop and trot.

Holmes decides to see what he can flush out with some carefully placed disinformation. At the Fighting Cock Inn, close to the duke's home, he lets it be known that he is anxious to meet with the duke, for he has news of the missing boy. The innkeeper, Reuben Hayes, appears most surprised to hear this piece of information.

Of course Holmes registers the man's reaction, and slowly a web of local intrigue begins to draw tight. James Wilder, the duke's personal secretary, is involved—it was his bike tracks, Holmes discovers, that led to the tangle of not-quite-cow prints. The cows, of course, were horses to which cow-shaped horseshoes have been affixed.

The innkeeper, Hayes, whose horse shows signs of having recently been re-shoed, was in on it, too. And so was a fourth unwitting player, the duke himself, sucked into this intrigue through the machinations of Wilder, who turns out to be the duke's own illegitimate son. The missing boy is being held in the inn.

"The Adventure of the Priory School" is a delicious mystery, a tale that takes so many twists that even Holmes is unable to unravel all of its intricacies. Certainly, for anybody reading the stories in order of publication, it more than

Holmes in Denmark.

makes up for the disappointment of its predecessor, and as this latest story cycle neared its halfway point, this particular yarn established *The Return of Sherlock Holmes* as a truly worthwhile successor to the inviolate favorites of old.

The Adventure of Black Peter (February 1904)

Although it merely referred to the red cliffs that led down to the marshland and river, the Ratcliffe Highway's very name conveys its stink.

A long, poorly maintained, and badly lit road that linked the easternmost reaches of the city of London with the docks and points farther east to Limehouse, the Ratcliffe Highway was synonymous with vice and crime even before the notorious Ratcliffe Highway Murders of December 1811 shook the newspaper-reading world to the core.

Thomas De Quincey's *Murder Considered as One of the Fine Arts* was set on the highway, while the great chronicler John Stow visited in 1600 and described it as "a continual street, or filthy straight passage, with alleys of small tenements or cottages builded, inhabited by sailors and victuallers."

David Cordingley, author of *Women Sailors and Sailors' Women* (Random House, 2001), notes that "most sailors . . . were looking for women and drink, and the establishments along the Ratcliffe Highway provided for their needs." There is even a folk song, "The Deserter," aka "As I Was A-Walking Down Ratcliffe Highway," that tells of a sailor so horrified by all that befalls him on the highway that he considers himself fortunate to go back to sea, no matter how leaky the tub might be.

But the Ratcliffe Highway murders surpassed all these terrors. Two vicious attacks, two families torn apart, seven blameless bodies rendered to mutilated flesh, and so close to Christmas, as well—the first killings took place on December 7, the second on December 19. A draper and his family in the first instance, a publican and his kin in the second.

The Ratcliffe Highway, already a byword for the worst in human nature, now became synonymous with the worst in inhumanity, too. And a legend in the annals of law enforcement. The murders were instrumental in the eventual foundation of the Metropolitan Police and even gave pause for thought to a *Daily Telegraph* editorial, referenced in *A Study in Scarlet*. After alluding airily to the Vehmgericht, aqua tofana, Carbonari, the Marchioness de Brinvilliers, the Darwinian theory, and the principles of Malthus, the article singled out Ratcliffe Highway murders as a stick with which to admonish a government that simply didn't keep a close enough watch over foreigners in England.

It was on the highway that the author James Greenwood was warned, in the early 1870s, that the local womenfolk would "have the hair off a man's head if they could get a penny a pound for it." It was here that pubs with such names as the Globe and Pigeons the Malt Shovel and the White Swan (although the locals called it Paddy's Goose) spat drunkenness and smuggled tobacco fumes out into the fog. It was here that a fully grown Bengal tiger escaped Jamrach's Animal Emporium and, just by the entrance to Tobacco Dock, seized in its jaws the small boy who had never seen such a big pussycat before, and attempted to pet the beast.

And it was here that Sumner Shipping Agents had their offices, in "the Adventure of Black Peter"—a story that also opens our eyes to the existence of "Captain Basil," a *nom-de-guerre* that Holmes employed in his dealings with the denizens of that particular part of London.

"He had at least five small refuges in different parts of London, in which he was able to change his personality," marveled Watson, and this Captain Basil was clearly well known along the highway.

A good old-fashioned murder mystery hinges around the fatal impaling of "Black" Peter Carey, a violent man who does not seem to have had a friend in the world, not even among his own family, and certainly not among the men he marshaled during his years as master of the whaler, *Sea Unicorn*.

Certainly his wife and daughter seem almost glad that he is dead, and as Holmes—who has been asked to investigate by a clearly bewildered local policeman—delves deeper into the victim's personal habits, he does not find it hard to agree with them.

The dead man had some most peculiar quirks, though. Rather than sleep in the family home, he preferred an outhouse that he had arranged as a perfect replica of a sailor's cabin. He rarely smoked, but in a sealskin pouch emblazoned with his initials, he kept a supply of tobacco.

A booklet turns up, issued by the Canadian Pacific Railway and packed with stock-exchange information.

No footprints led to or from the scene of the crime, that quaint little cabin, beyond those of the deceased.

But a nearby stonemason named Slater swore he had seen a strange silhouette on the blinds of the cabin the night before the murder, and two dirty glasses were found by the body, as though the dead man had been entertaining company. And finally, sometime after the crime scene was sealed, some unknown person attempted to break into the cabin.

Sensing a break in the case, Holmes, Watson, and police inspector Hopkins lie in wait for the burglar to return—which he does. He is arrested and reveals himself to be John Hopley Neligan, whose initials match those found in the mysterious stock booklet.

He is not the murderer, however. Rather, he is a private investigator in his own right, pursuing the man who he believes murdered his, Neligan's, banker father and made off with a box of valuable securities.

Hopkins is not convinced; Holmes, on the other hand, takes just one look at the slight frame of Neligan and pronounces it impossible that such a man could have driven a harpoon with sufficient strength to pin the dead Carey to the wall. And he is correct. Returning to 221b, Holmes places an advertisement in the newspaper, describing himself as a sea captain who is need of a new harpooner. Three applicants include one man, Patrick Cairns, whose initials match those on the tobacco pouch—and who was a former shipmate of Carey.

He had also witnessed the murder of the banker, Neligan, and when he found himself on hard times, he had decided to resort to blackmail. Carey fought back, and Cairns killed him. It all was as simple (or otherwise) as that.

The Adventure of Charles Augustus Milverton (March 1904)

Of all the common criminals with whom Holmes tangled over the years, few filled him with so much loathing as Charles Augustus Milverton, a man who describes himself as "King of Blackmailers," although Holmes prefers the epithet "the worst man in London."

> Do you feel a creeping, shrinking sensation, Watson, when you stand before the serpents in the Zoo, and see the slithery, gliding, venomous creatures, with their deadly eyes and wicked, flattened faces? Well, that's how Milverton impresses me. I've had to do with fifty murderers in my career, but the worst of them never gave me the repulsion which I have for this fellow. And yet I can't get out of doing business with him—indeed, he is here at my invitation.

The business on this occasion, it transpires, is to conclude a transaction into which the debutante Lady Eva Blackwell has entered with Milverton. Pay him £7,000 or he will publish some letters that would arouse scandal enough to destroy the woman's happiness forever.

She, however, can afford no more than £2,000, and this is the offer that Holmes gives to Milverton. He turns it down. He is not a man to be trifled with, after all. If he offers one victim such a discount, then they all will be demanding one, and then where would he be? No, if Lady Eva can afford only a couple of grand, then we will see how grand she feels once her precious letters have been made public.

Now, theoretically, this is the point where Holmes and Lady Eva should have simply gone to the police, explained what was happening, and convicted Milverton for blackmail. But that would involve the letters being read by the police, news of their contents slipping out, and the eruption of a scandal regardless.

Holmes has but one alternative. He must turn criminal himself.

Disguised as a plumber, he visits Milverton's home and gets to know its routine. He cultivates the friendship of Milverton's housemaid and soon becomes engaged to her—while remaining confident that her heart belongs to another, and he will be freed of his obligation soon enough. He discovers the location of Milverton's safe, and that night, he and Watson break into the house to steal the letters. At which point Milverton walks into the room.

Just in the nick of time, the two would-be burglars hide themselves behind the sofa, listening in while Milverton and a woman, a maidservant to another potential victim, discuss his next crime. Except she is not a maidservant. She is one of the wily blackmailer's former victims, come to avenge the husband who died brokenhearted as a result of Milverton revealing her darkest secret.

She produces a gun, fires, and Milverton falls dead to the ground. Then she stamps on his face and leaves, while Holmes and Watson emerge from their hiding place, open the safe, and throw its entire contents onto the fire

They escape, but they are seen. The following day, when Lestrade visits 221b to request Holmes's assistance in solving the mystery of Milverton's death, he delivers a description of one of the men who are wanted for the murder.

"They were as nearly as possible captured red-handed. We have their foot-marks, we have their description, it's ten to one that we trace them. The first fellow was a bit too active, but the second was caught by the under-gardener, and only got away after a struggle. He was a middle-sized, strongly built man—square jaw, thick neck, moustache, a mask over his eyes."

"That's rather vague," Holmes muses to himself. "My, it might be a description of Watson!"

But he turns down Lestrade's entreaties. "The fact is that I knew this fellow Milverton, that I considered him one of the most dangerous men in London, and that I think there are certain crimes which the law cannot touch, and which therefore, to some extent, justify private revenge. No, it's no use arguing. I have made up my mind. My sympathies are with the criminals rather than with the victim, and I will not handle this case."

This serves as a reminder that Holmes was not created to uphold the law. He was created to uphold justice, and there is frequently a difference between the two.

The Adventure of the Six Napoleons (April 1904)

Although Inspector Lestrade is frequently regarded among Sherlock Holmes's closest allies, and one of his adventures' most oft-recurring characters, in fact—like Mycroft and Moriarty—his actual appearances in the original stories are very limited. And this is the last in which he plays a personal role. Subsequent mentions will be just that, either offhand references to him as one of Scotland Yard's finest, or retrospective tales from Holmes's past ("The Adventure of the Second Stain," for example). He will play no further active part in the Holmes canon, and at first he appears to be going out with something of a whimper.

For the mystery he brings to Holmes is scarcely one of national, or even local, import. Someone is wandering around town smashing plaster busts of the French emperor Napoleon. A crime, yes, at least in the eyes of those who own the busts. But a riddle demanding the keenest detective brain in the land? Scarcely.

Often, however, it is the most apparently mundane problem that gives the brain the most vigorous exercise, and Holmes swiftly dismisses Lestrade's belief that the felon is simply someone who hates Napoleon. That, after all, was scarcely a rarity in nineteenth-century England—at the time in which the Holmes stories are set, even the Battle of Waterloo had been fought just eighty years previous, meaning that the Little Emperor's dream of uniting the whole of Europe beneath his personal banner was scarcely more distant than Adolf Hitler's ambitions are today.

Men still lived whose fathers had fought against the Frenchman, men whose lives had taken inexorable turns for the worse as a result of that long conflict at the other end of the century. Add sundry nihilists, anarchists, Spaniards, and even descendants of the fallen Frenchman's final jailer and yes, a lot of people hated Napoleon.

Holmes, however, looked beyond the obvious facts, to those that underlay them. Each of the busts had been sold from the same shop. Each was made from the same mold. Even before Lestrade returned to 221b to report a startling new development—another busted bust, accompanied by an unsolved murder at the same location—Holmes suspected more than a historical grudge.

Geese come to mind. A Christmas goose, into which a prized jewel, a precious carbuncle, for example, has been secreted. Did Holmes's memory flash back to that long-ago case? Did Conan Doyle's? Either way, no matter how convoluted the ensuing mystery may be, and how brilliant Holmes's step-by-step deductions may seem, the astute reader has cracked the case long before Holmes gives the first indication that he has. A point, one suspects that scriptwriter Giles

The Strand delivers the best news of the month.

Cooper was well aware of as he prepared the tale's adaptation for the BBC's 1965 series of TV adventures.

With Sherlock—Douglas Wilmer—hamming it up to magnificent degrees, a supporting cast combines lunacy, stupidity, and comic exaggeration in equally absurd doses, so much so that even Holmes and Watson are reduced to fits of laughter by some of the characters they encounter.

Thus is one of the least intriguing cases in the canon transformed into an absolute romp, one that is solved by Holmes's realization that a precious jewel, the long-lost Black Pearl of the Borgias, was secreted within one of the busts. It was simply the criminal's bad luck that out of the six possible busts in which it might be, it should be in the sixth and final one. Because that is the one that Sherlock Holmes has just purchased, and he would be cracking it open. And cracking the case, as well.

The Adventure of the Three Students (June 1904)

Sometimes, Conan Doyle's gift for describing a landscape is so precise that one could find it in one's sleep. Other times, it is so infuriatingly vague that when he says that Holmes is visiting "a university town," the greatest minds in Holmesiana cannot agree whether it is Oxford or Cambridge, the two English cities one is most naturally inclined to think of when hearing that term.

The mystery is equally perplexing, albeit in a rather schoolboyish manner. A lecturer at St. Luke's College, Hilton Soames, has discovered somebody has been looking through the galley proofs of an examination he is about to set.

Nothing is missing, nothing has been disturbed. But the papers have clearly been inspected, and Soames is convinced that one of his students is the felon, a cheat and a scoundrel who intends to pass the exam no matter how low he must stoop.

But which of them was it?

The "adventure," such as it is, is extraordinarily underwhelming, more akin to the "whodunnit"-style stories that were already popular in British children's literature and comics of the day. Indeed, excise Holmes and the entire tale could have fallen from the pages of *The Boy's Own*. That it should exercise the mind of Holmes still seems baffling today.

Whodunnit? Well, there are only three students sitting the exam, and all three live in the same building.

One, Giles Gilchrist, is a lanky, athletic lad, a hard worker whose sole misfortune in life is that his father is a reckless gambler.

Another, Miles McLaren, is himself a gambler.

And the third, Daulat Ras, is just a nice, quiet boy who gets on with his work in a painstaking manner.

The only other person on the scene was Soames's own servant, Bannister.

Holmes gathers up the clues. A pile of pencil shavings, a broken pencil lead, a small hollow blob of black clay with sawdust on it, and an unexplained three-inch cut in the lecturer's desk. Nothing else.

He interviews the suspects and talks to Bannister, too. Then he delivers his findings. The cheat had to be tall enough to see through the window and determine that the papers had been left on the desk. The scratch in the desk was caused by the spikes on a pair of running shoes, and the clay came from the soles of those shoes, impacted upon the spikes and then falling away again.

The locked office was opened by someone with access to the key and who had a close relationship with the cheat himself. Bannister, before coming to work for Soames, had been butler for Gilchrist's father. Gilchrist was tall, he was athletic. He wore running shoes and had that afternoon been training in the long-jump pit, the source of the mysterious clay. And, as soon as Holmes confronts him, he confesses.

Gilchrist was last heard of joining the Rhodesian police force. There, one fervently hopes he had more exacting mysteries than this to solve.

The Adventure of the Golden Pince-Nez (July 1904)

Murder most foul!

Inspector Stanley Hopkins has a case that he simply cannot see a solution to. Willoughby Smith is—or, rather, was, for he is now dreadfully dead—secretary to an invalided old professor, Coram, out in that most picturesque part of southern England, the gently rolling hills above the River Medway near Kent.

A naval town, much like Conan Doyle's beloved Portsmouth, Chatham is (and remains) the centerpoint of a growing conurbation that also includes Gillingham and Rochester, once the home and forever the muse of Charles Dickens. His final, unfinished novel, *The Mystery of Edwin Drood*, was set there, an apparent murder mystery that over a century's worth of subsequent authors and scholars have been unable to crack.

Sherlock Holmes may have, and had Conan Doyle only allowed him to extend his visit to the Medway for a little longer, what a triumph that would have been. Instead it was left to other authors—Andrew Lang in 1905, Harry B. Smith in 1924, and doubtless others besides—to truly match a Holmesian solution to the Dickensian mystery. (The latter's unequivocally titled *Sherlock Holmes Solves the Mystery of Edwin Drood* is the best.)

Conan Doyle's Holmes, on the other hand, was in and out of town like a flash.

The murder was committed at (the fictional) Yoxley Old Place, the murdered man stabbed with a sealing-wax knife that belonged to the professor. Footprints leading to (or from . . . it was hard to tell) the house were found in the muddy lane outside, and it appears the killer entered the premises through the back door. Nothing has been stolen, nothing disturbed.

The professor was asleep; the maid was in another room hanging curtains. But she heard a scream and rushed to the room to discover Smith dying. His final words, she reported, were, "The professor—it was she." But the professor was a man.

The killer's gender is no secret to Holmes, of course, not after he discovers something that was left behind at the scene of the crime. A pair of gold pince-nez glasses, from which the detective swiftly draws his conclusions. The murderer was indeed a she. A well-bred, well-dressed one with a thick nose and close-set eyes. A puckered forehead, a squinty gaze, and rounded shoulders completed his portrait. And she had visited her optician at least twice in the past few months.

None of this squares with the old professor's insistence that Smith simply committed suicide. The professor has a long history of unsuitable secretaries, after all—Smith is his third in a fairly short time, and neither of the others worked out at all satisfactorily. Why should this one be any different?

But Holmes has his own ideas and proceeds to compile his customary litany of seemingly irrelevant clues. Including the fact that the corridor that runs from the back door, and that which leads to the professor's bedroom, are both lined with coconut matting.

He spends time with the professor, and having ascertained that the house-keeper is not due to sweep the floors that day, he proceeds to drop cigarette ash all over the old man's bedroom floor. Then, returning later, he drops his cigarettes on the floor and, while making a show of slowly collecting them, takes a good look at the old ash. A woman's footprints are clearly visible.

The remainder of the mystery appears simple.

"A lady yesterday entered your study," he tells the professor. "She came with the intention of possessing herself of certain documents which were in your bureau. She had a key of her own . . . . She came, so far as I can read the evidence, without your knowledge to rob you."

She was discovered by Smith and, in the ensuing struggle, stabbed him with the first weapon that came to hand. Holmes did not believe she intended to kill him.

"Horrified by what she had done, she rushed wildly away from the scene of the tragedy. Unfortunately for her, she had lost her glasses in the scuffle, and as she was extremely shortsighted she was really helpless without them. She ran down a corridor, which she imagined to be that by which she had come—both were lined with cocoanut matting—and it was only when it was too late that she understood that she had taken the wrong passage, and that her retreat was cut off behind her. What was she to do? She could not go back. She could not remain where she was. She must go on. She went on. She mounted a stair, pushed open a door, and found herself in your room."

The professor appeared unimpressed. "Where is she now?" he asked, dismissively, and Holmes pointed to a large bookcase in the corner.

"She is there."

At which point the bookcase creaked open and out she stepped, "brown with dust and draped with . . . cobwebs."

Her name was Anna, and she was the professor's wife. Or former wife. "We were reformers—revolutionists—Nihilists," she explained.

> He and I and many more. Then there came a time of trouble, a police officer was killed, many were arrested, evidence was wanted, and in order to save his own life and to earn a great reward, my husband betrayed his own wife and his companions. Yes, we were all arrested upon his confession. Some of us found our way to the gallows, and some to Siberia. I was among these last, but my term was not for life. My husband came to England with his ill-gotten gains and has lived in quiet

ever since, knowing well that if the Brotherhood knew where he was not a week would pass before justice would be done.

She had not returned to exact that justice, however. A friend, a good man, was in prison, and the professor possessed documents that would lead to his immediate release. She had come to retrieve those, and had succeeded too. The documents were already in her possession when she was discovered by the unfortunate Smith. She passed them to Holmes.

"Here is the packet which will save Alexis. I confide it to your honour and to your love of justice. Take it! You will deliver it at the Russian Embassy. Now, I have done my duty, and . . . ."

And with that she collapsed to the ground, poisoned by her own hand.

The Adventure of the Missing Three-Quarter (August 1904)

Another of those tales that one feels Conan Doyle might have dashed off almost distractedly, simply to fulfill his quota. Certainly one hopes that he was actually pleased with it. There are a few stories in the canon that one can dismissively sniff are not particularly good. But this one is an absolute stinker.

Holmes is contacted by Cyril Overton of Trinity College, Cambridge, concerned over the fate of his star rugby player, the three-quarter Godfrey Staunton. There is a big match the following day against a rival Oxford team, but Staunton is missing, last sighted leaving his hotel at 10:30 at night in the company of a bearded man who had apparently delivered bad news. They were last seen heading toward the Strand, and only one word of their conversation was overheard by the porter. That word was "time."

Holmes visits the young man's room. He had received a telegram earlier in the evening, and Holmes is able to read his reply impressed into the blotting pad on the desk.

Kidnapping is briefly suspected, and so is the man to whom that last telegram was sent, a Cambridge academic and former doctor named Leslie Armstrong. But neither is the case, for by following the doctor, Holmes delivers the solution.

Staunton was back in Cambridge, at the bedside of his dying, consumptive wife.

Yawn.

The Adventure of the Abbey Grange (September 1904)

The tale begins not with a visitor, but with another of the most frequently quoted (and this time, accurately so) remarks in Holmesian lore.

"It was on a bitterly cold night and frosty morning, towards the end of the winter of '97, that I was awakened by a tugging at my shoulder. It was Holmes. The candle in his hand shone upon his eager, stooping face, and told me at a glance that something was amiss. 'Come, Watson, come!' he cried. 'The game is afoot.'"

The game is afoot. What a wonderful expression, and what a redolent one, too, alive with possibility, drama, and excitement, and heralding aloud the sheer joy with which Holmes approached his vocation.

It was all a game, a great game of wits and wisdom, and a new round was about to commence. The Randall Gang are already among the country's most notorious and wanted burglars, long before Inspector Hopkins fingers them as the prime suspects in a murder at the Abbey Grange, near Chiselhurst.

Sir Eustace Brackenstall lies dead; his wife, the Australian-born Lady Mary, was struck over one eye and is nursing a large purple swelling. But when Holmes, called in by the perplexed Hopkins, queries two strange red marks on her Ladyship's arm, her maid Theresa explains that Sir Eustace was responsible for them.

He stabbed her with a hatpin.

The Brackenstalls' marriage was not a happy one. Sir Eustace was a violent and abusive man, an alcoholic who regularly beat and tormented his wife, her maid, and even her pet dog, whom he ultimately killed in an especially sadistic manner.

But still she is horrified by the brutal death of her husband, killed with a single blow from a poker while she lay helpless, stunned by a blow to the head, tied to a chair with a bell rope, and gagged.

Neither were the raiders in a hurry. Drifting in and out of consciousness, Lady Mary awoke at one point to see the intruders sitting, carelessly helping themselves to some wine. The men—one older, two younger—then left with just a few pieces of silver plate.

Holmes is intrigued by her story. The bell rope, for instance. The very act of cutting it down should have set bells clanging in the kitchen, yet nobody had heard a thing. He notes a few details about the wine bottle and the glasses, but the matters that concern him the most have more in common with what *didn't* happen than what did.

The Randall Gang had just undertaken a major job elsewhere; normally they would have lain low to avoid capture, not set out again on an even more audacious raid. And having done so, why did they then take so little from the scene?

Nothing else had been disturbed, yet the Randalls were notorious ransackers.

Holmes pointed out that the wine bottle they opened had been left half full. That the crime was committed at 11:00 p.m., an early hour for any burglar. That the knots in the bell rope that bound Lady Mary were uncommonly well tied for a landlubber. That Sir Eustace's blood was spattered on the seat of the chair that his wife claimed to have already been seated in when he entered the fray.

The murderer, Holmes declares, is not a member of the Randall Gang. The murderer is a 6-foot-3-inch-tall sailor who fell in love with Lady Brackenstall when she sailed to England from Australia eighteen months earlier. The missing silver will be found in the lake, close by the hole that was recently broken in the ice.

And by the time he arrives home to 221b, another piece of evidence has turned up. The Randall Gang has just been arrested in New York City.

Soon, Holmes is hearing the entire story from the sailor himself, Captain Crocker, and it becomes clear that the murder was committed in self-defense after he foolishly tried to visit Lady Mary that night and was instead greeted by her drunken husband. The story of the raid was concocted with the maid, Theresa, and Crocker is quite willing to accept the consequences of his actions.

Instead, the noble Holmes sets him free.

The Adventure of the Second Stain (December 1904)

Sherlock Holmes was absent from the next two issues of *The Strand*, dated October and November 1904. But he returned in December with a tale that sharp-eyed readers quickly recognized as a blast from the past, an adventure that was first alluded to in "The Adventure of the Naval Treaty" eleven years earlier.

At the time, Watson explained the case was of "such importance and implicates so many of the first families in the kingdom that for many years it will be impossible to make it public."

Presumably, those years had now passed.

More than that, however, Holmes, too, was in a very different place from where he had been just three issues earlier. As the adventure of the Abbey Grange ended, the reader is left in no doubt that he will return, full of vigor, in due course.

But the opening lines of this new tale speak of a very different future.

Watson drops the bomb in his opening sentence. "I had intended 'The Adventure of the Abbey Grange' to be the last of those exploits of my friend, Mr. Sherlock Holmes, which I should ever communicate to the public."

No dramatic death, no much-heralded horror. No cliff-hanging ending. Just a plain and simple statement of fact.

> This resolution of mine was not due to any lack of material, since I have notes of many hundreds of cases to which I have never alluded, nor was it caused by any waning interest on the part of my readers in the singular personality and unique methods of this remarkable man. The real reason lay in the reluctance which Mr. Holmes has shown to the continued publication of his experiences. So long as he was in actual professional practice the records of his successes were of some practical value to him, but since he has definitely retired from London and betaken himself to study and bee-farming on the Sussex Downs, notoriety has become hateful to him, and he has peremptorily requested that his wishes in this matter should be strictly observed.
>
> It was only upon my representing to him that I had given a promise that 'The Adventure of the Second Stain' should be published when the times were ripe, and pointing out to him that it is only appropriate that

The British love of remembering historical personages with blue plaques is extended to
the world of literature.   © *Steve and Betsy Mortensen*

this long series of episodes should culminate in the most important
international case which he has ever been called upon to handle, that I
at last succeeded in obtaining his consent that a carefully guarded
account of the incident should at last be laid before the public. If in
telling the story I seem to be somewhat vague in certain details, the
public will readily understand that there is an excellent reason for my
reticence.

Holmes has retired?

A thousand questions immediately spring to the reader's mind. But Watson
does not care to answer them. For now, he is concerned only with wrapping up
the saga of Sherlock Holmes with, indeed, "the most important international
case which he has ever been called upon to handle," and he does so with swag-
gering aplomb.

A rare excursion into the realms of politics and the affairs of state, "The
Adventure of the Second Stain" is one of the very few stories in the canon that
loses a soupçon of its veracity by the need to insert fictional characters into
prominent positions: there never was a prime minister named Lord Bellinger,
nor a secretary of state for European affairs named Trelawney Hope.

Of course, their existence in this story was necessary; the modern penchant
for introducing real-life politicians into fictional escapades had yet to dawn,
and that approach can bring its own storytelling problems, as well. So Conan
Doyle was right to do as he did. Particularly as neither of the invented politicians
actually comes out of the story looking especially brilliant.

Hope is the biggest fool, as he contrives to lose a crucial document from
the dispatch box that he kept with him at all times. Crucial indeed—were this

document to fall into the wrong hands, war might well explode around it. And with typical governmental bullishness, the authorities really don't want Holmes to know anything more than that.

It is only when he points out that it will be very difficult for him to find a particular document if he doesn't know what the document actually is that they admit it is a somewhat incendiary letter penned by a foreign ruler.

We welcome Inspector Lestrade back to the fold, returning from the void into which more recent Holmesian adventures had cast him to take an active role in this latest mystery. And, of course, to allow Holmes to outmaneuver his best suspicions once again.

Holmes has two initial lines of inquiry. First, who knew that Hope had the letter in his possession? Nobody; not his wife, not his servants. No one. And second, what can Holmes's contacts within the espionage world tell him? Not much. Especially after Holmes learns that one of the most reliable of them all, a gent named Eduardo Lucas, was found murdered the previous night. It is not, Holmes is sure, a coincidence, and for a time it is the mystery of Lucas's death that preoccupies him.

Lucas's valet was the initial suspect, but he was able to provide an alibi. Lucas's wife, Madame Henri Fournaye, is linked to the crime (Fournaye was one of Lucas's other identities), but she is insane and cannot be relied upon for any statements whatsoever. What is apparent is that the killer had enough time in the room where Lucas died to move both furniture and the carpet around—the "second stain" alluded to in the story's title refers to the fact that while Lucas was stabbed to death on one side of the room, the bloodstain was on the other. And beneath the carpet, there is a secret hiding place.

Sadly, it is empty, but it has clearly been recently used.

The constable stationed outside the murder scene acknowledges that he had allowed somebody into the room, a woman whom he intended to accompany throughout her visit but who fainted at the sight of so much blood. The constable left to get her some brandy, and when he returned she had recovered and gone.

Holmes produces a photograph of Trelawney Hope's wife, Hilda. It was she.

The story flows out from there. Lucas had been blackmailing Mrs. Trelawney Hope, demanding the contents of her husband's dispatch box to maintain his silence—a spy in the politician's own office had informed Lucas of what was in there. She delivered the papers, but before she could leave again, Lucas's insane wife appeared, accusing the pair—Lucas and Hilda—of being lovers.

Hilda left; when she returned, Lucas had been murdered. She retrieved the papers while the constable was fetching her the brandy and had now returned them to the dispatch box. Which was where, Holmes told the prime minister and the secretary, they had been all along.

The secretary had made all that fuss for nothing.

12

The Adventure of the Not Especially Retiring Retiree

In which Conan Doyle is Widowed, Holmes Bestrides the silver screen, and we Begin to Suspect that the Business about Beekeeping was all a Bunch of Malarkey

F reed once again from the demands of Sherlock Holmes, Conan Doyle continued his novel-writing career, while all the time conscious that his wife's health was finally faltering.

She had long outlived the gloomy prognoses with which her initial sickness had been greeted, but on July 4, 1906, aged just forty-nine, Touie passed away.

The effect that her death had on Conan Doyle has long been argued over. Some biographers and writers have argued that he went into a steep decline, both as an author and as a thinker. Others see him embracing life—and death—even more fully than he had before, throwing himself into a dizzying whirl of social engagements, while using his renown and success to promote any number of causes.

He became a champion for what he perceived as victims of injustice; he became an avid proponent of spiritualism and the supernatural. He married his beloved, and so patient, Jean Leckie; and in August 1908, he gifted readers of *The Strand* with a brand-new Sherlock Holmes story, the first in what was described as an "occasional series"—meaning Conan Doyle would tell a story only when he believed he had a story to tell.

Holmes had not been totally absent from the world. Late 1905 saw the release of the first-ever narrative Holmes movie, an American production titled *Adventures of Sherlock Holmes, or, Held for Ransom*, produced by the Vitagraph Company of America and, apparently, fully licensed from Conan Doyle's American publisher, McClure, Phillips & Co.

Little of the movie survives today—just a fourteen-foot paper print deposited for copyright purposes with the U.S. Library of Congress in September 1905. The full movie, revolving around the kidnapping of a child and Holmes's attempts to rescue her, has long since been lost, and so thoroughly that there is no certainty as to whom even played Holmes. Attempts to revisit the movie from period press clippings and reviews, therefore, have involved historians in a mystery as pronounced as any Holmes ever investigated.

What of the real Holmes, however? Well, he sprang back into action in a tale so gripping that it was perforcedly spread over two issues of *The Strand*, to emerge as one of the great detective's most satisfying adventures.

A Reminiscence of Mr. Sherlock Holmes, aka The Adventure of Wisteria Lodge (part one: The Singular Experience of Mr. John Scott Eccles—August 1908; part two: The Tiger of San Pedro—September 1908)

Holmes remained in retirement, as Watson explains at the outset of the new tale.

"I find it recorded in my notebook that it was a bleak and windy day towards the end of March in the year 1892. Holmes had received a telegram while we sat at our lunch, and he had scribbled a reply. He made no remark, but the matter remained in his thoughts, for he stood in front of the fire afterwards with a thoughtful face, smoking his pipe, and casting an occasional glance at the message."

A gentleman named John Scott Eccles wishes to discuss something that he describes as "grotesque" with Holmes; he is invited to visit 221b but has barely arrived when the police show up, too. Eccles has been implicated in a murder that occurred the previous evening—one Aloysius Garcia has been beaten to death, and a note in his pocket suggested he would be meeting with Eccles that night.

Eccles has nothing to hide. He spent the night at Garcia's home, Wisteria Lodge, and had been most perplexed when he awoke in the morning to find the house deserted. Neither Garcia nor his house staff were around, and that included the servant who had interrupted an already awkward evening (Garcia seemed strangely ill-at-ease the whole night) with what appeared to be a most ominous note.

Inspector Baynes already had the note in his possession. It seemed meaningless. "Our own colours, green and white. Green open, white shut. Main stair, first corridor, seventh right, green baize. Godspeed. D."

It was written by a woman, and Baynes suggested a jealous husband might have been involved. Holmes, however, kept his own counsel. The murderer was a local person, he said. Was an Englishman. And he or she lived in a large house.

The first, enthralling part of the story ends with the arrival of a telegram and a gloating Holmes's explanation.

We have already arrived at the conclusion that the message received by Garcia at dinner was an appointment or an assignation. Now, if the obvious reading of it is correct, and in order to keep the tryst one has to ascend a main stair and seek the seventh door in a corridor, it is perfectly clear that the house is a very large one. As the number of large houses close to Oxshott must be limited, I adopted the obvious method of . . . obtaining a list of them. Here they are in this telegram, and the other end of our tangled skein must lie among them.

They arrive in Esher to discover the constable assigned to guard Wisteria Lodge reeling from a sighting of a particularly brutish-looking man.

It was just about two hours ago. The light was just fading. I was sitting reading in the chair. I don't know what made me look up, but there was a face looking in at me through the lower pane. Lord, sir, what a face it was! I'll see it in my dreams.

Dark deeds to discuss in Wisteria Lodge.

Paget explores Wisteria Lodge.

It wasn't black, sir, nor was it white, nor any colour that I know but a kind of queer shade like clay with a splash of milk in it. Then there was the size of it—it was twice yours, sir. And the look of it—the great staring goggle eyes, and the line of white teeth like a hungry beast. I tell you, sir, I couldn't move a finger, nor get my breath, till it whisked away and was gone. Out I ran and through the shrubbery, but thank God there was no one there.

Footprints, however, prove that somebody *had* been there, and touring the house, a number of other disquieting oddities are discovered. A dead and dismembered bird. A plate of burned bones, a bucket of blood, a mummified baby. All signs, Holmes declares, of voodoo.

Inspector Baynes makes an arrest. The awful face that the constable saw at the window that day resolved itself into a perfect description of Garcia's cook, who is now in custody. Holmes does not for a moment consider the man guilty of the crime, but the arrest preoccupies Baynes and allows Holmes to continue his own investigations.

He focuses upon High Gable, home to a Mr. Henderson, whose staff include an English governess named Miss Burnet and a dark-skinned, patently foreign servant; and he is promptly rewarded when Henderson attempts to flee, taking a clearly unwilling Miss Burnet with him.

She is rescued in the nick of time, for when Henderson's description reaches Baynes, it becomes clear that this is no simple case of murder.

Henderson is Don Juan Murillo, former dictator of the Central American nation of San Pedro, and so cruel and violent that he was better known as an animal: the Tiger of San Pedro. And so unspools a gripping tale of hotblooded Latin politics spilling out on the quiet green of England, and a worthy return to the game for Sherlock Holmes.

The Adventure of the Bruce-Partington Plans (December 1908)

Amid all the references to the London underground that can either be discovered or inferred from within Conan Doyle's writings, the best known of all Holmes's subterranean investigations was that which took him along the train tracks between Gloucester Road and Aldgate (not to be confused with Aldersgate) stations.

No pleasure jaunt this, however. No early morning commute. Rather, he was tracing the journey taken days earlier by the luckless corpse of Arthur Cadogan West, a clerk at the Royal Arsenal in Woolwich, across the river in south London.

The mystery opens at Aldgate, a station opened in 1876 and, by the time Conan Doyle came to write "The Adventure of the Bruce-Partington Plans," one that offered a straight shot from Richmond in the west to Tower Hill in the east. The corpse could have joined the train at any point along that route.

"The body was found at six on the Tuesday morning," Watson explains. "It was lying wide of the metals upon the left hand of the track as one goes eastward, at a point close to the station, where the line emerges from the tunnel in which it runs."

There was no train ticket in the corpse's pocket, suggesting he had not entered the underground network through any conventional or legitimate means. There was no blood on the scene, suggesting his head must have been bashed in someplace else. And there was nobody who could tell how the body—alive or dead—had come to be deposited where it lay. Regardless of whether or not the case was solved, poor Arthur's remains remain at the heart of one of the most alluring and atmospheric of all Holmes's latter-day mysteries. All the more so since, had he been alive, he would have seen the London Underground from a vantage point that very few other people can ever have managed. From *atop* the train.

How did he get there?

Well . . .

Among the many peculiarities of the underground system, the network's habit of rising out of the ground to run in the open air is one of its most charming. Unless, of course, you happen to live in one of the houses that actually border the tracks—of which, around the city, there are many. These include one, on the Cromwell Road hard by Gloucester Square Station, and still visible on the tracks today, from which it would have taken a matter of moments to move a body from the window ledge to the roof of a train as it waited at the signal outside the station itself. This house Holmes isolates, and one end of the mystery is solved.

At the other end, the body's sudden fall from its lofty perch, the dense concentration of points just outside of Aldgate bore sole responsibility for that. The Underground has indeed starred in many stories, by many authors. But rarely has it played such a hands-on role in the action.

As for the story, it's another of Conan-Doyle's "missing secrets" tales. The titular plans are those of a top-secret submarine, stolen and only partially recovered—seven of the ten pages were found on Cadogan West's body.

Sadly, it is the three missing pages that are the most important ones, for it is from these that one of Britain's many international enemies could discover the means to build its own submarine.

The obvious conclusion is that Cadogan West stole the plans, intending to sell them, and then either fell or was pushed from a train. Holmes disproves that, just as he sorts out the rest of the mystery. Far from being a treacherous dog, Cadogan West was actually a national hero, the bold lad who tried to recover the stolen plans from the foreign agent who had snatched them in the first place, and who was murdered for his pains. And with that sorted out, now the authorities could get on with tracking down the real criminal.

The Adventure of the Speckled Band Revisited

First published in 1892, the popularity of "The Adventure of the Speckled Band" (or "The *Spotted* Band," as it was titled in America) has established it among the best-loved of all the Holmes stories. It was certainly Conan Doyle's personal favorite, and perhaps rightfully so. The mystery is one of his most ingenious, its solution one of his most triumphant, and its conclusion one of his most just.

It was also precisely the kind of panacea he required, that spring of 1910, as he reflected upon the not-quite-abject failure of his latest attempt to break into the world of theater, with an adaptation of his *Rodney Stone* novel.

The House of Temperly: A Melodrama of the Ring was well received critically, but bums on seats were at such a premium that Conan Doyle grasped the first available opportunity to cut short its proposed six-month run.

On May 6, 1910, King Edward VII passed away after just a decade on the throne, and all of London's theaters closed their doors as a sign of respect. Conan Doyle's show at the Adelphi simply didn't reopen afterward. Instead he set to work on an adaptation of the Holmes story, making sufficient changes to the plot and characters to allow him to give it a new title, *The Stonor Case*, and then reverting to the original name shortly before the play opened.

Which was not very far off. With the actor H. A. Saintsbury taking the role of Holmes, *The Speckled Band* was in rehearsal within just two weeks of its predecessor's closure, and on June 4 it opened to the public, first at the Adelphi, and then the Globe. It ultimately ran for a very respectable 169 performances before closing on October 10 and could well be termed a success.

Conan Doyle, however, had had enough of the theater and immediately announced his retirement from ever venturing into those waters again. Anxious not to prejudice anybody who did make their livelihood, or extract enjoyment, from the medium, however, he was swift to explain, "I am not leaving stage work because it does not interest me. It interests me too much. It's so absorbing that it draws your mind away from the deeper things of life. I recognize my own limitations. I make an absolute pledge that I will not write for the stage again."

Instead, he wrote for Sherlock Holmes instead.

The Adventure of the Devil's Foot (December 1910)

The furthest-flung of all Holmes's canonical adventures, at least so far as the English mainland is concerned, "The Devil's Foot" is also responsible for some of the most breathtakingly designed of all his televisual tales.

One of the most dramatic and baffling of all Holmes's later cases, and arguably one of his finest altogether, "The Adventure of the Devil's Foot" finds the dynamic duo of Holmes and Watson vacationing in Cornwall, the arm of land that sees southwest England stretching out toward the Atlantic.

Both the 1965 BBC series with Douglas Wilmer, and that of Jeremy Brett twenty years later, made great use of the natural rugged beauty of Cornwall; indeed, in the case of the latter adaptation, the cost of transporting all concerned down to the location took such a great bite from the budget allocated to the series *The Return of Sherlock Holmes* that two entire episodes had to be cut from the season, while two more were filmed on the barest sets possible.

It was worth the sacrifice, however.

It is here, among the desolate cliffs and tiny fishing villages, that we first find Holmes, recovering from a recent breakdown by only begrudgingly following his doctor's orders, as Watson wryly notes.

"The state of his health was not a matter in which he himself took the faintest interest, for his mental detachment was absolute, but he was induced at last, on the threat of being permanently disqualified from work, to give himself a complete change of scene and air. Thus it was that in the early spring of that year we found ourselves together in a small cottage near Poldhu Bay, at the further extremity of the Cornish peninsula."

Scarcely have they arrived, then, and Holmes is already growing restless. Searching for a diversion, he settles upon untangling the roots of the Cornish language, even then considered a dying tongue, and the puzzling origins from

Basil Rathbone enters *The House of Fear*. *Photofest*

which it sprang. As Watson put it, "He had, I remember, conceived the idea that it was akin to the Chaldean, and had been largely derived from the Phoenician traders in tin."

Mercifully for Watson's clearly exhausted attention span, his ruminations into this fascinating topic are interrupted by the arrival of the local vicar, wild-eyed and frenzied, bursting into the room with shocking news. Three members of a local family have been discovered seated around a table at their home—two brothers insane, their sister dead.

They had been playing whist and were discovered with "the cards still spread in front of them and the candles burned down to their sockets. The sister lay back stone-dead in her chair, while the two brothers sat on each side of her laughing, shouting, and singing, the senses stricken clean out of them. All three of them, the dead woman and the two demented men, retained upon their faces an expression of the utmost horror—a convulsion of terror which was dreadful to look upon."

"Many of my readers," Watson continues, "may retain some recollection of what was called at the time 'The Cornish Horror,' though a most imperfect account of the matter reached the London press. Now . . . I will give the true details of this inconceivable affair to the public."

The expressions on the victims' faces suggest that no human agency could possibly have been involved. Which is, of course, a red rag to Holmes. "I fear," he replied, "that if the matter is beyond humanity it is certainly beyond me."

But he is willing to seek a natural explanation, and so unfolds a fascinating saga of deadly poison, jealous rage and icy revenge, a curmudgeonly explorer and a misdivided family fortune—layer upon layer of plot that not only takes Holmes's mind far away from his linguistic researches, but also distracts him from his illness.

As for the medical suggestion that he enjoy a change of air to go with the change of scenery, Holmes takes that instruction too literally, as he tests the suspected poison upon himself, an excuse for the Jeremy Brett–era detective to undertake one of the greatest sequences in all of Holmes's television adventures, a wild hallucination that brings chilling reality to an observation that Watson merely dispassionately recorded.

"In every direction upon these moors there were traces of some vanished race which had passed utterly away, and left as it sole record strange monuments of stone, irregular mounds which contained the burned ashes of the dead, and curious earthworks which hinted at prehistoric strife. The glamour and mystery of the place, with its sinister atmosphere of forgotten nations, appealed to the imagination of my friend, and he spent much of his time in long walks and solitary meditations upon the moor."

With the nature of the deaths and insanity solved, Holmes swiftly roots out the truth behind the mystery, long before his deductions are borne out by the confession of the explorer Doctor Sterndale. And with that, Holmes announces, "I think we may dismiss the matter from our mind and go back with a clear conscience to the study of those Chaldean roots which are surely to be traced in the Cornish branch of the great Celtic speech."

The Adventure of the Red Circle (March/April 1911)

Another two-parter, published in *The Strand* the following spring, "The Red Circle" opens with a visit from Mrs. Warren, a landlady who has serious qualms about her lodger, a young, bearded foreign chap who offers her double the rent for a room, provided she accede to certain requests.

Such as: not saying anything when he comes home at all hours of the night. Having a copy of the *Daily Gazette* delivered to his door every morning. Little things, trifling things, but they all mount up, and she's puzzled. So puzzled that she has purloined a cigarette end and some spent matches from the young man's ashtray, and brought them to Holmes for his inspection.

At which point we should mention one of Sherlock Holmes's proudest achievements, a monograph titled *Upon the Distinction Between the Ashes of the Various Tobaccos*. (In the twenty-first-century reinvention, this is the subject of his own attempt at a blog.) Using this evidence, as he frequently reminds Watson, he is able to determine no less than 140 different brands of cigar, pipe, or cigarette ash.

And having mentioned it, move on.

He has no need for such expertise here, after all. One look at the cigarette end is sufficient to tell him that the smoker does not use a cigarette holder—a very unusual feature in a gent so heavily whiskered.

What else can Mrs. Warren tell the detective? Not much. In fact, aside from the first day that the lodger moved in, she has not spoken to nor even seen the man. His requests are left as notes by the door; he moves around the house only when confident he will not be seen. In fact, Holmes wouldn't be surprised if the person living in the house now was a completely different man than the one Mrs. Warren had let the room to. He probably didn't have a beard, either.

He makes one of those logical leaps that seem somewhat bewildering to modern readers: that the mysterious lodger's attachment to the *Daily Gazette* can be attributed to the fact that he is sending and receiving messages through its classified advertisements—a method that was actually very common in those days before telephones, emails, and Facebook. It appears, too, that he is correct. Watson explains:

> He took down the great book in which, day by day, he filed the agony columns of the various London journals. 'Dear me!' said he, turning over the pages, 'what a chorus of groans, cries, and bleatings! What a rag-bag of singular happenings! But surely the most valuable hunting-ground that ever was given to a student of the unusual! This person is alone and cannot be approached by letter without a breach of that absolute secrecy which is desired. How is any news or any message to reach him from without? Obviously by advertisement through a newspaper. There seems no other way, and fortunately we need concern ourselves with the one paper only.'

Holmes treats Watson, and therefore his readership, to a few choice examples of what he finds there. Complete with bitter interjections of his own.

"'Lady with a black boa at Prince's Skating Club'"—that we may pass.

"'Surely Jimmy will not break his mother's heart'"—that appears to be irrelevant.

"'If the lady who fainted on Brixton bus'"—she does not interest me.

"'Every day my heart longs . . .' Bleat, Watson—unmitigated bleat!"

But then he begins to uncover those notices that seem more promising. One is from just two days after the mystery man arrived: "Be patient. Will find some sure means of communications. Meanwhile, this column. G.'"

Three days later, "Am making successful arrangements. Patience and prudence. The clouds will pass. G."

A week more, "The path is clearing. If I find chance signal message remember code agreed—One A, two B, and so on. You will hear soon. G.'"

Holmes is certain. "If we wait a little, Watson, I don't doubt that the affair will grow more intelligible."

He is correct. The following morning, the next message appears. "High red house with white stone facings. Third floor. Second window left. After dusk. G."

Before Holmes can do more than plan his next move, however, he is interrupted by the return of a most distraught Mrs. Warren. Her husband was kidnapped by ruffians . . . and then unceremoniously unkidnapped, pushed out of the cab onto the roadway up on Hampstead Heath.

What could it all mean?

A case of mistaken identity, decides Holmes. Mr. Warren was snatched by men who believed him to be the mysterious lodger, and then released when they realized their mistake.

Now things begin to fall into place. Hiding out in the boardinghouse, Holmes and Watson discover that the lodger is a woman. They realize that the "high red house with white stone facings" stands at the bottom of the road. And that night, they watch as the lodger and her confederate, presumably the mysterious G, exchange messages by lantern signal. In Italian.

"Beware!"

"Danger!"

And then—an interruption! Holmes and Watson hurry to the house, there to discover . . . the police! Inspector Gregson and Leverton, a detective with the American detective agency Pinkerton's, are hoping to ambush one of the most vicious killers it has ever been London's misfortune to harbor, a wicked man named Giuseppe Gorgiano. He is, they have reason to believe, in the house. But they will have a long wait. Neither man paid much attention to three other men who left the house a little earlier, because none of them matched Gorgiano's description. Now they effect an entry and discover their prey is dead. Murdered.

Somebody at the door! It is the woman from the boardinghouse, and isn't she pleased to see Gorgiano lying cold and stiffening on the floor? Pleased because the man had been pursuing her and her husband Gennaro,

Classic Comics give the hound his lurid walkies.

the bearded foreigner who so baffled Mrs. Warren, for months, out for blood after they betrayed a secret Italian crime ring, the Red Circle. From Italy to New York, from New York to London, Gorgiano was relentless. But now he was dead, now they were free.

Or they would be, once they had finished helping the police with their inquiries.

The Disappearance of Lady Frances Carfax (December 1911)

When an English aristocrat, Lady Frances Carfax, vanishes from her hotel in Lausanne, Switzerland, Holmes's suspicions and fears go into overdrive. Although not so much that he can take the time to investigate the matter himself. It is Watson who is dispatched to foreign climes to see what he can deduce about the disappearance.

Not much. The lady is alone, and her luggage is packed with valuable jewels. Five weeks have elapsed since she was last heard of—she had always made a point of writing weekly letters to her former governess, but none has been received for over a month. Neither has any trace of her been found through other means. Just two checks have been written on her account, one to the last hotel she stayed in, the other to the young French maid she had in her service.

There are two clues. The first is that she was spending a lot of time in the company of another couple at the hotel, the Schlessingers; the second is that she appeared to be in fear of a distinctively large, bearded Englishman whom she met while out on a walk one day. Holmes, while scarcely impressed with Watson's information, at least is content that the lady's life is in danger.

But not from the bearded man. He, Holmes quickly discovers, is her former fiancé, Philip Green, and his only desire is to be reunited with Lady Frances—years earlier, their union had been prohibited by her family because he was so poor. But now he is wealthy and wants her back.

No, it is the Schlessingers that Holmes is worried about, for he has information that places their entire identity in doubt. Mr. S is a well-known Australian confidence trickster named Henry Peters, and his wife is a brutal woman named Fraser. Together, posing as a disabled professor and his doting wife, they win the trust of young, unsuspecting women and then take them for every penny they can.

So it is with the luckless Lady Frances. Deducing that the trio are now in London, Holmes circulates the pawn shops with which he is acquainted and swiftly discovers that a man matching Peters's description had recently pawned a pendant identical to one of Lady Frances's. Days later, with Philip Green keep watching, Fraser visits the same store to pawn the pendant's twin. Worse still, when Green follows her as she leave the store, it is to an undertaker's, where she has placed an order for an "out of the ordinary" coffin. The funeral for which this item is required will take place the following morning.

Acting fast, Holmes and Watson visit Peters's home, demanding to see the body. They have no search warrant, and Peters is swiftly able to evict them with the assistance of a none-too-willing passing policeman. Not, however, before he has shown the duo the object of their curiosity, a very small, very emaciated, and very dead old lady. His wife's childhood nurse, he explains.

"Rose Spender by name," continues the rogue, honey dripping from his fangs.

> Whom we found in the Brixton Workhouse Infirmary. We brought her round here, called in Doctor Horsom, of 13 Firbank Villas—mind you take the address, Mr. Holmes—and had her carefully tended, as Christian folk should. On the third day she died—certificate says senile decay—but that's only the doctor's opinion, and of course you know better. We ordered her funeral to be carried out by Stimson and Co., of the Kennington Road, who will bury her at eight o'clock to-morrow morning. Can you pick any hole in that, Mr. Holmes? You've made a silly blunder, and you may as well own up to it. I'd give something for a photograph of your gaping, staring face when you pulled aside that lid expecting to see the Lady Frances Carfax and only found a poor old woman of ninety.

Holmes is baffled—until he spends a sleepless night going over every aspect of the case, and suddenly the significance of the "out-of-the-ordinary" coffin dawns on him. Even with a normal-sized corpse, it would have been large enough for two bodies. It is far too vast for the tiny frame of the nurse.

Back to the house, back into the parlor where the coffin has now been closed. The police are on their way, hopefully bearing the search warrant that Holmes has been promised. But there is no time to wait. The coffin is forced open, and there, chloroformed and unconscious, is Lady Frances, her body unceremoniously dumped on top of the old woman's.

Of course Watson is able to revive her, but what of the dastardly duo that intended to bury her alive? They escaped, and Holmes strangely does not seem to especially mourn their disappearance. Their plan, after all, was "a clever device, Watson. It is new to me in the annals of crime. If our . . . friends escape the clutches of Lestrade, I shall expect to hear of some brilliant incidents in their future career."

The Adventure of the Dying Detective (November 1913)

Well, here we go again, and once again Watson, who really ought to know better, is utterly taken in. He is called to 221b, where Sherlock Holmes, the greatest detective who ever lived, is preparing to breathe his last. He has contracted a rare Asian disease, picked up not in Asia itself, but while on a case in the mean streets of Rotherhithe, out in east London in one of those areas that had experienced an influx of Chinese immigrants. He has not taken food or water in three days, and the disease is so contagious that Holmes forbids anybody to approach him, for fear that they might also contract it.

Mrs. Hudson is at her wits' end:

'He's dying, Dr. Watson . . . . For three days he has been sinking, and I doubt if he will last the day. He would not let me get a doctor. This morning when I saw his bones sticking out of his face and his great bright eyes looking at me I could stand no more of it. 'With your leave or without it, Mr. Holmes, I am going for a doctor this very hour,' said I. 'Let it be Watson, then,' said he. I wouldn't waste an hour in coming to him, sir, or you may not see him alive."

Holmes does indeed look deathly, but when Watson attempts to help, Holmes rebuffs him. Only one man

Sidney Paget mourns the Dying Detective.

can help him, he insists, but Holmes will not name him until six that evening. Then, to ensure Watson does not creep out and fetch further assistance of his own, Holmes leaps out of bed, locks the door, and takes the key.

And so they waited, Watson in several states of despair, Holmes drifting in and out of delirium but alert enough to snap at his friend when he felt the occasion deserved. Such as when Watson moved to pick up a small black and white ivory box with a sliding lid.

Finally, the appointed hour arrives. Holmes tells Watson to turn on the gaslight but to keep the light low. He then gives the doctor the name he has waited all day for, a Mr. Culverton Smith of 13 Lower Burke Street. The man is not a doctor, Holmes explains. But he is an expert in the disease from which

Holmes is suffering. Oh, and one final thing. The two men, Smith and Watson, are to return to Baker Street separately.

It swiftly transpires that there is no love lost between Holmes and this man Smith; apparently, Holmes once had cause to investigate Smith regarding the looming death of a nephew. "There is no good feeling between us. His nephew, Watson–I had suspicions of foul play and I allowed him to see it. The boy died horribly. He has a grudge against me. You will soften him, Watson. Beg him, pray him, get him here by any means. He can save me—only he!"

Smith initially refuses to even see Watson, but his attitude changes when he learns that Holmes is dying. He agrees to visit Baker Street, while Watson—pleading another engagement—hurries back there himself and, as Holmes directs, hides behind a decorative screen. There he watches as Smith taunts the dying man, jabbing at him over his monstrous insistence that he, Smith, could possibly have murdered his nephew. No, it was pure coincidence, the *purest* coincidence, that poor Victor should have succumbed to

"an out-of-the-way Asiatic disease in the heart of London—a disease, too, of which I had made such a very special study. Singular coincidence, Holmes. Very smart of you to notice it, but rather uncharitable to suggest that it was cause and effect."

And coincidence, too, that Holmes should now be dying from the exact same contagion?

No, not exactly. There is nothing whatsoever amiss with Holmes. He is not ill; he is not dying. He is peckish, of course, and thirsty, and he is gasping for a cigarette. But otherwise he is as healthy as a horse. He just wanted to get Smith to confess, which in his arrogance and triumph, he had, that he was responsible for Victor's death. And to do so in front of two witnesses, Doctor Watson, of course, and the equally well-hidden Inspector Morton.

13

The Adventure of the Valley of Fear

In which Conan Doyle Publishes his Fourth and Final Sherlock Holmes Novel, while Contemplating Anew the Possibility of Doing Away with the Detective Altogether

"There's an east wind coming, Watson."

"I think not, Holmes. It is very warm."

"Good old Watson! You are the one fixed point in a changing age. There's an east wind coming all the same, such a wind as never blew on England yet. It will be cold and bitter, Watson, and a good many of us may wither before its blast. But it's God's own wind none the less, and a cleaner, better, stronger land will lie in the sunshine when the storm has cleared."

(from His Last Bow*; published September 1917, set in August 1914)*

Great Britain was at war. No, the world was at war. On August 4, 1914, just days before the latest issue of *The Strand* hit the streets, the storm clouds that had been rolling across Europe for so many months finally broke. War was declared on Germany, and the nation mobilized.

Conan Doyle mobilized with it. On the very day that hostilities were declared, he hosted a meeting in his local Oddfellows Hall "to discuss the feasibility of forming a Local Company or Companies for Purposes of Drill and Efficiency, that we may be of service to our Country in this crisis."

The Crowborough National Reserve Company would be armed and drilled; a private army made up of men whom the regular military would never conceive of calling up—the old, the young, and the infirm, of course, but also those whose occupations would establish them as essential personnel on the homefront.

Conan Doyle fell into the first category; at fifty-five years of age, he was far beyond even the upper limits of military service. But he wanted to do his bit, and how furious must he have been when the War Office responded to his patriotism by demanding the immediate disbandment of all and any unauthorized armed bodies. Instead, the military itself established a national volunteer service, and Private A. C. Doyle would serve with as much distinction as the constant marching, drilling, and rifle practice permitted.

Of far greater value to the war effort was his journalism, based not around the events of the war itself, but on their consequences. When three British warships were sunk, in the course of one hour, by a roaming German submarine, with the loss of almost fifteen hundred lives, it was Conan Doyle who launched a media campaign for all seamen to be equipped with lifejackets—incredibly, at that time, they weren't. But they soon would be, as the admiralty acknowledged the wisdom of Conan Doyle's words and agreed that never again should "a young German lieutenant with twenty men . . . [cause] us more loss than we suffered at [the Battle of] Trafalgar."

Not all of Conan Doyle's ideas met the same response. The authorities shrugged off his suggestion that fighting men should be equipped with body armor, sensible though the idea was; ignored, too, was his farsighted visualization of the modern minesweeper.

He suggested a postwar boycott of Germany, whatever the outcome of the war, and recommended that for every British town that was bombed by a German Zeppelin, three German towns should be obliterated in response. A quarter of a century later, in August 1940, Adolf Hitler passed similar judgment on the British following a raid on Berlin and ignited what Londoners still call "the Blitz." The British in 1915 were not so reactionary, although that did not calm Conan Doyle's rhetoric. He continued to preach escalating retribution, speaking aloud the thoughts and conversations of the average man on the street, and certainly increasing his own popularity as he did so.

The Valley of Fear (September 1914–May 1915)

If the authorities regarded him as just one of many influential rabble-rousers, however, there was one area in which Conan Doyle had no peer whatsoever. In keeping up morale with his talents as a storyteller. That same month that war erupted across Europe, and across the first nine months of what would ultimately stretch on for a wearying four years, *The Strand* launched *The Valley of Fear*, a new full-length Holmes adventure that . . . well, in truth, it was only half a Holmes adventure, as "part two" of the tale flashed back to the adventures of the Pinkerton detectives in the days of the Molly Maguires—Irish secret societies who wreaked havoc across the Pennsylvania mining district some fifty years before.

"Part One," however, "The Tragedy of Birlstone," was classic Holmes.

Set prior to the events at Reichenbach Falls, the story fills in some of the gaps in the Holmesian chronology which that story so infuriatingly opened up—namely, the nature of Holmes's investigation into Professor Moriarty's criminal activities that led up to that final crisis.

It opens with a coded letter sent to the detective by Fred Porlock, a member of the Moriarty gang, warning (once it has been decoded, of course) of the imminent murder of one John Douglas of Birlstone House. Unfortunately, the letter arrived too late. No sooner has Holmes finished deciphering it than a knock on the door announces Inspector MacDonald of Scotland Yard, come to ask Holmes's assistance in the mystifying murder of . . . one John Douglas of Birlstone House.

Mystifying because four other people were known to be in the house at the time: his wife, his butler, a servant, and an American friend named Cecil Barker. Longstanding Holmes readers no doubt raised their eyebrows at that revelation. Another perfidious colonial? But the detective does not take the bait, for there are other intriguing elements to the case. Douglas lived in a moated home; that is, it was completely surrounded by water, accessible only via a drawbridge. And he raised it every night at 6:30 p.m.

An exciting new card game!

The body itself is all but unidentifiable; a shotgun blast to the face at close range will have that effect. Douglas was identified by a peculiar branding on his arm, and by the nugget ring he wore. His wedding band, however, was missing.

As for clues, there was a single bloody footprint on the windowsill, and a card reading "VV 341." There is also the strange presence of a bicycle and a bag that have been traced to a guest at a nearby hotel—a guest whose physical description matches the dead man.

Holmes swiftly ferrets out further oddities. One of the dead man's dumbbells is missing. It is found in the moat, where it was used to weigh down a bundle of clothes. He replaces it, however, and then sets a trap, letting it be known that the moat is to be drained in search of evidence. Sure enough, that night, a figure is spotted furtively retrieving the bundle. It is Barker.

But was he the killer? No! No sooner has he been arrested than Mrs. Douglas rushes in, declares the American innocent, and then opens up a secret compartment in the fireplace. John Douglas, the supposedly murdered man, steps out. For it was not he who was killed. It was the intruder, a man named Baldwin whom he knew when he, too, was in the United States, running with a gang in Vermissa Valley, Lodge 341. A gang whose members all wore the same distinctive brand.

Baldwin had come to England expressly to murder Douglas, for reasons that he would go on to reveal in part two. Which we will read because we are halfway through the story, and because Conan Doyle can always spin a good yarn when he has the storytelling bit between his teeth. But, as with *A Study in Scarlet* thirty years before, the remainder of the story is mere background to the events that led up to the investigation, and background, too, to Moriarty's role in the action.

Until we reach the epilogue. It appears that fate caught up with Douglas after all. Traveling to South Africa with his wife, he disappeared from on board ship during a storm. Officially, he seems to have simply fallen. But Holmes believes he knows better. Moriarty always hated leaving lose ends lying around.

The Stirring Adventure of the Real-Life Detectives

You know how it goes. You wake up, there's a mystery on the doorstep. You don't want to call the police in yet, because all they'll do is laugh at you, but you need someone who will take it seriously immediately. There's only one place to turn. A private detective.

Throughout the years during which Conan Doyle was writing and Sherlock Holmes was active, there was one detective agency that everybody had heard of. The Pinkerton Detective Agency.

Like Conan Doyle, the titular Pinkerton was Scottish, born on August 25, 1819. Allan Pinkerton was a cooper by trade, and when he immigrated to the United States and settled in Dundee, Illinois, in 1842, he intended on maintaining that profession. Indeed, he quickly established himself as one of the finest coopers around, famed not only for the superior quality of his workmanship, but also for the low prices that he charged.

It was during one of Pinkerton's regular trips out of town, looking to source fresh materials, that the notion of the detective agency first struck him. A major counterfeiting ring had been operating in the area for some time but had baffled all attempts by officialdom to discover its headquarters. Pinkerton did, stumbling upon the gang's hideout on a supposedly deserted island. He contacted the local sheriff, and together they staked out the area until the gang showed itself. They were arrested; their ringleader, absent from the initial raid, followed his henchmen into custody, and Pinkerton suddenly found himself fêted as a detective par excellence.

Pinkerton founded his detective agency in 1850, building its staff, its reputation, and indeed its entire operation upon his own principles of law and justice. Cases flooded in to the office, taking operatives far, far afield in pursuit of their quarry, and when the Civil War broke out, Pinkerton was swiftly recruited by the Union to head up their own spying operation.

Then it was back to his own agency until his death on July 1, 1884, after which the Pinkerton National Detective Agency continued to grow and prosper.

The Strand tells it like it is.

Not every operation that the agency was brought in to investigate was popular. The government frequently hired Pinkerton's to work against the nascent labor movement, leading many people to regard them as an unofficial arm of the government itself. But still their reputation as a firm that got things done was untarnished, and though Pinkerton's itself no longer exists (it was subsumed into the vast Securitas organization in 2003), its name remains as potent a synonym for detective work as Holmes's own.

With as much history behind it, no particular eras can be described as Pinkerton's "golden age." But the 1880s and 1890s, the years during which the first Holmes stories were being written, certainly saw the company's name writ large in the headlines of the day.

In 1892, Pinkerton men were in the frontline of the Homestead Strike, called in to protect the Pittsburgh mining industry from striking workers. Two years later, a Pinkerton operative, Frank Geyer, brought to justice one of America's first documented serial killers, a Chicago hotelier known as Dr. Henry Howard Holmes, whose hotel was expressly built with murder in mind. After preying on visitors to the Chicago World's Fair in 1893, Holmes would confess to twenty-seven slayings but may well have been responsible for almost two hundred more. And yes, commentators of the time did remark upon the irony of a real-life detective catching a man named Holmes, at the same time as a fictional detective named Holmes was apprehending criminals of his own.

Conan Doyle was acutely aware of Pinkerton's and may even have drawn some of his inspiration from published reports of the company's activities. The second half of *The Valley of Fear* was firmly based around one of the agency's operations, against a secret organization of Irish coalminers called the Molly Maguires; and a Pinkerton agent has a small role in "The Adventure of the Red Circle." Indeed, Leverton is described by Holmes as "the hero of the Long Island cave mystery"—and how we wish Conan Doyle had written that tale down!

In the years since then, fiction has rarely shied away from invoking the name and the activities of Pinkerton's; a legion of books, articles, and movies have told tales that draw the agency's detectives into play, not least of all, among recent publications, Seattle author Cherie Priest's *Clementine*, an installment within her Clockwork Century series of Steampunk novels.

There, a former Confederate spy named Maria Isabella Boyd finds circumstances pushing her to work for Pinkerton's, in pursuit of a stolen top-secret dirigible—a gripping adventure that successfully melds a strong sense of Pinkerton morality to the electrifying universe of Steampunk itself. And so another Victorian-age detective steps onto a modern fictional stage that, quite frankly, is now so lousy with the things that it's a wonder there's anyone left for them to investigate.

SHERLOCK HOLMES & DR. WATSON "THE REIGATE SQUIRE"   SHERLOCK HOLMES & SIR HENRY "THE HOUND OF THE BASKERVILLES"   SHERLOCK HOLMES & LESTRADE "THE SIX NAPOLEONS"   SHERLOCK HOLMES & MYCROFT "THE GREEK INTERPRETER"   SHERLOCK HOLMES & MORIARTY "THE FINAL PROBLEM"

You can even ask Holmes to post a letter for you!

Rathbone and Bruce in pursuit of The Secret Weapon.   *Photofest*

His Last Bow (September 1917)

Increasingly preoccupied by his war writing, Conan Doyle penned just one further Sherlock Holmes story during the Great War, and we should not perhaps be surprised that it too was heavily flavored by current affairs.

It is an unusual story in many ways. It is told in the third person, with Watson simply a partner, as opposed to the narrator of the story. It reflects back a little on past Holmesian tales of deduction and spycraft but is concerned not simply with the retrieval of missing documents, but with the capture of a dangerous German spy. And, had it been the work of any other author, with any other protagonist, it would today be regarded as just one more in the long, long line of propagandist fictions foisted upon the reading public as the war dragged on.

It is a good one, to be sure; a clever one, too. But even today, read as the final tale in the fourth collected edition of Sherlock Holmes adventures, *His Last Bow: Some Later Reminiscences of Sherlock Holmes*, it stands apart from the six other stories in the volume, those that were first published prior to the war.

"His Last Bow" is set in mid-1914, on the very eve of the Great War. A German agent, Von Bork, has been in Britain for some time now, gathering information that will surely be put to good use once hostilities are declared. His wife and family have already returned to Germany; Von Bork is simply awaiting one final piece of intelligence from one of his most reliable sources, an Irish-American agent named (in tribute to Conan Doyle's father) Altamont.

After much to-ing and fro-ing, and the extraction by the American of all manner of secret German information, Altamont is revealed to be Sherlock Holmes, playing the final hand in a game that has seen him feed false information to Von Bork for the past two years. His chauffeur, of course, is Doctor Watson. And the information he had to pass on? A copy of the *Practical Handbook of Bee Culture*. Yes, it appears that when Holmes said he was retiring to raise bees in the countryside, he meant every word.

The German is chloroformed and taken to Scotland Yard. And Holmes returns to his retirement, this time for good. There would be more Sherlock Holmes stories in the future. But they would be memories of past cases, rather than recountings of current adventures.

The Great Detective had taken his final bow.

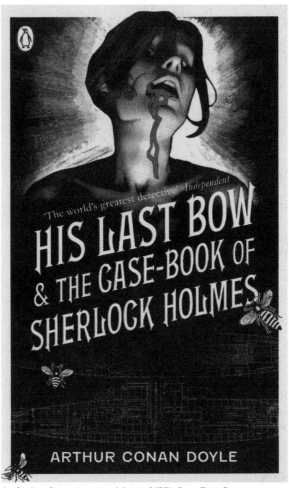

A gloriously gruesome vision of "His Last Bow."

were fakes, conjured up with nothing more than a few paper doll cutouts, there were others equally adamant that they weren't. Doyle, with the erudite support of theosophist Edward Gardner, fell face-first into the latter category.

The Coming of the Fairies, published that same year, is perhaps the best known of all Doyle's many spiritualist writings. Selling respectably at the time, it has since acquired a degree of notoriety ensuring that even tattered copies rarely stay on bookshelves for long; even today, there is something utterly irresistible about the idea of Doyle, the brain behind the most analytical mind in literary history, falling for such a simple childish prank.

For it was a prank. While Doyle and his friends launched themselves into a serious debate over the true nature of the photographs (did they depict real fairies? Or were they another manifestation of spirit photography?), other figures readily demonstrated precisely how a simple childish game had so spectacularly backfired upon the adult world.

Time and science (borne out by the elderly Elsie Wright's own confessions in the 1980s) prove those cynics to have been correct, but Doyle was not appeased. Still he adhered to the words that had rung so loudly from another of his spiritualist tomes, *The New Revelation*: "The objective side of it ceased to interest . . . . The religious side . . . was clearly of greater importance."

This shifting of interests and, indeed, purpose shows through many of the Sherlock Holmes stories that appeared throughout the 1920s. A dozen new tales, purporting to be adventures that Watson had not hitherto documented, were published in *The Strand*, but almost without exception they are as weak as any in the canon, their failings as both mysteries and even pieces of writing only amplified by their being bound together in a single volume.

TS Eliot, the poet, mourned the "mental decay" that seemed to have affected Holmes. *Punch* magazine declared, "every phrase is like a dirge." Nobody reading the stories at the time could doubt that Conan Doyle was writing them on autopilot; nobody flicking back to earlier (prewar) stories could have argued that the standard of his work now was in any way comparable to that which had been so effortlessly attained ten or twenty years previous.

Conan Doyle had never been especially secretive of the fact that he wrote the Sherlock Holmes stories for money; the outrageous fees he was able to command for each adventure were, in fact, a point of pride for him. But this final dozen, with just a handful of exceptions, felt as though the check were all that he cared about, and any old story would suffice if it brought in the cash he required. He was self-publishing many of his spiritualist writings, and that was not an inexpensive endeavor. Sherlock Holmes was his financier.

Which is one way of looking at it. On the other hand, however, doubtless each of these stories is somebody's favorite (including Conan Doyle, who once insisted that they were at least the equal of past tales), and there is not one that is quite so asinine as "The Three Students," nor as implausibly convoluted as "The Solitary Cyclist." In fact, more than a few of them are actually rather good.

The Adventure of the Mazarin Stone (October 1921)

"The Adventure of the Mazarin Stone" follows in the footsteps of "The Last Bow" in being written in the third person, with Watson an active player in the drama, as opposed to its narrator. Which This is a better fate than that which initially lay in store for him; the tale was originally written as a stage play, *The Crown Diamond*, in which the doughty doctor scarcely appeared. Even here he spends most of the story on an errand, but it's an important one, so he probably didn't mind.

Besides, there are other matters to consider.

While we the reader, and often Watson, too, seemed to expect every trick that Sherlock Holmes employed and every device he developed to be new, exciting, and utterly brilliant, the old boy really wasn't averse to repeating himself. When he hears, for example, that an attempt will be made on his life one night, he has no hesitation in dragging out the old waxwork dummy that he'd propped up by the window in "The Adventure of the Empty House," and doing so for the same purpose. (And, originally, to fool the same man—the original antagonist in *The Crown Diamond* was our old friend Colonel Sebastian Moran.)

Holmes is in the midst of one of his most dangerous cases ever, hot on the trail of the Mazarin Stone, a diamond stolen from the Crown Jewels of England, and if its financial value, £100,000, is staggering, that is nothing when compared to its prestige and importance within the Royal Regalia.

Powerful politicians have visited, entreating him to increase his efforts. He has unearthed every disguise in his repertoire, everybody from an unemployed laborer to a tired old lady. But the jewel has eluded him.

The jewel thief, on the other hand, has not. He is Count Negretto Sylvius of 136 Moorside Gardens—the very man whom Billy the Page (a young manservant whom we met fleetingly in *The Valley of Fear*) is now announcing as a visitor. Neither is he a man who, at close quarters, is likely to be confused by a waxwork. Holmes was expecting to be shot at through the window. The count clearly has a more intimate fate in mind, as is evidenced by his companion, a boxer named Sam Merton.

Watson hurries out the back way with a message for Scotland Yard; and Holmes . . . where is Holmes? The count enters the room, spots the effigy, and is just about to whack it with his cane when Holmes appears from another direction entirely and greets him.

The count is exasperation itself. Why, he demands to know, is Holmes having him followed by a multitude of dubious-looking characters? Holmes assures him that only one person is shadowing the count's movements, and that is Holmes himself, aided of course by his manifold disguises. As for why he is doing it, that should be obvious. Because the count is a jewel thief.

This is where things fall down. Both men are armed, but neither draws his weapon. Holmes relies on his powers of persuasion, and the count, having been smart enough to figure out how to steal one of the most precious and, presumably, securely safeguarded jewels in the land, relies on . . . well, nothing, really.

He simply sits with his boxer friend in Holmes's study, listening as the detective plays violin in another room, and they ponder the offer he left them with: reveal the whereabouts of the jewel and go free, or remain silent and go to jail.

Beside them, the waxwork sits impassively—right up until the moment when the count explains to his henchman how he has the diamond in his pocket; he takes it out to show the man and is astonished when the waxwork turns around and snatches it from his hand. It was Holmes all along. The violin they've been listening to was a gramophone recording.

Watson returns with the police; the count and the boxer are arrested. Lord Cantlemere, one of the political figures who doubted that Holmes could ever crack this particular case, is forced to eat humble pie . . . and the whole thing kind of dribbles out from there.

The Problem of Thor Bridge (February/March 1922)

A-ha! Now we know where all these stories are coming from. "Somewhere in the vaults of the bank of Cox & Co., at Charing Cross," writes the doctor, in the "travel-worn and battered tin dispatch-box with my name, John H. Watson, M.D., Late Indian Army, painted upon the lid," there lurks a box that is "crammed with papers, nearly all of which are records of cases to illustrate the curious problems which Mr. Sherlock Holmes had at various times to examine."

What caused Watson to delve back into these cases is never explained. But delve he did, and this month he emerges with the taxing tale of . . . yes! An American! So we know right away that he did it. Whatever it is.

Murder! Maria, the wife of Neil Gibson, the so-called Gold King and a former senator for one of the western states, has been slain. His children's governess, Grace Dunbar, is the number-one suspect, and it does look rather bleak for the girl. The dead woman was discovered in a pool of blood on Thor Bridge, a bullet through the head and a note in her hand, asking her to meet the governess at that very spot.

But add that to the discovery of a recently fired revolver casually thrown into her wardrobe, and the fact that the senator is in love with Ms. Dunbar, and Holmes is right to overlook the most obvious evidence. Especially after he finds a mysterious chip in the stone on the underside of the bridge. Almost as if someone had rigged up an extraordinarily complicated contraption involving one of a pair of matching revolvers, and a piece of string . . .

Yes, the American did it. But it was the female American, Maria Gibson, committing suicide to escape her abusive, unfaithful husband, but deciding that if she couldn't have the man, neither could the governess. Yes, the revolver in the wardrobe had indeed been fired. But the one that released the fatal bullet now lies in the water, dislodged when Maria triggered her contraption. The whole thing was set up to frame the lovely Ms. Dunbar, and, but for Holmes, it might have succeeded.

The Adventure of the Creeping Man (March 1923)

This is one of the most unusual of all Sherlock Holmes's adventures, and one of the most intriguing, given Conan Doyle's medical background. The entire tale is predicated not on the mystery for which Holmes is summonsed (elderly employer acting extraordinarily strangely), nor for the wealth of what transpires to be irrelevant background with which it is window-dressed (impending nuptials and recent engagements).

It all comes down, with a twist that just proves that there is nothing new under the sun, to an old man who is about to marry a younger woman and fears that he will disappoint her on their wedding night. So he goes to see a doctor . . . in Prague, in what is now the Czech Republic . . . and is given some little pills (are they blue?). Which, he is assured, will put an end to all his worries.

Unfortunately—for this is what they were derived from—they also make him behave like a langur, a species of South Asian ape that spends most of its time on all four feet. Creeping. The dangers, in other words, of taking unlicensed medicines . . . .

The Adventure of the Sussex Vampire (January 1924)

We have already noted Conan Doyle's occasional predilection for a good tale of the supernatural, but the old master's most redolent tale must be *The Adventure of the Sussex Vampire*, a story that has been cited by more than one learned Holmesian scholar as Conan Doyle's personal tribute to (or perhaps, parody of) *Dracula*.

It features all the necessary ingredients for a good vampire tale. A child, mysteriously weakening and bearing twin telltale fang marks on his throat. His mysterious South American mother, who is seen by the nurse with her mouth sucking at the boy's throat. And Holmes, the master of logic and common sense, apparently battling with the realization that here, for once, is a case that defies all of his learning and erudition.

But what, he asks his faithful sidekick Doctor Watson at the outset of the tale, "what have we to do with walking corpses who can only be held in their graves by stakes driven through their hearts? It's pure lunacy."

And so it proved, as the vampire turned out to be a fifteen-year-old boy, jealous of the half brother his newly remarried father has just foisted upon him, and amusing himself by firing poison darts into the infant's neck—poison that his stepmother then dutifully sucked out of the wounds, to prevent her husband from discovering just what a nasty little brat he had sired during his first marriage.

Such a down-to-earth (if, simultaneously, utterly fanciful) solution to what could have been a very jolly romp through the undead denizens of the English countryside has not, of course, stilled the voices of those who will seek out arcane meaning from every word Conan Doyle wrote.

Modern London can still find a place for Holmes to practice   © *Steve and Betsy Mortensen*

Wryly, we note, there has even been a volume published devoted wholly to Conan Doyle's "vampire stories," without one of the tales therein actually involving anything remotely resembling a vampire. And other writings that not only discuss Holmes's relationship with the characters in Stoker's novel, but even suggest that the detective and the vampire had come to a certain arrangement, under whose terms neither would do anything that impinged upon the other's territory.

Loren D. Estleman's 1978 novel *Sherlock Holmes Versus Dracula; or the Adventure of the Sanguinary Count* is a profoundly authentic-feeling romp through one such encounter that notes, very imaginatively, that Holmes and Dracula took their respective bows onto the streets of London more or less simultaneously, and that one could not have helped but notice the existence of the other. Where that notice led, however, is another matter entirely.

The Adventure of the Three Garridebs (October 1924)

Beyond being an anagram of "RI Badger," which is utterly meaningless, the name "Garrideb" is scarcely one that would have sparked even a glimmer of recognition among the readership of *The Strand*. Which means it was possibly the most mysterious element in this entire story.

There are, initially, just two Garridebs. One is named John, claiming to be a wealthy American lawyer (uh-oh); the other is Nathan, who comes to Holmes bearing news of a remarkable offer. A third, now deceased Garrideb, a millionaire land tycoon, bequeathed his entire fortune, some $15 million, to John, on the understanding that he will share it equally with two other bearers of the family name. John contacted Nathan, Nathan contacted Holmes: help me find the third.

Holmes is immediately suspicious, although beyond a variety of minor discrepancies in the lawyer's story, he cannot quite put his finger on why. Nathan is an elderly eccentric with a variety of interests and collecting passions, but he is scarcely a rich man, and, besides, John has said or done nothing to make the older man distrust him. Although he clearly does.

The plot thickens when John announces that he has finally discovered a third Garrideb, a Birmingham-based businessman named Howard, who recently placed an advertisement in the newspaper.

Holmes is not impressed; the ad is so littered with Americanisms that it is clear John placed it himself. But when John insists that Nathan travel to meet the man, all becomes clear—for hadn't Holmes himself employed a similar deception before, in the case of the missing Naval Treaty? And wouldn't he do it again, in the Adventure of the Retired Colourman? John wants Nathan out of the way, so he can visit the old man's rooms himself.

Holmes decides to involve Scotland Yard and quickly learns that he could have saved himself a lot of thinking had he only done this before. John Garrideb is actually James Winter, sometimes known as James Morecroft and at other times referred to as Killer Evans. Three men died at his hand in America, and after he busted out of prison and escaped to London, another was murdered here: Rodger Presbury, a Chicago forger who just happened to have lived in Nathan's home before him.

A trap is laid and Killer is captured, but not before he shoots Watson in the leg and is himself knocked cold by the butt of Holmes's revolver. Off he goes to prison, and down in the basement of the house, of course they find the dead Presbury's counterfeiting equipment. Oh, and poor Nathan never gets his $5 million and winds up in a nursing home, depressed beyond all measure.

The Adventure of the Illustrious Client (November 1924)

Berkeley Square is one of the jewels of what was once London's most desirable residential districts, laid out by the architect William Kent and named for the family whose London home, Berkeley House, stood nearby. Beautiful four-story brick homes originally towered around the central square, overlooking Alexander Munro's sculpted fountain and the London Plane trees that are among the oldest still standing in central London. By the late nineteenth century, however, smog and pollution had transformed the homes into what Doctor Watson shudderingly described as "those awful grey London castles which would make a church seem frivolous."

Gunter's Tea Shop, one of the Victorian city's most cherished institutions, stood at numbers 7 and 8; and at number 104, Conan Doyle placed the opening scenes of "The Adventure of the Illustrious Client."

For the modern sightseer touring Holmes's London, the luxuriously appointed home of the war hero General de Merville concerns us only briefly on our perambulation, for another of the square's residents has caught our imagination. Number 50 Berkeley Square is the headquarters of the renowned antiquarian bookseller Maggs Brothers, onetime owners of Napoleon Bonaparte's penis; it is also widely known as the most haunted house in London, the preserve of what at least one anthologist described as "the Nameless Horror of Berkeley Square."

The house's history was respectable enough, the London residence of the politician and statesman George Canning from 1770 until his death in 1827, just 119 days after he became prime minister of England. Yet it already had an uncanny reputation. Canning, not a man subject to wild flights of imagination, told friends that he was often disturbed by strange noises in the house and that he had experienced sundry phenomena that he was pained to comprehend. But it was during the tenancy of a Mr. Myers, renting the house from its next owner, the Viscount (later, Lord) Bearstead, that number 50 truly took on the mantle that still clings to it.

Myers was not what one would call a conscientious tenant. Jilted by his fiancée, he all but permanently retired to one of the attic rooms, and as the house crumbled into disrepair around him, so his mind crumbled within. Visitors to the house certainly felt a change in the atmosphere, even after Myers's departure. In 1872, no less a personage than Lord George Lyttelton, former undersecretary of state for war and onetime president of the British Chess Association, spent a night in the attic—apparently for a bet. He took the wager seriously, too—he was accompanied by a shotgun and, the following morning, chilled many a soul with his tale of the ghastly apparition that appeared to him in the night, impervious to the shotgun shells that he blasted at point-blank range into it.

Seven years later, shrugging off the attic's reputation, the house's latest owner converted the attic into a bedroom for one of the family's maids. Nobody knows for sure what happened next, but the poor girl was discovered the next morning raving mad, and she died the following day in an asylum.

A friend of the family, a nobleman by all accounts, promptly offered to spend a night in that same room—and the following morning was found stiff and lifeless. The coroner said he died of fright. On a separate occasion, another nobleman was struck dumb by whatever he saw in that same room; a third, the author Edward Bulwer-Lytton, was at least sufficiently impressed by the legends to revisit them in his short story "The Haunted and the Haunters."

The horror was last seen in 1887. A party of sailors on shore leave from HMS *Penelope* were staying at the house, in the attic. And whatever occurred was terrifying enough that, fleeing from the building in the middle of the night, one of their number tripped and was killed. The others could swear only that whatever they had seen was terrible enough that they could not even give it a name.

Rathbone . . . Bruce . . . Lupino . . . Marshall! The cast is almost as great as
the hero.   *Photofest*

Sherlock Holmes, as he passed through Berkeley Square en route to visiting
General de Merville, could not have failed to be aware of the house's reputation
and doubtless could not have resisted glancing up at the darkened house as the
carriage slowly passed it by.

Personally, he had no time for what lesser intellects termed the supernatural;
he regarded them, with or without a nod toward Charles Dickens's Ebenezer
Scrooge, as the product purely of some other, utterly earthly agency altogether—
as Dickens himself had his immortal miser mumble, most supernatural visita-
tions were caused by "an undigested bit of beef, a blot of mustard, a crumb of
cheese, a fragment of an underdone potato. There's more of gravy than of grave
about you."

All of which, sadly, is a polite way of saying that "The Illustrious Client" is an
astonishingly routine . . . nay, mundane . . . tale, less a mystery and more a matter
of discrediting a suave but certainly dangerous Austrian baron, Adelbert Gruner,
who has won the heart of General de Merville's daughter Violet.

It permits, however, Conan Doyle to make some remarkable detours into
the underworld of contemporary London, enlisting its denizens to assist him
in gathering information against the perfidious Gruner, and also for him to
comment on a topic that many other chroniclers of contemporary crime seem

to overlook: that the best criminals are often as smart as the best investigators ranged against them. Sometimes more so.

"'A complex mind,'" Holmes explains. "'All great criminals have that. My old friend Charlie Peace was a violin virtuoso,'" and one is astonished to hear either of these things—that such a common housebreaker and murderer could have even known what a violin was (beyond the fact that it was probably worth stealing), or that Holmes counted him among his friends.

There again, a lot of people admired Peace, a crook whose career, and notoriety, had only just been brought to a close when the first of one hundred installments of his biography, *Charles Peace, or the Adventures of a Notorious Burglar*, appeared in 1879—a penny dreadful of the most dread variety! Peace was hanged that same year for the murder of one of his mistresses' husband, but his legend lived on. He remained infamous enough that he could be blithely mentioned in a Holmes story almost fifty years after his death, and forty years on from that, a comic strip version of his life debuted in the British children's comic *Buster*. Like Holmes himself, so disparaged by his own creator, immortality strikes often where we least expect it to.

The Adventure of the Three Gables (September 1926)

What would you do if you wanted to make sure Sherlock Holmes stayed as far out of your business as it was possible for him to do?

There are lots of ways of keeping yourself off his radar, redoubtable though it is. But probably the least effective would be to saunter up to 221b, knock on his door and introduce yourself, and then tell him not to go to Harrow.

Because of course, it means he will. It also means you will be interrogated by Watson before the message is even delivered, and if you are as dumb as Steve Dixie seems to be, then you will basically spill the whole story before the adventure has even begun. All Holmes then has to do is make a few assumptions, a few deductions, the odd informed guess, and what do you know? Case solved.

The Adventure of the Blanched Soldier (October 1926)

Set in the immediate aftermath of the Boer War, the story begins with what appears to be a simple missing-person case. James M. Dodd, once of the Imperial Yeomanry, is anxious to trace a friend and fellow soldier, Godfrey Emsworth. Letters to the family home elicited only a terse and seemingly unwilling explanation that Emsworth has set off to travel around the world, but Dodd has his doubts.

A visit to old Colonel Emsworth only makes him more uneasy, especially after one of the servants seemed to speak of Godfrey in the past tense. Dodd asked if that meant his friend was dead; the butler said no. But he might have been better off if he were. And that night, up in his bedroom, Dodd saw Godfrey at the window.

He left the next day, essentially driven away by the colonel. But he caught one final clue before he departed: a man walking away from an apparently deserted outbuilding, and a second man within. That, he seemed certain, was Godfrey.

Stranger and stranger! But Holmes has his own theories, although the manner in which he explains them does seem to run absolutely contrary to all that he has learned in the past.

Why, he asks, would any family shut up one of its own?

Well, if you're Jephro Rucastle, late of the Copper Beeches, it would be to keep your daughter from a persistent fiancé. If you are Mr. Culverton Smith, in the case of the dying detective, it is because you have infected your son with a deadly Asian disease. If you are . . . and so and so forth.

No such sinister machinations here. Silly ones, maybe, but sinister, no. Young Godfrey is suffering from leprosy, and his family are too embarrassed to tell anybody. Holmes, on the other hand, knows exactly what to do. With him to the Emsworth estate travels the world-renowned dermatologist Sir James Saunders, who is able to put everyone's mind at rest by explaining the boy merely has ichthyosis, an easily treated skin condition that only looks and feels like leprosy. He will be as right as rain in no time . . .

Unlike anybody reading these adventures as they continue to unfold. A sense of weariness must certainly be creeping in by now . . . .

The Adventure of the Lion's Mane (November 1926)

Holmes, firmly in the thrall of his retirement home beside the Sussex beach, is chatting with a friend of his, Harold Stackhurst, headmaster of a nearby preparatory school. Suddenly their idyll is interrupted by another man, the school's science master McPherson, who collapses and dies in agony before them. His last words are indistinguishable, beyond two of them: "Lion's mane."

His body is examined. Vicious red welts decorate his back, shoulder, and ribs, and as Holmes and Inspector Bardle of the Sussex Constabulary investigate the death, it seems evident that they are dealing with a particularly cruel and sadistic murder. Possibly involving a cat o'nine tails, possibly a mesh of red hot wires. And possibly engendered by a jealous rival for a particular young lady, the school math teacher, Murdoch. In fact, Bardle is on the point of arresting the man when Holmes—who has never forgotten the dying man's last anguished words—has a thought.

McPherson had been in the habit of bathing in a nearby lagoon, created following a recent storm. So had Murdoch, who now appears, hideously scarred by the same dread weapon that dispatched McPherson. Or not. No manmade instrument of torture caused these searing wounds. They are the distinctive stings of *Cyanea capillata*, a deadly species of gelatinous zooplankton whose common name is . . . "lion's mane."

Holmes kills the beast with a rock—which is actually quite an accomplishment, given the creature's natural ability to squish and squelch itself beneath all such blows—and clearly nobody murdered anybody. In fact, as Holmes most certainly wouldn't have said, the whole affair turned out to be jellyfish-mentary.

William Gillette prepares for action.   *Photofest*

The Adventure of the Retired Colourman (December 1926)

"Oh dear. Chateau Liverpool Street."

Thus does Nigel Stock, Watson to Douglas Wilmer's 1965 Holmes, pass judgment on the lunch hamper he picks up at the railroad station, as he and the aggrieved art-supply dealer Josiah Amberley embark upon a wild goose chase. Holmes himself devised it (or, at least, borrowed it from the adventure of the Three Garridebs) to ensure Amberley was well out of the way while he, the great detective, turned his house upside-down.

And why? Because while everyone else believes Amberley's sorrowful saga of a perfidious wife, a treacherous friend, and the theft of £7,000 from his private safe, Holmes has other ideas entirely.

Why is the ordinarily miserly old man suddenly repainting a home that has not seen a stroke of work done to it in decades? Could he be trying to cover something up? An unsightly stain . . . an unseemly smell?

Why did the man, again out of character, purchase a single ticket for the theater and then claim he'd bought two, one for his wife, on the night she disappeared?

And why does he seem so unwilling to avail himself of every opportunity he is offered to regain his wife and his fortune?

Because pitiful, pathetic, and broken though he seems to be, Amberley is a coldblooded murderer who lured his wife and her lover into a sealed, airless room and then gassed them to death while he stood outside laughing. The bodies he dumped in a disused well; the disappearance he thought he could camouflage with his tale of adulterous woe.

That, however, was before he met Holmes . . . and before Holmes met Barker, a private detective hired by the missing man's family, to pursue their own suspicions regarding their kinsman's fate. A rival detective? Barker was not the first man to set himself up as a rival to Holmes, either in fiction or in reality. But he was, apparently, one of the most impressive. As we shall see later in this book.

The Adventure of the Veiled Lodger (January 1927)

You never know where you are with lodgers. Not if you're living in a Conan Doyle story, anyway. If they're not heavily bearded men who turn out to be chainsmoking ladies, mixed up with mysterious red circles, then they are sinister American gangsters, prone to leaving coded messages on their ex-girlfriend's sundial. Or you could be poor Mrs. Merrilow, who rented a room to an unusual lodger who has never once shown her face. Not knowingly, anyway. But, with that keen eye, sharp nose, and merciless curiosity that so many private landladies seem to nurture, she did catch a glimpse of the woman's face once. All horribly scarred it was, mutilated and ghastly.

None of which was Mrs. Merrilow's concern, of course. What her tenants want to walk around looking like is their concern, not hers. But now the young lady has taken to waking up the household with her deathly screams. Cries of "murder, murder," ring through the night. "You cruel beast! You monster!"

Her health, too, is suffering. The poor girl is wasting away, but when Mrs. Merrilow offers to call the police, the lodger begs her not to. If she must involve anybody, it should be Sherlock Holmes. In fact, it *must* be Sherlock Holmes, and to make sure he knows what it all involves, here's a message for him: "Abbas Parva."

The words mean nothing to the landlady, but Holmes understands immediately. It refers to a terrible case involving a circus lion who got loose and attacked two people, a husband-and-wife team that regularly performed with the beast, and who cared for it and fed it. The husband was killed, the wife was savagely scarred, and though the police had wondered why the animal should have so shockingly turned on two people it trusted, they accepted that wild animals remain wild, no matter how sweet and cuddly we may think they are. Look at that poor jellyfish in the last-but-one story!

Holmes hastens to the rooms of the woman, Mrs. Ronder, to find her preparing to die. She is clearly contemplating suicide, but she wishes to do so with a clear conscience. Her husband had been a monster, she explains, cruel to her, cruel to the animals. She had taken a lover, the circus strongman, and together they plotted her husband's demise: a fake lion attack, using a club with five nails in it. They bashed in the man's head, and then to complete the facade, she released the lion. Who promptly attacked her. At which point the strongman ran away screaming.

Holmes cannot help but feel pity for the woman. He will not inform the police, but she must not give up. Life is always worth living, no matter how lousy the hand one has to play it with. Even when she lifts the veil and shows him the awful remains of her face, Holmes remains calm. She is beautiful inside.

Mrs. Ronder appears to believe him, as well. Two days later, a package arrives for him from Mrs. Ronder. It contains the bottle of prussic acid with which she planned to do the deed. She has chosen life.

The Adventure of Shoscombe Old Place (March 1927)

The last-ever new Sherlock Holmes story returns to a scene familiar from one of the greatest-ever old ones, a racing stable, Shoscombe Old Place, whose master, Sir Robert Norberton, has apparently gone mad.

Mason, the head trainer, explains the situation to Holmes, adding a few extra details. The stable is actually owned by Lady Beatrice Falder, Sir Robert's sister, and all have high hopes for their horse, Shoscombe Prince, in the upcoming derby. Even mad Sir Robert.

Has anything else strange happened lately, asks Holmes. Well, it so happens, quite a few things.

For instance, when Lady Beatrice takes the air in her carriage, though she used to stop to greet her favorite horse, now she just rides by. Neither did she did put up a fuss when Sir Robert gave her favorite dog away.

Then there's Sir Robert, spending his nights hanging round the old family crypt and meeting a mysterious man there.

And finally, there is the discovery of burned human bones inside the Shoscombe furnace, which is probably the tale this story should have started with. But no matter. Holmes is on the case, and he soon has things sorted out.

The dog was given away so it would not go looking for its mistress. She died about a week ago from a nasty case of dropsy and has since been impersonated by the man whom Sir Robert meets by the crypt every night. The crypt, incidentally, is where the lady's body has been laid, and the burned bones are the ones that were removed to make way for her corpse. Her death needs to be covered up until after the horse race, because her will leaves the stable to her late husband's brother.

If Shoscombe Prince wins the derby, Sir Robert will be set up for life independently. If the horse loses, on the other hand, his debts will swallow him whole. And we bid farewell to Sherlock Holmes with a most gratifyingly happy ending. The horse wins the race, Sir Robert (who wasn't mad, after all) is saved, and Holmes can return to his retirement, his bees, and his books, and not one of us will give a backward glance. After forty years of solid detective work, the old boy deserves to rest.

15

The Curious Case of the Multitudinous Sherlocks

In which we ask Who was the Greatest Holmes of all, and put a few Watsons under the Microscope, too

From high school productions to Hollywood extravaganzas; from nineteenth-century theatrical ventures to twenty-first-century animation, there have probably been enough different Sherlock Holmeses to populate a small city. Like Shakespeare and Dickens, those other authors whose work is as familiar to someone who has never read one of their stories as it is to someone who has read nothing else, Sir Arthur Conan Doyle's Sherlock Holmes has transcended the realm of mere fictional devices and become a genre in his own right. For an actor to be invited to play Holmes, then, is as grand an achievement as being asked to become Hamlet or MacBeth, Oliver Twist or Nicholas Nickleby.

Not every recipient of the honor has succeeded, of course. Some astonishingly leaden performances have spooled out over the past 125 years—some appalling mismatches, some ghastly miscastings. But when an actor gets it right, even an absolute neophyte knows it.

The following all got it very right indeed. Perhaps it is familiarity and repetition that has lodged them so securely in the hearts and minds of the viewing public; perhaps even Basil Rathbone, generally regarded as cinema's most perfect Holmes of all, would now be forgotten had his career as Sherlock begun, and not ended, with the abysmal *Dressed to Kill.*

But it is repetition that made Holmes so compulsive in the first place—had Conan Doyle allowed his adventures to end at the point they began, with *A Study in Scarlet,* Holmes would be just one more in a so-lengthy series of one-off fictional detectives, no more or less remarkable than any other who grasped the popular imagination for the length of a single story.

Only by answering the demand for a second story, and then by fashioning a dozen more for *The Strand*, did Conan Doyle raise his creation to immortality, and so it is with the actors who have portrayed him. John Barrymore was an excellent Sherlock Holmes once, but would we have felt the same way over a dozen further pictures? We cannot answer that. But we can hold up no less than half a dozen other performers and, rewatching their adventures today, agree that all six truly were a remarkable Holmes.

The Unparalleled Genius of the Shakespearean Star

Basil Rathbone is the template from which all future portrayals of Sherlock Holmes would be drawn.

Born in Johannesburg, South Africa, on June 13, 1892—that is, in the same month as "The Adventure of the Copper Beeches" brought the first volume of Sherlock Holmes stories to an end in *The Strand* magazine—Philip St. John Basil Rathbone was the son of a mining engineer, Edgar, and a violinist, Anna.

He arrived into a violent world. The Boer War that would soon be captivating Arthur Conan Doyle was already percolating as the Dutch settlers, the Boers, prepared to rise up against their British overlords, and the Rathbones were not to be immune to the conflict. In 1895, the family returned to England, fleeing their home after Edgar was accused of being a British spy by the Boers. They never returned.

Schooled at Repton, one of Britain's most storied public schools, Rathbone's aptitude for the stage saw him join Sir Frank Benson's Shakespearean repertory company, and in Ipswich on April 22, 1911, he made his debut playing Horatio in *The Taming of the Shrew*. The following year, again with Benson, he visited the United States for the first time; and when war broke out in August 1914, Rathbone was performing at London's Savoy Theatre, a fast-rising star on the theatrical circuit.

Enlisted to the army in 1915, Rathbone served with the London Scottish Regiment,

Basil Rathbone at his best.   *Photofest*

rising to the rank of lieutenant (and later, captain) when he became an intelligence officer. He was decorated in 1918, receiving the Military Cross, and back home at the end of the conflict, he would entertain friends by detailing how his acting abilities served him in such good stead throughout the conflict. He was a master of disguise and such a dab hand with camouflage that on more than one occasion, he was out scouting the enemy German lines in broad daylight, without the enemy having any idea whatsoever that he was nearby.

He returned to Shakespeare and the stage, both at home and abroad. In 1923, co-starring with Eva Le Gallienne, he took Broadway by storm with *The Swan*, and by the early 1930s, his American fame was secured both on stage and on film. Rathbone made his movie debut in 1925 in a film called *The Masked Bride* and five years later won much acclaim for his role as the detective Philo Vance in *The Bishop Murder Case*, one of the series of crime novels with which author S. S. Van Dine gripped the late 1920s.

Over the next decade, Rathbone was ubiquitous. His filmography includes starring roles in such well-remembered epics as *David Copperfield, A Tale of Two Cities, Anna Karenina, Captain Blood, The Adventures of Robin Hood, The Last Days of Pompeii, Son of Frankenstein,* and *The Mark of Zorro.* But his crowning glory, at least in terms of his future reputation, arrived in 1939, when he was cast as Sherlock Holmes in 20th Century Fox's upcoming production of *The Hound of the Baskervilles.*

Still regarded among the definitive retellings of Holmes's best-known adventure, the movie was only ever intended as a one-off. Its success, however, prompted the studio to swiftly follow up with *The Adventures of Sherlock Holmes*, a movie ostensibly based upon William Gillette's original play but scarcely recognizable in any form. Indeed, Rathbone's second Holmes movie retains only a handful of that earlier piece's characteristics—a bit of subplot, a couple of characters, and a nice piece of sparring between Holmes and Moriarty. Like so many of Rathbone's performances, however, his very presence overcomes any attempt to contextualize the story in terms of the original Holmes; he is just such a great actor, with such a formidable grasp on the role, that one is instantly sucked into this tale of fiendish ne'er-do-welling, while admiring the fresh insights into a genuinely Holmesian mind that it delivers.

It is *The Adventures of Sherlock Holmes*, for instance, that introduces moviegoers to the detective's attempts to discover the most potent insecticide ever known; having trapped some bluebottles inside a brandy glass, he is now plucking his violin at them, "observing the reaction on the common housefly of the chromatic scale." It is his belief—or, at least, hope—that somewhere within the range of notes, there will be one that will strike such horror into the heart of the pest that it will leave the room directly.

Both of these movies were set in Victorian London, as the modern viewer might expect. At the time, however, this was regarded as a somewhat daring departure from the norm; most past Holmes movies, including the series of five made earlier in the decade with Arthur Wontner in the lead role, updated the

Rathbone is *Dressed To Kill.*   *Photofest*

adventure to "the present day," and this would become the setting for all of Rathbone's future excursions.

Fox made just the two Holmes movies, with Rathbone and his trust Watson, Nigel Bruce, then taking their adventures over to the radio instead, for a weekly serial that remains one of the best loved of all time. By 1942, however, the movie franchise (as the modern tongue insists we term it) was in the hands of Universal Studios, and both Rathbone and Bruce were recalled to the silver screen for a series of twelve films that would keep them occupied until 1946.

The present-day setting for the movies was not established purely for the "modern" feel that it conveyed. It also allowed Holmes to set his formidable intellect against the greatest enemy the United States had ever confronted as the country entered into World War II (in December 1941).

Three successive movies, *Sherlock Holmes and the Voice of Terror, Sherlock Holmes and the Secret Weapon,* and *Sherlock Holmes in Washington,* placed Holmes in implacable opposition to the Nazi foe, battling a radio propagandist, pursuing a top-secret bombsight, and unraveling the mystery of a missing microfilm—the first two films loosely adapting, respectively, the original stories "His Last Bow" and "The Dancing Men"; the third, despite a very vague similarity to "The Bruce-Partington Plans," being an original story by writer Bertram Millhauser.

Sherlock Holmes in Washington was also the first disappointment in the sequence. No matter that more than a few of Conan Doyle's original stories feel like makeweights in comparison to the leviathans of the canon, the fact is even

Sherlock's weakest adventure remained Holmesian. This, on the other hand, is simply an espionage-themed adventure movie, whose heroes happen to be named, and dressed like, Sherlock Holmes and Watson.

Such was Rathbone's (and Bruce's, for this was a true double act) strength, however, that such failings register only if one watches from the viewpoint of a confirmed Holmes fanatic. To the moviegoing public of the age, Rathbone could probably have restaged *Gone with the Wind* (which rumor insists he almost did—Margaret Mitchell is said to have suggested him as her ideal Rhett Butler) and, so long as he wore his deerstalker, cape, and pipe, it would have become a Sherlock Holmes movie.

Sherlock Holmes Faces Death was next, restructuring "The Musgrave Ritual" around Doctor Watson's service as a doctor at a military hospital. When his assistant is found murdered, he calls upon Holmes to solve the mystery—for it is plain that Lestrade, who is happily seeking his suspects from among the hospital's patients, never will.

The Spider Woman, another Millhauser creation (albeit one that is delightfully littered with Conan Doyle–isms), followed, and this one is an absolute classic, probably the best of all the Universal Holmes movies and arguably one of the finest Sherlock films ever. Provided you don't take it too seriously. Alan Barnes, author of *Sherlock Holmes on Screen*, describes it as "Holmes . . . on acid," and it is true. If a late 1960s underground filmmaker had ever decided it was time to match Sherlock Holmes with the counterculture, *The Spider Woman* would have been the result.

It begins with "the pajama suicides," the mysterious deaths of sundry Londoners who apparently get out of bed and, without bothering to dress, throw themselves out of their bedroom windows. Holmes is reported dead in an unrelated fishing accident. then resurfaces as a wealthy Indian gambler who ultimately flushes out the cause of the suicides: *lyconsa carnivora*, a vicious little African spider whose venom fills its victim with an uncontrollable urge for self-destruction. Owned, of course, by the titular Spider Woman.

Packed with thrills, littered with laughs (Watson's attempts to unmask the apparently fraudulent entomologist Gilflower is especially amusing), *The Spider Woman* is Sherlock Holmes *in absurdia*. Compulsory viewing, and it was not alone.

The Scarlet Claw, early in 1944, was a supernatural thriller that is just as enjoyable as its predecessor, but for very different reasons. Not a million miles divorced from *The Hound of the Baskervilles* in terms of atmosphere or plotting, *The Scarlet Claw* oozes as much atmosphere as the very best of the hound's many adaptations, a dark, foreboding Canadian swamp that holds a terrible secret, a murderous marsh monster whose presence has been rumored for a century . . . since the last time it went on the rampage.

Like *The Spider Woman*, *The Scarlet Claw* reveals everything that was great and that remains legendary about Rathbone's Holmes, and a triptych of jewels was completed with *The Pearl of Death*, later in 1944. But Rathbone was tiring of the role; would grow to hate Sherlock Holmes; believed that the role had typecast

Ronald Howard is the world-famous sleuth.

him and irredeemably hamstrung his career. Which may be true, because it often is the case that when an actor becomes so associated with a single role, nobody can imagine him portraying any other.

Equally damaging, however, is an audience's insistence upon blaming an actor for any perceived shortcomings in a new movie, without giving the writer, producer, or director a thought. And here come the game changers.

The House of Fear (1945) was a middling adaptation of "The Five Orange Pips" but scarcely showed Holmes at his most incisive; *The Woman in Green* (1945) recruited Mycroft and Moriarty to share in an adventure that wanted to be a violent slasher movie but contented itself with merely slicing off a few fingers; and then came the series' stultifying denouement, in the form of *Pursuit to Algiers*, *Terror by Night*, and *Dressed to Kill*.

Pursuit to Algiers was the first unquestioned indication that Universal's Sherlock Holmes series was running out of steam now, and no, that is not a dreadful pun based around the fact that most of the action takes place aboard the *SS Friesland.*

Basil Rathbone and Nigel Bruce are as watchable as ever, and there is certainly some drama when word reaches Watson, aboard the ship, that Holmes has just perished in a plane crash. We also learn that Moriarty was a virtuoso on the bassoon and that Watson likes to relax by singing traditional Scottish airs. Sadly, however, neither of these nuggets disguises the fact that the story is an abject plodder.

Terror by Night followed barely memorably after, but it was left to *Dressed to Kill* (released in the UK as *Sherlock Holmes and the Secret Code,* so please don't buy it twice) to take the inglorious final bow. Indeed, it seems to declare its finality with almost every frame, although even it contains a few moments of supremely Holmesian irony. Fans of Holmes's famous fascination with cigarette ash will especially enjoy seeing it used against its own creator. But overall, this was a sad, sad end to an enthralling movie series and, indeed, one of the most enthralling Holmeses of them all.

Rathbone ended his run as radio's Sherlock Holmes around the same time as the movies ceased; he was replaced in the series by Tom Conway and, with Nigel Bruce remaining at the microphone as Watson, the adventures marched on for another two seasons, until the final broadcast in July 1947. The mantle of portraying Holmes then passed to Ronald Howard, who took the role across thirty-nine adventures made (and newly written) for American television during 1954–55.

Rathbone himself made a handful of Holmesian reappearances; in full cape and deerstalker drag, he appeared as a guest on Milton Berle's TV show, and he dressed up again for some TV commercials for the Getz pest exterminator during the 1960s. But attempts to relaunch his Holmes onstage in a play penned by his wife Ouida in late 1953 were doomed after illness forced Nigel Bruce to pull out; and when his faithful Watson passed away on October 8, Rathbone's enthusiasm for the project died with him. The play ran for just three performances before Rathbone called a halt.

Rathbone remained an active performer on television, movie, and stage until the late 1960s, albeit with ever-diminishing returns. His final role was a Mexican B-flick called *Autopsy of a Ghost,* released a few months after the grand old man's death on July 21, 1967.

The Extraordinarily Well-Spoken Adventure of a Frightfully British BBC Holmes

With his distinctive nose and chin tracing back to Sidney Paget's very first drawings of Holmes for *The Strand,* coupled with his matinee-idol good looks, cultured charm, and so-English bearing, Basil Rathbone became, and remains, the model for every future Sherlock Holmes. Every good one, anyway—even Benedict Cumberbatch's portrayal, for all its twenty-first-century mannerisms (and distinctly un-Holmesian hair) retains the essence of the classic imagery's physique.

Twenty years, however, would elapse between Rathbone's abdication and the coronation of a new "ideal" Holmes, when BBC television in Britain set to work adapting "The Speckled Band" for television as the precursor for a possible full series of twelve adventures.

The corporation had addressed Holmes just once in the past, when 1951 brought the long-windedly titled *We Present Alan Wheatley as Mr Sherlock Holmes in* . . . , a series of six stories commissioned as part of the BBC's Festival of Britain celebrations. (The same festival's Holmesian exhibition is now to be found at the Sherlock Holmes pub in London.)

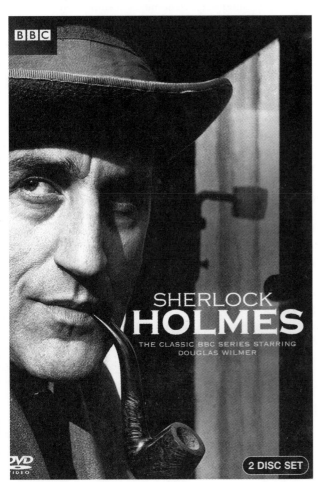

That series no longer exists; it was broadcast live without any reliable means of recording, and we have only photographs and reviews to remind us of actor and newscaster Wheatley's performances in "The Empty House," "A Scandal in Bohemia," "The Flying Detective," "The Reigate Squires," "The Red-Headed League," and "The Second Stain." All suggest that Wheatley did an admirable job, however, and his role model would surely have been on the production team's mind as they cast around for a new Holmes.

They selected Douglas Wilmer, a Shakespearean actor who was already into his midthirties before he came to public notice in Olivier's *Richard III* in 1955. He made up for lost time, however, snagging supporting roles in sufficient movies to be a familiar face,

Douglas Wilmer—a dynamic successor.

even if his was not a household name. That situation, however, would be remedied by Holmes.

The pilot for the proposed series was aired on May 18, 1964, a one-off episode within a series of eighteen adventures in the *Detective* series. Itself conceived as a replacement for the tremendously popular *Maigret* series, starring Rupert Davies as Georges Simenon's French detective, *Detective* ranged through the criminal canon for singular adventures starring some of literature's most enduring sleuths: DCI Alleyn, Father Brown, Philip Trent, and, in week eight, Sherlock Holmes. It is an indication of just how successful the series was that, within a year, no less than three new series had spun out from it: *Cluff*, *Thorndyke*, and *Sherlock Holmes*.

"The Speckled Band," the tale of the murderous stepfather and his foreboding menagerie of exotic pets, was Holmes's contribution to *Detective*, and it proved so popular and so well received that the episode was repeated just four months later. Work now was under way on the full series of twelve episodes, and on February 20, 1965, Wilmer's Holmes and Nigel Stock's Watson again strode prepossessingly onto the cathode tube.

Placing Holmes firmly back in the late Victorian firmament in which he is at his traditional (non-Rathbone) best, *Sherlock Holmes* has survived the intervening years largely intact and is readily available today on DVD. There, eleven episodes (all but two installments of the full series plus the pilot) step readily out of their black-and-white, set-bound milieu, and it is fascinating to watch.

Early reviews (including the actor's own) feared that Wilmer's Holmes, as he himself put it once, was "too smooth, urbane and civilized." Swiftly he remedied this, becoming, again in Wilmer's own words, "ruthless . . . primitive . . . savage." He has little pity, he has no sentimentality. At the end of "The Speckled Band," as Holmes reflects upon his direct role in the death of the evil stepfather, a soupçon of reason, if not regret, hangs over his words. There would be no room for that in the future, as Wilmer marches through case after case, dispatching all humanity from the room in favor of the only thing Holmes truly cared for: the clues, the deductions, the work.

"The part interested me very much because I'd never really, I felt, seen it performed to its full capacity," Wilmer later reflected. "There's a very dark side to Holmes, and a very unpleasant side to him. And I felt that this was always skirted round which made him appear rather sort of hockey sticks and cricket bats and jolly uncles . . . a kind of dashing Victorian hero. He wasn't like that at all. He was rather sardonic and arrogant, and he could be totally inconsiderate towards Watson. I tried to show both sides of his nature."

Select your own favorite from the thirteen episodes, and another viewer will argue convincingly a different tale. No matter that the original story is one of Conan Doyle's weakest; "The Illustrious Client," the first in the series proper, is absolutely gripping, its riot of cacophonous cockneys in a smoky music-hall setting exquisitely capturing a taste of period working-class entertainment. Debuting the series' sharp grasp on supporting characters, Rosemary Leach is unimpeachable as the fallen Kitty Winter, and Norman Mitchell likewise as the lovable rogue Shinwell Johnson, so memorably described by Watson:

> Johnson, I grieve to say, made his name first as a very dangerous vil-lain and served two terms at Parkhurst [one of the so-called modern prisons opened as Newgate was phased out of use]. Finally he repented and allied himself to Holmes, acting as his agent in the huge criminal underworld of London and obtaining information which often proved to be of vital importance. Had Johnson been a 'nark' of the police he would soon have been exposed, but as he dealt with cases which never came directly into the courts, his activities were never realized by his companions. With the glamour of his two convictions upon him, he had the entree of every night-club, doss house, and gambling-den in the town, and his quick observation and active brain made him an ideal agent for gaining information.

Such a dramatic opener was followed by a brilliant rendering of "The Devil's Foot," "The Copper Beeches," "The Red-Headed League," "The Abbey Grange" (the first of the missing episodes), "The Six Napoleons," "The Man with the Twisted Lip" (the first in the series to be filmed, and therefore the one that shows Holmes at his most urbane), "The Beryl Coronet," "The Bruce-Partington Plans" (also sadly missing), "Charles Augustus Milverton," "The Retired Colourman," and "The Disappearance of Lady Frances Carfax."

All are true to the Conan Doyle originals in terms of storytelling; all take sufficient license to dismiss any weaknesses inherent in the original stories. All also are remarkable in the pains taken to present Holmes and Watson as their own men, as opposed to the sometime-cyphers that any attempt to ape the old Rathbone/Bruce double act might become. Indeed, no matter how triumphant Wilmer's Holmes might be, Nigel Stock's Watson is truly superlative, a cross between affable sidekick and excitable fool blessed with such a range of expressions that he often did not even need to speak in order to convey his true thoughts about whatever was happening.

Which—his talent, his believability, his all-round unsung magnificence—is often regarded as the reason why it was he, and not Wilmer, who was recalled when Sherlock Holmes returned to the screens in 1968, three years after the BBC decided against giving Wilmer's detective a second series. In fact, it was Wilmer who chose not to continue, after learning that a second series would be granted considerably less rehearsal time than the actor believed the role merited.

He departed, but he would return to the role. A decade later, Wilmer was cast as an admittedly scarcely seen Holmes in *The Adventure of Sherlock Holmes's Smarter Brother*, written and directed by Gene Wilder and opening with the still-shocking sight of Queen Victoria exclaiming a heartfelt "shit" as she sits on the throne.

Peter Cushing—Dracula's worst nightmare becomes London law's
best friend.   *Photofest*

Holmes's scarcity in the movie is explained by its title. *The Adventure of
Sherlock Holmes's Smarter Brother* introduces a brand-new character to the universe,
a younger but, indeed, breathtakingly brilliant brother named Sigurson. Holmes
turns to him when he is forced to abandon another case, having been called
upon to serve the queen's needs instead; and Sigurson is forced to deal with the
returning Moriarty—by now a familiar face from past movies, despite his scarcity
in the original canon.

One of American cinema's most inspired and irreverent comedians, Wilder
himself was a huge fan of Holmes, and when the notion of making such a
movie first arose, his initial concern was that he could not bring himself to
make fun of his hero. The creation of an insanely jealous younger brother
immediately relieved him of that concern, yet wildly amusing as the movie is, it
is also a very affectionate tip of the hat to the original stories, alive with all the
intrigue and mystery that Conan Doyle created . . . just seen through a very
different, very funny prism.

This was a far cry indeed from the role that made Wilmer a star and that, thanks to the aforementioned DVD, allows us again to experience the magnificence of his Sherlock Holmes.

The Fang-Baring Adventure of the Holmes who was also Van Helsing . . . Doctor Frankenstein . . . Doctor Who . . . Whoever!

Nigel Stock, too, would return as Watson, and did so even sooner than his erstwhile partner in crime fighting. In 1968, with a new series of *Sherlock Holmes* under way, he was cast alongside Peter Cushing, then at the very height of his career as one of Britain's most recognizable yet utterly untypecast-able actors.

Cushing was born on May 26, 1913, in the small town of Kenley, Surrey; was raised in Dulwich, south London, and then Purley, back in the county of Surrey, where home was a striking Art Deco house built by his Quantity Surveyor father on St. James Road.

Originally pointed toward his own career in his father's line, Cushing won a scholarship to the Guildhall School of Music and Drama, worked in local rep for a few years, and then, audaciously, took himself off to Hollywood to become a star. He landed a role in *The Man in the Iron Mask* in 1939 and also appeared alongside Laurel and Hardy. But it was with that other great man of the British stage, Laurence Olivier, that Cushing made his mark, appearing as Osric in 1948's *Hamlet*.

Another actor whose face was oftentimes more familiar than his name, thanks to the amount of work he was undertaking, Cushing nevertheless established himself. In 1952, a BBC production of *Pride and Prejudice* cast him as Fitzwilliam Darcy; in 1954, he appeared as Winston Smith in an utterly spellbinding adaptation of Orwell's *1984*, scripted by Nigel Kneale and so unanimously applauded that the BBC was forced to air it again within a week of the original broadcast—which was good news for posterity. Because otherwise, we'd never have been able to see it again. Although the technology to record the corporation's live broadcasts was now in place, it was not always employed—and even when it was, it could often prove temperamental. The initial performance of *1984* indeed vanished into the ether as soon as it was broadcast, so the entire cast was assembled again for the repeat, and they went through the performance once again. This time it was recorded, and while contemporary critics insisted that the second go-round was inferior to the first, still the performance exists today, and it remains one of the Orwell's masterpiece's most masterful retellings.

In 1957, Cushing entered into what is probably his best-known association, joining the stable of actors at the Hammer film studio and, over the next fifteen years, establishing himself alongside Christopher Lee as *the* face of the studio's horror output. He is Van Helsing in the Dracula movies, he is the Baron in the Frankenstein films, and he appears to have loved every moment of it. "Who wants to see me as Hamlet?" he once asked. "Very few. But millions want to see me as Frankenstein, so that's the one I do."

Typecasting could, and indeed should have, devoured him now. But Cushing never fell prey to lazy audience expectations, primarily because he was so versatile. When 1965/66 brought the decision to bring television's *Doctor Who* to the big screen, Cushing stepped as effortlessly into that role as any other, eschewing comparisons with the show's TV doctor, William Hartnell, by playing him as an entirely different kind of person—and, in so doing, setting the stage for what has since become one of the TV series' own signatures, the titular doctor's regular "regeneration" (actually, a change of lead actor).

He appeared in *The Avengers* and in later years would guest in that show's 1970s reincarnation as *The New Avengers*. He was excellent in the first (1977) *Star Wars* movie (the one that has since been retitled *Star Wars IV*,

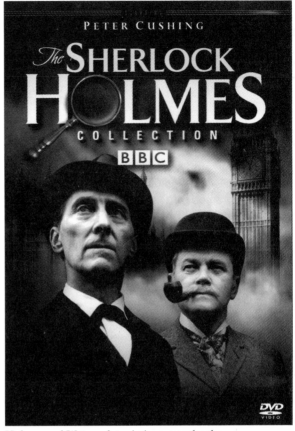

Holmes and Watson, late sixties super-sleuths.

and what a daft notion that was), and into the 1980s, he was Colonel William Raymond in the *Adventures in Time* movie version of the British children's favorite W. E. Bigglesworth—Biggles, for short. And in every role, one's initial thought of, "Oh, look, it's Van Helsing/the Baron/the Doctor, *whoever*," would immediately be subsumed beneath the sheer believability that Cushing brought to every role.

Sherlock Holmes, then, was just one more icon for Cushing to absorb, and of course, he did it magnificently. The presence of Nigel Stock as his faithful Watson lent the new series sufficient continuity with the old that it can almost be regarded as that long0overdue second series. But whereas Wilmer required a few episodes to truly bed himself into the part, Cushing knew from the outset what he needed to do, and he delivered it with gusto.

We curse the BBC's gift for false economy, recording over existing shows with new ones in order to save on buying new videotape. Just five of Cushing's sixteen adventures survive today: "A Study in Scarlet," "The Boscombe Valley Mystery," "The Sign of Four," "The Blue Carbuncle," and the two-part "Hound of the Baskervilles." Everything about them is superlative, including the fact that they were to be shot in color, at a time when even *Doctor Who* (not to mention most TV sets in Britain) was still black-and-white.

For fifty minutes a night, between September 9 and December 23, 1968, Cushing and Stock brought period England into modern Britain, with scripts, sets, and manners that may (as usual) have deviated from the Conan Doyle originals when they needed to but also nodded toward Cushing's own reputation as a master of English filmic Gothic for more than a soupçon of atmosphere. One of his earliest jobs for Hammer, after all, had been an adaptation of *The Hound of the Baskervilles*, in 1959, and the Holmes he played there had much in common with that he was to enact now.

As with the Wilmer series, it is hard to play favorites among the episodes, although the fact that only five stories survive to bear witness to the team's brilliance does narrow the field somewhat. The festive romp of "The Blue Carbuncle," aired just two days before Christmas 1968, has to be high on any list, however, and it is impossible not to be charmed by Watson's blundering courtship attempts throughout "The Sign of Four." As for the remainder of the series highlights, a quick look at the full series of sixteen titles allows us to at least guess at what we have lost:

- "The Second Stain" (missing episode)
- "The Dancing Men" (missing episode)
- "A Study in Scarlet"
- "The Hound of the Baskervilles" (two parts)
- "The Boscombe Valley Mystery"
- "The Greek Interpreter" (missing episode)
- "The Naval Treaty" (missing episode)
- "Thor Bridge" (missing episode)
- "The Musgrave Ritual" (missing episode)
- "Black Peter" (missing episode)
- "Wisteria Lodge" (missing episode)
- "Shoscombe Old Place" (missing episode)
- "The Solitary Cyclist" (missing episode)
- "The Sign of Four"
- "The Blue Carbuncle"

Cushing would return to the role of Holmes in 1984's *The Masks of Death*, a British TV movie that also reunited the now seventy-one-year-old with his old Hammer studios director Roy Ward Baker. It is a fascinating view, in that Cushing makes no attempt to deny his age—he is as crotchety and ill-tempered as any man in his seventies has earned the right to be, unswayed even by the appearance of Irene Adler, played by sixty-two-year-old American actress Anne Baxter in one of her last-ever roles. Watson (John Mills, seventy-six), meanwhile, is so arthritic he can no longer even chronicle Holmes's adventures, and the entire affair has the distinct ring of a macabre spin-off of *Golden Girls* to it.

Which is not to deny its entertainment value, nor the storied rank it holds in the annals of Peter Cushing's filmography. *The Masks of Death* was not quite his final major role, as is often said—*Biggles: Adventures in Time* followed it in 1986, and Cushing's performance is as magisterial there as one could wish. It was, however, his last work to receive praise for both Cushing's performance and for the production itself, a ranking that the *Biggles* movie, no matter how excellent it actually is, was singularly unable to attain.

Cushing's Holmes was the last to feature as a series on British television for some sixteen years (America had not seen one since the end of the Ronald Howard series in 1955).

Not that 221b Baker Street lay empty, of course; annually for the next decade, at least one Holmes movie or television special would be aired in either the US or the UK, with the title role going to actors as far apart as Stewart Granger (*The Hound of the Baskervilles*, 1972), John Cleese (*Elementary, My Dear Watson*, 1973; and *The Strange Case of the End of Civilisation as We Know It*, 1977), Larry Hagman (*The Return of the World's Greatest Detective*, 1976), Roger Moore (*Sherlock Holmes in New York*, 1976), Peter Cook (*Hound of the Baskervilles*, 1978), and Christopher Plummer (*Murder by Decree*, 1979).

The year 1979, however, saw the focus for Holmesian brilliance shift away from its traditional heartland, to the Soviet Union.

Замечательный пример советского Шерлока

Holmes had never been an exclusively Anglo-American phenomenon. As far back as 1908, Danish director, writer, and actor Viggo Larsen shot the silent *Sherlock Holmes i Livsfare*, the first in a series of some half a dozen films.

Germany was also very early onto the Baker Street bandwagon, and with his adventures being translated ever farther afield, Holmes became a truly international attraction.

Priklyucheniya Sherloka Kholmsa i doktora was a Soviet Russian production, launched in 1979, a few years after a local adaptation of *The Hound of the Baskervilles*, starring Nikolay Volkov, became one of the television hits of the decade. Eleven episodes would ultimately be shot, with Vasily Livanov portraying Holmes and Vitaly Solomin as Watson.

So far, so nothing unusual here. Until one fast-forwards some quarter of a century to the collapse of communism and the ensuing flood of DVDs that poured out of the former Soviet Union, making the nation's once super-secretive entertainment industry available to all. *Sherloka* was among the first beneficiaries of this unexpected largesse, and it proved one of the most savage surprises that the western television critic, so secure in his belief that "we do it best," has ever received.

Sherloka is brilliant. It doesn't matter that everybody rabbits away in Russian, and the English subtitles are eccentric to say the least. It doesn't matter that

ПРИКЛЮЧЕНИЯ
ШЕРЛОКА ХОЛМСА
и доктора ВАТСОНА

Based on the Works by Sir Arthur Conan Doyle
THE ADVENTURES
OF SHERLOCK HOLMES
AND DOCTOR WATSON
Sherlock Holmes and Doctor Watson
The Adventures of Sherlock Holmes and Doctor Watson
The Hound of the Baskervilles The Sign of Four His Last Bow

ДЛЯ ПРОДАЖИ ТОЛЬКО НА ТЕРРИТОРИЯХ США И КАНАДЫ

GOLD COLLECTION OF RUSSIAN CINEMA

COMPLETE VIDEO AND AUDIO REMASTERING

DVD
VIDEO
6 DISCS

The Soviet Holmes.

one's enjoyment of the show is occasionally tripped up by the subtle politicking that may or may not have been the maker's original intent. It doesn't even matter that the pace of the stories is relaxed, to say the least. Across five seasons, 1979–86, the best of the original canon was adapted and arranged into nine stories (including two two-parters) whose very titles cannot help but thrill: "The King of Blackmail" (revisiting "Charles Augustus Milverton"), "Mortal Fight" ("The Final Problem"), "Tiger Hunt" ("The Empty House"), and "The 20th Century Begins," conflating no fewer than four original stories into one gripping, seamless adventure.

Yet all of that only begins to capture the sheer joy of the series, for there is another crucial aspect, too. Russia loved Sherlock Holmes, but it loved his literature. The past eighty years' worth of Anglo-American film, television, and radio had not infiltrated the country in any way, shape, or form. Perhaps some people were aware of the fact that Holmes was a visual goldmine in the west, but opportunities to see the treasure with their own eyes would have been seriously restricted. The powers that controlled the Soviet Union were scarcely more interested in importing western entertainment than they were concerned with exporting their own.

Soviet television, like every other aspect of the arts, did not grow up in a vacuum, however, any more than the first American or British excursions into the medium could be said to have done so. It simply developed along its own path, with no care for the conventions of the decadent west and no interest in trying to emulate them.

Russian television was made for Russian viewers, and the Russian Sherlock Holmes was made for Russian Sherlock Holmes fans. And they had their own interpretations of his life, style, methods, and appearance that had nothing to do with Basil Rathbone, Peter Cushing, Ronald Howard, or even John Cleese. There was no formula to their interpretation, no sense that "this is how it should be done." Holmes was Holmes, and *Sherloka* will astonish any viewer who expects anything else.

Vasily Borisovich Livanov was born in Moscow on July 19, 1935, the son of actor Boris Nikolaevich Livanov. A student at both the Russian Academy of Arts and the B. V. Shchukin Drama School, the younger Livanov made his acting debut in 1960 as a geologist in the movie *Neotpravlennoye Pismo* (*The Unposted Letter*). Over the next two decades he maintained regular appearances on both the small and big screen, but it was *Sherloka* that confirmed his stardom, just as it did for Vitaly Mefodyevich Solomin, six years his junior, who was cast as Doctor Watson.

Reviewing *Sherloka* through western eyes is a waste of time. Commentaries on the series, once it made its way to the west, remarked upon Holmes's slight appearance. He was shorter than we expect, scrawnier. He wore spectacles. His face was more rounded than the Sidney Paget ideal that has become so essential for western actors to emulate. While Solomin's Watson does adhere to type in many respects, Holmes looks wrong. Which is what makes him so right. It is like meeting the old boy for the first time . . . again.

The sets are amazing. Victorian London may not be re-created with the same eye for detail and easy cliché as it is in western television, but it is convincing enough, even if St. Petersburg's ornate beauty does occasionally impose itself on a shot. Dark sets dominate, bringing precisely the right amount of atmosphere to the sets, with even Holmes's study at 221b looking more like the scene of some looming, desolate gothic horror than a pleasant room in the center of a bustling metropolis.

But again, this is what we want to see—how cripplingly disappointing it would have been had Sherlock come sweeping out of the east, looking and behaving exactly like every other one we've ever seen. The performance was reason enough for Conan Doyle's daughter Dame Jean to describe Livanov as a Holmes of which her father would have wholeheartedly approved (suggesting,

Jeremy Brett and Edward Hardwicke—the Eighties' greatest double act.

Photofest

perhaps, that all the others would have disappointed him?); reason, too, for Livnov to be awarded an Honorary MBE by the Queen of England, for "service to the theater and performing arts" in general, but—unspoken officially, but surely plain to see—for service to Holmesiana in general.

Readily available on DVD today, *Sherloka* might well be the crowning glory of Holmesian television, at least so far as its first half century was concerned. Its initial legacy and impact, however, were perhaps not as lost to western attentions as popular belief now insists. For in 1984, some ten years before the first Soviet DVDs reached our shores, a new series of Holmes was commissioned in the UK, and *Sherloka* was surely a shining influence.

The Heartbreaking Case of the Detective whom the Tabloids Said Was Mad (and We All Believe the Tabloids, don't we?)

Jeremy Brett was the quintessential western Holmes, just turned fifty when he landed the part and powerfully pointy in all the right places. He was familiar enough from his earlier career for audiences to accept him in the new role, but obscure enough to both devour and be devoured by the part. Plus, he was an heir to the Cadbury chocolate empire, and an Old Etonian, whose father, a deputy lord lieutenant of Warwickshire, was so disappointed that the boy wanted to become an actor that he forced him to change his name to preserve the family honor. Peter Jeremy William Huggins became Jeremy Brett, naming himself for the maker of the first suit he ever owned.

Accomplished on both stage and screen, a member of the National Theatre Company, a Broadway veteran, and a reliable Shakespearean, Brett made his cinema debut in the 1956 Audrey Hepburn version of *War and Peace* (he and Hepburn were later reunited in *My Fair Lady*) and was a solid supporting character in a variety of 1960s/70s British TV action series. He also appeared on stage as Doctor Watson in Los Angeles in 1980, with Charlton Heston a most unlikely Holmes, in *The Crucifer of Blood*.

It was Holmes that brought Brett stardom, however. Initially accompanied by actor David Burke as Watson, but more famously by Edward Hardwicke, Brett described Holmes as "the hardest part I have ever played—harder than Hamlet or Macbeth." Nevertheless, he sleuthed sophisticatedly through no less than forty-one episodes over the next decade, in a series that all concerned adamantly proposed would be the greatest adaptation ever produced.

They came close, too. Drawing upon members of the same team that produced the previous decade's period drama smash *Upstairs Downstairs*, everything about the series is noteworthy, but still Brett rose above his surroundings.

According to legend, he spent close to a year before shooting began immersing himself in everything Holmesian, noting it all down in a seventy-seven-page Baker Street File that became as invaluable to him as the script. For it was there that he noted every last characteristic of the original Holmes that he wished to replicate, and from there that he drew his objections to anything, no matter how tiny, that deviated from what he considered authentic behavior.

It was a grueling routine, and as the series marched on, it took its toll on Brett. Utterly obsessed with the role, Brett "became" Sherlock Holmes, adopting his mannerisms off stage as much as on, borrowing his speech, even dreaming about him. The fictional Holmes's disregard for his own personal safety when the clue-hunting bit was between his teeth became a part of Brett's personality, as he threw himself into the stunts that the television demanded, but he had no intention of letting it go.

Diagnosed with manic depression in 1986 and prescribed lithium, Brett absorbed the drug's side effects, physical and emotional, into his portrait of Holmes. A lifelong smoker, he was puffing his way through sixty cigarettes a day at the height of the Holmes series, and when his doctors warned him to slow down the frenetic pace of his double life (he suffered from an enlarged heart and frequently needed oxygen on set), he responded by doubling his workload. When playwright Jeremy Paul produced the play *The Secret of Sherlock Holmes* in 1988, Brett and Hardwicke stepped straight out of their television roles and into the rigors of the theater.

Yet if Holmes could be said (as many did) to have been killing Brett, life without Holmes proved even more fatal. He died from heart failure just two years after the show left the screens, shortly after making a brief non-Holmesian appearance in the 1996 movie version of *Moll Flanders.*

The Adventures of Sherlock Holmes, as the first series of thirteen broadcasts was titled, debuted in the UK on April 24, 1984, with "A Scandal in Bohemia"—establishing from the outset, then, that Conan Doyle's original chronology was of no concern, despite the series makers' insistence upon absolute accuracy.

It is of no import. The fifty-minute episode effortlessly reestablished Holmes and Watson in the viewing public's minds, simultaneously serving up an Irene Adler (Gayle Hunnicut) whose efficacy would remain unchallenged until Lara Pulver commandeered the role over a quarter of a century later.

Hunnicut's seemingly effortless portrayal of extreme grace under extraordinary pressure is as dynamic in such a short space of time as Brett's introduction of Holmes's touchstones—his drug addiction, his egotism, and his brilliance. Three qualities honed to a degree that would be remarkable in three separate men. To find them all so convincingly bound up in one single persona left even the hard-to-please UK press of the day breathless at the prospect of more adventures to come.

"The Dancing Men" and "The Naval Treaty" followed; "The Solitary Cyclist" allowed the cast to relax into a more lighthearted atmosphere than hitherto; "The Crooked Man" shook off its general reputation as a somewhat substandard Conan Doyle story to become one of the best in the entire series; and "The Speckled Band" introduced another dimension to the Holmesian personality, as he became almost pleasant . . . concerned . . . even friendly.

Concluding the first half of the series on June 5, 1984, "The Blue Carbuncle" was watched by a best-yet eight million viewers on its first airing, and it was apparent to all concerned that Granada TV, the series' makers, had a major hit on their hands. So much so that the yearlong break that preceded the series' resumption served only to excite anticipation further, and its return on August 25, 1985, attracted a staggering eleven million viewers (approximately 20 percent of the country's population) for "The Copper Beeches."

"The Greek Interpreter," "The Norwood Builder," "The Resident Patient," and "The Red-Headed League" followed, all of them leading up to the series finale, "The Final Problem." And throughout every episode, further facets of Holmes's character and world would be revealed.

Joss Ackland, in "The Copper Beeches," firmly establishes Jepho Rucastle as one of Holmes's most formidable, if cruelly underrated, opponents. We encounter Mycroft in "The Greek Interpreter"; we meet Lestrade in "The Norwood Builder." "The Resident Patient" lurks just a little to the left of an Edgar Allen Poe–style shocker, reminding us of the gothic undertones that our best impressions of Holmes should always develop from; and the final two tales, linked amidships by the utterly unexpected (in canonical terms) presence of Moriarty, lead to a death plunge that is no less shocking (and extraordinarily well executed) here than it must have appeared in 1893.

Certainly one's knowledge of Holmes's survival does not even cross the viewer's mind as that startling conclusion unfolds, and when the credits flow it seems as unlikely that either Holmes or Moriarty (played with devastating intent by Eric Porter) will ever return. In fact, it is poor old Watson who is destined for a form of retirement, as David Burke was replaced in the role by Edward Hardwicke, and on July 9, 1986, *The Return of Sherlock Holmes* got under way with "The Empty House."

After so much character and background had been packed into the first series, what could possibly be added to the second? A lot. You will read in many places, the booklet accompanying the series' DVD box set included, that "the first seven episodes of *The Return of Sherlock Holmes* are arguably the finest Granada ever produced."

This is true, assuming one wishes to forget all that came before, and much of what would follow. "The Empty House," "The Abbey Grange," "The Musgrave Ritual," "The Second Stain," "The Man with the Twisted Lip," "The Priory School," and "The Six Napoleons" probably rank as few readers' favorite tales, especially *en masse*.

Somehow, though, it is these lesser-rated stories that allowed Brett and the newly arrived Hardwicke to truly spread out, not only in their own right, but also as members of what was now a fairly well-established team: Colin Jeavons (Lestrade) and Rosalie Williams (Mrs. Hudson) were not prominent, or even present, in every episode. But still there is an ensemble feel to the performance that prompts the viewer to raise a silent cheer whenever one or other of these beloved characters makes another appearance.

The joy of the production masked tragedy in Brett's private life. The actor's second wife, Joan Wilson, died of cancer in July 1985, during the filming of *The Return of Sherlock Holmes*. Grief-stricken, Brett suffered a nervous breakdown that led to him being hospitalized for close to three months. Depression and lithium followed, and of course all work on the series was postponed. The seven episodes that are so loudly lauded today were complete and broadcast on schedule. But it would take a Christmas 1987 one-off presentation of *The Sign of Four* to announced Brett's return in fine form, and it would be April 6, 1988, before the series proper resumed with the moody malignancy of "The Devil's Foot."

The scars of the recent past were plain to see in Brett's demeanor and performance. Not that he was no longer brilliant; nor that the four stories that completed the series ("The Devil's Foot" was followed by "Silver Blaze," "Wisteria Lodge," and "The Bruce-Partington Plans") were not of the highest quality.

True, budgetary miscalculations did necessitate reining in much of the proposed action and location footage planned for the final two stories and were responsible, too, for the series running to just eleven episodes instead of the projected thirteen. But Brett's health was a concern, and the lithium had caused him to bloat (water retention is a common side effect).

His performance was as powerful and his acting as sharp as ever. But appearances will always influence perceptions, particularly coupled with the general, tabloid-fed public perception of Brett's malaise—"TV Sherlock in Mental Home" was the headline in *The Sun*, Britain's favorite litterbox liner, when Brett's illness was made public, and long after the rest of the story had been forgotten, the possibility that the actor had gone insane did cloud some viewers' judgment. And, apparently, still does. Do not believe them. Those final four stories in *The Return of Sherlock Holmes* are as gripping as any among the first seven, with the series finale, featuring Charles Gray returning as a memorable Mycroft, an absolutely mesmeric production.

A two-hour TV-movie-style retelling of *The Hound of the Baskervilles* in August 1988, contrarily, ranks among the entire series' low points; but February 1991 brought the regular series back to the screens, this time under the umbrella title of *The Casebook of Sherlock Holmes*, and for the next month and a half, we thrilled to "The Disappearance of Lady Frances Carfax," "The Problem of Thor Bridge," "The Boscombe Valley Mystery," "The Illustrious Client," "Shoscombe Old Place," and "The Creeping Man."

This time around, however, some of the old magic did seem to have dissipated, although it is difficult to say whether it was the show that had run out of steam or the viewers that had run out of patience. A new decade always brings with it new fascinations, and *Sherlock Holmes* had so guilelessly dominated the 1980s that it suddenly felt like a relic in the 1990s.

Plus, British television has never wanted for weekly hourlong detective series, and the past few years had overflowed with the things, many of them dipping into the same idealized vision of a past halcyon era that was one of Sherlock Holmes's greatest charms and cramming nostalgia down its audience's throat. As Holmes declared to Watson in "His Last Bow" back in 1917, "you are the one fixed point in a changing age." At the time, it was intended as a compliment, a symbol of constance and reliability. Now it felt like an epitaph.

TV movies briefly became the order of the day: *The Master Blackmailer* (retitled "Charles Augustus Milverton") in January 1992; *The Last Vampyre* ("The Sussex Vampire") twelve months later; and *The Eligible Bachelor* ("The Noble Bachelor") in January 1993. And that did appear to be it. Reviews for all three were poor, but *The Eligible Bachelor* was roundly panned from even further afield.

Dame Jean Conan Doyle weighed into the fray, denouncing the movie as an unworthy blot. But plans were already afoot for one further series of six one-hour stories, and they could not be abandoned. With heavy hearts all round, it seems, 1994 would see the team reunite one last time, for *The Memoirs of Sherlock Holmes*.

Fact: including the four novels, there are just sixty original Sherlock Holmes stories to adapt.

Fact: the series so far had covered thirty-five of them, more than any other team had ever managed before, and naturally incorporating not only the best of the batch, but also the second- and third-best.

Which meant . . . .

Nobody really wants to say that, out of the twenty-five stories that remained to be televised, that there was not one that could be ranked among Conan Doyle's finest. But the fact remains, even the stories that were ultimately selected for adaptation scarcely number among Holmes's most memorable excursions. "The Three Gables," "The Dying Detective," "The Golden Pince-Nez," "The Red Circle," "The Mazarin Stone," and "The Cardboard Box" passed through spring 1994 to low viewing figures and an increasing sensation of multiple dead horses being soundly flogged.

Holmes and Watson seemed to have drifted apart; they remained partners, of course, but they talked at and around one another, rather than to. Excellent supporting actors of the caliber of Peter Wyngarde, Frank Finlay, and Kenneth Connor felt wasted in their assigned roles, and even today, viewing these final stories as the last stage of devouring the entire forty-three-hour DVD box set, it feels more of a chore than a pleasure: "I own the entire series, therefore I must watch the entire series. But I will be jolly pleased when it's over."

In and out of treatment for his continuing mental health problems, increasingly beleaguered by physical ailments, the last decade of Brett's life—which means the lion's share of his time as Sherlock Holmes—was not a happy one, and it seems cruelly ironic that such great fame should have grasped him at almost precisely the same time as such brutal tragedy. He died on September 12, 1995, and the world's media flocked to remember a man whom few would deny as the greatest Sherlock Holmes of them all.

So far . . . .

16

The Thoroughly Modern Adventure of the Twenty-first-Century Holmes

In which we Consider what might have Happened had Sherlock Holmes not Existed until Today

Across the century and a quarter since he first set foot on the printed page, Sherlock Holmes has been revised and revisited, rewritten and rewired, reinvented and redeployed. He has never, however, been so completely and absolutely reimagined that everything we think we know about him is presented for us to discover again, in a manner that establishes even the most familiar aspects of his life and adventures as something new and exciting.

When Conan Doyle first sat down to write about his pet detective, all he had before him was a blank sheet of paper. Yes, in his usual methodical manner, he had probably made some notes; and, of course, he had memories and experiences to draw upon, too. His time at sea, his years at school, his career as a doctor, his own intellectual development, all of these things were to become a part of this "Sherlock Holmes" character. But of Holmes himself, he knew no more than he wrote at the time, with every fresh line, every new idea, every twist in the plot and turn of the page not only building the story, but also building the personality of the man at its heart.

It was a work of absolute immediacy, spontaneous in some places, accidental in others, and no matter what ideas Conan Doyle may have had when he first picked up his pen, it was not until he reached the end of *A Study in Scarlet* that he could truly look back and shake hands with his creation. And only then could he get down to the serious business of getting to know the man.

Arguably, the Sherlock Holmes for whom we thank Conan Doyle was not wholly established until the author wrapped up the first series of short stories for *The Strand*. Equally arguably, the Holmes whom we all think we know today

Benedict Cumberbatch and Martin Freeman—the new Holmes and Watson.   *Photofest*

continued to grow through sundry rereadings of his story and rewritings of his adventures, and the efforts of so many great actors and scriptwriters. On screen, a bad Holmes is one that tells us nothing more than we already know about him. A good one, as we saw in the last chapter, is one who continues to open new vistas to the viewer.

But what if none of that had ever happened?

The Spellbinding Adventure of the Reinvented Classic

The Soviet TV series *Sherloka* introduces us to a world in which Conan Doyle's original remains the only Holmes, but necessarily refracts that uniqueness through the multifarious prisms of its own culture and society. The 2012 American series *Elementary*, with Holmes (Jonny Lee Miller) an expat English detective based in modern-day New York, solving crimes with a Holmesian demeanor and a female Doctor Watson, takes a similar notion but litters its journey with knowing winks and deliberate clues, as though challenging (albeit none too fiendishly) the viewer to determine who is the bigger fool: us for watching it, or Holmes, for not realizing that the Fox network's *Keen Eddie* went down a similar route a decade earlier and didn't need Sherlock's assistance either.

And smack in between the two of them, informed by the Russians and self-confessedly the impetus and inspiration for the Americans, lies *Sherlock*, a BBC TV series that so exquisitely redecorates every page of the original canon that one can imagine future researchers wondering which of the pair was truly created first: the twenty-first-century ADD sociopath with fewer people skills than a skipful of scorpions, or the nineteenth-century cokehead who at least was born with a few manners and scruples?

Sherlock was the brainchild of British TV writers Steven Moffat and Mark Gatiss, the former recently installed as executive producer of the monstrously successful *Doctor Who*, the latter one of his most reliable scriptwriters.

Even pre–*Doctor Who*, Moffat's track record was formidable. Two of the most exhilarating British comedies of recent years, *Joking Apart* and *Coupling* (the UK original, not the tragic stateside knockoff), were his work; so was the thriller *Jekyll*, effectively a reimagining of Robert Louis Stevenson's *Doctor Jekyll and Mr Hyde*, translated to modern-day Britain. In addition, three of Doctor Who's own most beloved recent adventures were his—the two-part *The Empty Child/The Doctor Dances*, *The Girl in the Fireplace*, and the ultra-terrifying *Blink*.

Gatiss, too, had a powerful résumé. As both an author and an actor, his *Doctor Who* credentials were peerless. As a comedian, he was a member of the much-praised League of Gentlemen team; as a scriptwriter, he played a major role in a modern reappraisal of yet another British icon, shifting the detective drama *Randall and Hopkirk (Deceased)* out of the late 1960s and into the early 2000s.

Now he and Moffat were discussing another of their shared loves, Sherlock Holmes, and regretting how every fresh imagining, even elements of the superlative Jeremy Brett series, had been so concerned with getting the setting correct, the character right, and the atmospheres just so that they forgot about what should have been the most crucial element of all. The story. They discussed, too, how a Holmes that stripped away all of the window dressing and just went back to Conan Doyle's blank page might well prove to be one of the most fascinating projects either had ever taken on.

If Holmes had never existed in the past, what would they have to write about? They started with a man named Sherlock Holmes who sets himself up as a consulting detective. He is introduced to a recently returned military doctor, John Watson, fresh from serving in Afghanistan. Watson, though wounded, is damaged more in emotional terms than physical. The London police force views Holmes with suspicion, not because they doubt his abilities, but because they deny they need somebody who possesses those abilities. A shared apartment in central London . . . Baker Street, convenient for the underground, but also within walking distance of so much of the city.

Stories that Conan Doyle developed from the times and trials in which he lived, and that—for all the intentions of sundry subsequent authors—remain largely locked in that universe of late Empirical mannerisms and propriety, would be resurrected around modern concerns and conceits. In the original "The Adventure of the Five Orange Pips," the pips are literally those of an orange. Nobody would employ such a signal today. But they might use the traditional beeping sound of the Greenwich Mean Time signal . . . *pip, pip, pip, pip, piiiiiiiiiiiip.*

Conan Doyle's Holmes and Watson were, simply, Holmes and Watson, colleagues. First names were for introductions and other people. The modern duo were Sherlock and John. Friends.

Conan Doyle's Holmes eschewed any technology he did not believe would assist him in his task, but he devoured any that would help, because that was the world in which we lived, the Victorian age of ever-greater feats of engineering and ingenuity. The modern Holmes is gadget-crazy, because that was the environment in which *he* was raised, one in which new and exciting electronic distractions seemed to rain down from heaven, and all had a purpose of some sort.

Conan Doyle's Holmes diced with popular opprobrium by nursing a cocaine habit, just at that point in time when society was beginning to distinguish between medicinal drugs and recreational abuse. The modern Holmes is a tobacco user, a smoker in an age when that particular vice seems to have actually overtaken cocaine on any truly health-conscious soul's litany of society's most ruthless scourges.

Conan Doyle's Holmes had his adventures chronicled in a monthly magazine. The modern Holmes is the subject of a blog.

The greatest difference of all, however, was the most intrinsic of the lot. Other writers took their ideas and shoehorned Conan Doyle's stories inside them. Moffat and Gatiss would reverse the process altogether. Conan Doyle's ideas would be grafted into their stories.

The Gripping Adventure That, Infuriatingly, Is Between Seasons at the Time of Writing

At the time of writing, three seasons of three stories apiece have been broadcast, time enough for Holmes to encounter Irene Adler, investigate the hound of the Baskervilles, and re-create his death dive with Moriarty. But Adler is no longer an opera singer; she is a high-class dominatrix. The hound is no longer an ancient family legend, but the outcome of experiments at a top-secret government laboratory. And Holmes and Moriarty perish not amid the raging torrents of a Swiss waterfall, but on the roof of a London hospital, in full view not only of a street full of people, but of Doctor Watson, as well.

Sherlock is a success not simply for the vivacious veracity with which every story is paced, and the ease with which even the most familiar tale is twisted into something fresh. Casting, too, plays a giant part in the show's celebrity, with the central role, the title role, being handed to an actor whose suitability as a traditional Holmes might never have crossed anyone's mind, but who makes such an appropriate modern one that it is already impossible to view anybody else in the part.

Thirty-four years old when 2010 delivered the first season of *Sherlock*, Benedict Timothy Carlton Cumberbatch already had five years of astonishingly eclectic acting behind him, impressing in roles as disparate as scientist Stephen

Benedict Cumberbatch as Sherlock in London's China Town.   *Photofest*

Hawking, eighteenth-century prime minister William Pitt, Victor Frankenstein and his monster (alongside Jonny Lee Miller, of *Elementary* fame), and a World War I major (in Spielberg's *War Horse* grotesquery). *Sherlock*, however, was to prove a cut above them all.

The series started life, as is the norm, as a pilot episode, rewiring the first-ever Holmes mystery, "A Study in Scarlet," around the discovery of a pink-clad woman's body in an abandoned house in London's Brixton neighborhood, the latest in a series of mysterious and inexplicable deaths that the police can only surmise are a rash of copycat suicides.

A shade shy of an hour in length, the pilot proposed a six-part series of similarly structured episodes; the BBC, enthused by the concept, responded by commissioning three ninety-minute stories, necessitating a complete rewriting and restructuring of what had been retitled "A Study in Pink," shot with the exact same cast and just enough of the original script for the viewer to watch the two side by side (the pilot is among the DVD's bonus tracks) and agree that the Beeb made the correct decision.

"A Study in Pink" makes all the necessary introductions, then launches into dramatic territory. The scene in which Holmes introduces himself to the investigation by interrupting Lestrade's latest press conference, contradicting the inspector's every pronouncement via text message, is classic. It also establishes this new Holmes's methodology. He doesn't care who he offends and is not, for the most part, even aware that they have been offended. He says and does what he deems appropriate. It is other people's concern if they don't like what they see and hear.

Lestrade allows Holmes into the investigation; Holmes responds not only by solving a most ingenious case, but also by introducing Watson (Martin Freeman)—whom he has only just met, through a mutual acquaintance—to what he, Holmes, has decided will become Watson's way of life. Poor John; desperate for adventure and affection he may be, and a willing accomplice he may become. But there are moments when he certainly wonders what on earth he has let himself in for.

Filming "The Blind Banker" for *Sherlock* season two.   *Photofest*

He relishes his new life regardless. "Watson is not an idiot," Mark Gatiss once pointed out, "although it's true that Conan Doyle always took the piss out of him. But only an idiot would surround himself with idiots." And Holmes may be a lot of things, but he is not an idiot.

A stunning debut was followed by two more tales, "The Blind Banker" and "The Great Game"—Holmesian titles indeed, and adventures wherein even the ghost of a Conan Doyle original could send the action flying off in other directions entirely. We see both canonical and noncanonical adventures referenced, sometimes as primary plot lines, other times as mere vignettes or even passing nods. But never in such a fashion that they feel forced, or thrust into the story.

Vagaries of plotting that Conan Doyle, whether through forgetfulness or carelessness, allowed to live on are neatly sewn up. Few readers at any point since 1893 have failed to wonder precisely how a villain so grand as Moriarty could have passed unmentioned through Holmes's adventures until the story in which they fight their final battle. This point, of course, was reinforced every time he was brought up in a later movie.

Sherlock addresses this by giving us a Moriarty who can be seen tracking Holmes long before their final denouement, and doing so with a cunning that really is the equal of Holmes's own. "We knew what we wanted to do with Moriarty from the very beginning," Moffat explained. "Moriarty is usually a rather dull, rather posh villain so we thought someone who was genuinely properly frightening. Someone who's an absolute psycho."

Brilliantly played by Andrew Smith, Moriarty certainly fits that billing, a master of disguise in his own right who ultimately succeeds in turning even

Holmes's greatest allies against him. But Rupert Graves as Lestrade is equally captivating; Una Stubbs is the ideal Mrs. Hudson, forever bustling around 221b while constantly reminding Holmes that she is his landlady, not his housekeeper; and then there is Molly (Louise Breeley), down in the mortuary of St. Bart's Hospital, and so clearly in love with an utterly oblivious Holmes that she allows him free rein of her office and facilities, just for the pleasure of having him close by.

Conan Doyle purposefully eschewed a love life for Holmes, a device that subsequent chroniclers have raged against to varying degrees of satisfaction. Molly is the first time a recurring character has recurred with such unrequited stubbornness, and she is all the more delightful for it.

The first season of three episodes ended with Holmes and Watson finally encountering Moriarty face to face at a swimming pool, alive with snipers and explosives. It is a magnificent scene, high drama offset by absolute absurdity—Moriarty's ringtone of the Bee Gees' "Staying Alive" has probably rewired that song for everyone who watched the episode. And, because it is a cliffhanger that has no parallel in the Conan Doyle stories, it ensured that a second series would be at least as avidly watched as the first.

Having toyed so successfully with, among others, *A Study in Scarlet* and "The Bruce-Partington Plans" in the first series, Gatiss acknowledged that "the natural order" for series two "would be to do three of the most famous [adventures]." Around that seemingly elementary premise, however, there was "the question of how to go out on a cliffhanger and then the thematic things of the three stories, where we were trying to get to, and what Sherlock and John's relationship is a little further on. You can't just go back to: 'You have no emotions.' 'I don't care.' You've got to move on somewhere and make sure the other characters have something of a journey too."

"A Scandal in Bohemia," repositioned in the fashionable London neighborhood of Belgravia, opened the second series, Holmes and Watson commissioned to retrieve some incriminating photographs of a British royal that Miss Adler has filed away on her cellphone and whose security she will safeguard with her life.

Adler's portrayal by English actress Lara Pulver arguably rates as her greatest ever. Born in Southend on September 1, 1980, Pulver first came to attention in the role of Lucille Frank in the West End musical *Parade* in 2008. The following year, she joined the cast of the BBC's latest, greatest adaptation of *Robin Hood*, playing the part of the fiendish Guy of Gisbourne's sister Isabella; 2010 brought her roles in *True Blood*, as Sookie Stackhouse's fairy godmother, and in *Spooks*, the final season of the BBC's long-running spy drama.

But it was as Irene Adler that she astonished the Holmesian community (and mortified the so-easily scandalized British gutter press) by appearing in sundry states of nudity in *Sherlock*. Certainly the *Daily Mail*, a mainspring of Britain's right-wing press, diminished now to a reactionary scandal sheet, clambered aboard the highest horse it could find to announce: "It's a mystery that Sherlock

Adler's portrayal by Lara Pulver arguably rates as the role's greatest ever.   *Alamy*

Holmes himself might struggle to solve—how could the BBC think that these scenes were appropriate for a pre-watershed audience?

"Families settling down to watch the Corporation's latest Sir Arthur Conan Doyle adaptation were shocked to see actress Lara Pulver . . . strolling around with no clothes on a full 25 minutes before 9pm" (the time is the so-called watershed, prior to which British programmers are obliged to be aware that not all little children go to bed early).

Naturally, the story was then illustrated with two photographs of the offending flesh, while "readers' comments" included the enraged Tweet, "How was Sherlock on pre-watershed with that slut walking round with no clothes on for most of it?!" Because that is precisely the kind of language you want your children reading in a family newspaper.

The BBC, for its own part, did not bat an eyelid. Some 9.5 million viewers watched the episode, and the ubiquitous spokesman told the paper, "We're delighted with the critical and audience response to the first episode, which has been extremely positive, and have received no complaints at this stage."

Nor, probably, would they.

The Hounds of Baskerville was next, a teasing reminder not only of past Holmes glories, but also of those wonderful 1950s-era B-movies in which something sinister is stirring down at the top secret laboratory—and it's going to make an awful mess of a lot of people before it's finally caught. In this case, the hound has just one victim, but the suspense laid down by the new storyline (and by our familiarity with the original), shot through with the truly atmospheric darkness and mists of the moor, readily places the Gatiss-penned retelling on an even par with any past adaptation.

Series two concluded with "The Reichenbach Fall," the death of Moriarty, and that of Holmes, as well. Only in this version, Holmes is *seen* to die, flinging himself off the hospital roof—only to reappear, still living, as Watson and Mrs. Hudson stand by his grave. And that was the cliffhanger. Not his death, but his miraculous escape from it.

The camera did not flinch as he fell, after all, and nobody could have mistaken the bloodied body that lay on the pavement. Certainly not Watson, whom we leave with even greater psychological scarring than when we initially met him; and not the show's Internet fans either, who then spent the entire hiatus preceding series three's "The Empty Hearse" curtain raiser by theorizing upon how Holmes did it.

As cliffhangers go—and everyone reading this could surely list at least a dozen that have truly kept them guessing—this one goes straight to the top of the pile. Just as *Sherlock* does when we discuss televised envisionings of the titular Holmes. Yes, envisioning. No "re-" prefix necessary.

He was back, though, and he was as brilliant as ever. As brilliantly punning, too, as "The Adventure of the Empty House" became "The Empty Hearse," The Sign of Four became "The Sign of Three," "His Last Bow" became "His Last Vow," and the shock of his survival at the end of series two was absorbed as effortlessly (and believably) into the new adventures as it had stunned everyone at the conclusion of the old.

"[Sherlock] cunningly avoided the pavement," Steve Moffat explained in the run-up to the new series. "That really is the only way to avoid dying. There's only a limited number of ways he can do this. He's got to interrupt his fall before he hits the pavement."

As for how he did it, however, that became one of the best-guarded secrets in recent TV history, with even Martin Freeman admitting, "Even we, on reading the script aren't quite sure [how Sherlock survived]." But to quote Moffat once more, "Now things are moving on, with John Watson getting married. Sherlock, being the way he is, wants everything to stay the same.

"But real life is flowing around him," and as the final episode approached its own conclusion, Holmes locked in conflict with Charles Augustus Magnussen (a Milverton for a new generation), the show runner spoke for every viewer when he gasped, ""You'll be watching the end of the last episode thinking, 'They wouldn't stop it there?! They wouldn't stop it there?! Oh my God, they wouldn't stop it there?!'"

17

The Peculiar Afterlife of All the Other Stories

In which we Spend several weeks Glued to the Television Screen and develop Carpal Tunnel from Constant Manipulation of the Remote Control

"The Adventure of Shoscombe Old Place" was Conan Doyle's final venture into the world of Sherlock Holmes. Even before that, however, there was no shortage of other writers and creators keen to pick up the deerstalker and pipe from where they were left and continue the life not only of Holmes, but also of his family and friends. And once technology introduced moving pictures to the equation, that life expanded even further.

Some of the ensuing tales are excellent; some of them are appalling. Some add much to the legend of the original Holmes; others suck the last ounce of joy from audience and subject matter alike. What follows is an opinionated but hopefully representative sampling of the best (and occasionally worst) of the manifold movies and television specials that have appeared across the past century or so, discussed alphabetically by title.

The Baker Street Boys (TV: 1983)

A very fondly remembered British children's series followed the adventures of the Baker Street Irregulars, the band of street urchins whom Holmes employed as his eyes and ears in the meanest corners of London life. Named here as Wiggins, Shiner, Beaver, Queenie, Rosie, and Sparrow, the six intrepid orphans enjoyed four hourlong adventures (each split into two parts): "The Adventure of the Disappearing Dispatch Case"; "The Ghost of Julian Midwife"; "The Adventure of the Winged Scarab"; and "The Case of the Captive Clairvoyant." Holmes, Watson, Moriarty, and Lestrade are all numbered among the supporting cast, but the adventures and mysteries are very much the children's own.

The series won several prestigious television awards, but hopes for a second series went unrealized, although the Baker Street Boys (and girls) lived on in a series of novelizations penned by the show's original writer, Anthony Read.

The Case of the Whitechapel Vampire (TV: 2002)

Matt Frewer played Holmes in no less than four movies: *The Hound of the Baskervilles* (2000), *The Sign of Four* (2001), and *The Royal Scandal* (2001), all of which were based upon original Conan Doyle tales (the latter merged "A Scandal in Bohemia" with "The Bruce-Partington Plans"), and this, a somewhat awkward but generally enjoyable cross between Bram Stoker's *Dracula* and Umberto Eco's *The Name of the Rose.*

The 1897 publication of Bram Stoker's *Dracula* is often regarded as a great landmark in the development of British literature equaling the arrival of Sherlock Holmes a decade earlier. Certainly the two veins of fiction that this pair of novels inspired, the detective story on the one hand, the vampire legend on the other, show no sign whatsoever of flagging in terms of popularity, and when one considers that HG Wells's *The War of the Worlds* was itself just twelve months away when Dracula first stalked, introducing science fiction to the realm, one can only marvel at the sheer ingenuity of the late Victorian mind. Has any other single ten-year period so rewritten our culture as thoroughly as that?

Conan Doyle and Stoker were already friends, and the former's kind words regarding *Dracula* were certainly as instrumental in its future success as any review can be. *Dracula*, Conan Doyle declared, was "the very best story of diablerie which I have read for many years."

Dracula himself is not a featured player in this movie. But his reputation, of course, precedes him. A monk is found dead at a Whitechapel abbey, with puncture wounds in his throat. The official verdict is heart failure, but the deceased's fellow brothers suspect a more ungodly agency—particularly after two further monks are slain by what appears to be a demon.

Aired on the Hallmark Channel—which, in all fairness, is seldom regarded as the natural home for first-run classic movies—*The Case of the Whitechapel Vampire* does a great job in conjuring up the requisite atmosphere, especially when the presence of Jack the Ripper is summoned up, as well, albeit more as a visual pun than any kind of plot device. Not a movie for true connoisseurs, then, but certainly one that is worth a late-night laugh.

Elementary, My Dear Watson—The Strange Case of the Dead Solicitors (TV: 1973)

An installment in the British BBC's long-running Comedy Playhouse Presents series, *Elementary, My Dear Watson* is very fondly remembered as "the one with John Cleese." *Monty Python*'s long-leggedly limber comedian was at the peak of his Pythonesque popularity at the time; indeed, this particular show was broadcast on the same day as Cleese's last-ever appearance in *Python*, January 18, 1973, and was touted accordingly as the actor's first role since that so-nurturing nest thrust him to fame.

Two mysteries face Holmes and Watson (played with singular brilliance by William Rushton). The first revolves around the reappearance of a deadly spectral rattlesnake, the ancestral curse of the Bellingham-Datchet family. Before the duo can truly investigate that matter, however, they are called in to solve the killings of five lawyers at an office in Cockfosters, north London. Naturally, they uncover the mystery in the most uproariously convoluted fashion, and Holmes even has time to cross swords with Moriarty. So all's well that ends well . . . unless you are a Bellingham-Datchet. The rattlesnake killed them all.

Doctor Watson and the Darkwater Hall Mystery: A Singular Adventure (TV: 1974)

Written by Kingsley Amis and starring Edward Fox as Doctor Watson, this seventy-three-minute BBC production takes place during a two-week hiatus in Holmes's usual routine. He is undergoing a rest cure in the country, but his latest would-be client, Lady Emily Fairfax, is desperate. She asks Watson to solve the case on his own. Which he does, rampaging across a set and script that are alive with reminders of past Holmesian adventures. We even, at one point, see him pick up a case folder titled "The Adventure of the Deadly Cobra" and retitle it "The Speckled Band."

That said, the story does demand a certain amount of patience, together with a general appreciation of Amis's own distinctive writing style—arguably, his peak as a parodist passed with the publication of the James Bond pastiche *Colonel Sun* in 1968, and *Darkwater Hall* struggles to match it.

The Great Mouse Detective (animated movie: 1986)

The Disney Studios turned their attention to Holmes with a cartoon that restates the entire Holmes legend behind the skirting boards of a London house in 1897. Based upon a series of books for children by author Eve Titus and illustrator Paul Galdone (the first, *Basil of Baker Street*, appeared in 1958), Basil is the titular sleuth, voiced by none other than Basil Rathbone; David Q. Dawson is his sidekick; and everything revolves not only around the fiendish machinations of Professor Ratigan, speaking in the measured, sinister tones of Vincent Price, but also around a host of visual puns borrowed from both Disney's own past and cinema history in general.

Hands of a Murderer (TV: 1990)

English actor Edward Woodward had already appeared in some of television's most iconic roles, including the British spy drama *Callan* and America's crimebusting *The Equalizer*, when he was recruited to this gripping Anglo-American co-production.

Okay, maybe "gripping" is not quite the word we should use—the story is threadbare, the action is episodic, and the writing is clunky. Plus, Woodward is so firmly established as a downtrodden antihero that it seems a little strange seeing him so happily cavorting with the cream of Scotland Yard, at the bidding of a script that seems curiously prescient of twenty-first-century television's overriding principle of "never mind the quality, feel the set pieces."

Anthony Andrews, once the heartthrob star of *Brideshead Revisited*, seems equally at odds with his role as Moriarty, and while there is a story to be followed here, if only one pays attention, *Hands of a Murderer* is perhaps better enjoyed as just a series of excellently visualized vignettes, interrupted by bathroom breaks of exposition and dialogue.

Plus, you keep waiting for Callan to kill someone.

The Hound of London (TV: 1993)

This Canadian TV movie is generally despised by serious Holmes fans but is actually a lot more fun that its secondhand (and, ultimately, distinctly non-Baskervillian) title might suggest. Patrick Macnee, John Steed of *The Avengers* fame, is Holmes, and what a cracking time he has of it, bringing all of his so-British bearing into play as he pursues the ever-scheming Moriarty once again and has another run-in with the beguiling Irene Adler—now performing onstage under her married name of Irene Norton.

Macnee had done his reputation few favors in his past encounters with the Holmesian legend (playing Watson alongside Roger Moore's unbelievably bad Holmes in *Sherlock Holmes in New York* and beside Christopher Lee's in *Incident at Victoria Falls* and *Sherlock Holmes and the Leading Lady*). He continues to divide opinion here. Certainly too much is made of his failings as a human being, because we simply do not need to see a cocaine-addled Holmes hallucinating snakes and contemplating suicide. But he quickly recovers, and if one can get past the sneaking suspicion that Conan Doyle has spent the past seventy-one minutes revolving in his grave, *The Hound of London* is well worth whistling up.

Incident at Victoria Falls (movie: 1990)

Christopher Lee shot two Sherlock Holmes movies in 1990, filmed back to back (just two days separated wrapping one and commencing the other), and both setting him alongside a disappointingly un-Watson-like Watson, played by Patrick Macnee. Indeed, given Lee's oft-quoted impatience with the multitude of bad movies he was invited to appear in (and which he unfailingly seemed to accept), neither *Incident at Victoria Falls* nor its predecessor *Sherlock Holmes and the Leading Lady* should be considered especially high on the totem of either man's filmography.

But the two stories told are at least on a par with some of Conan Doyle's more middling contributions to the canon, with Bosnian anarchists (in *The Leading Lady*) and the Victoria Falls both offering grandiose backdrops to any mundanities present in the plot. Thus, if the acting in this second movie lets the side down occasionally, perhaps the cast were as overcome by the scenery as the viewer should be.

The League of Extraordinary Gentlemen (movie: 2003)

British comic book author Alan Moore's often iconoclastic approach toward twentieth-century pop culture, most potent via *V For Vendetta* and most (im)pertinent across *Lost Girls*, reached an apex of sorts with *The League of Extraordinary Gentleman*, an ongoing series that commenced publication in 1999, rewiring a host of literature's most beloved (if unlikely) characters.

Allan Quatermain, Captain Nemo, Mina Harker, Tom Sawyer, Jekyll and Hyde, and Dante are among those who team up alongside Moriarty in the league, with the latter's own role in the Holmes canon given perhaps its most audacious (yet strangely satisfying) twist yet; that all along, he was working for the British secret service, controlling the country's underworld not, as Holmes assumed, for his own ends, but for the good of the empire.

In truth, the movie is fairly appalling, with Richard Roxburghe certainly lining up among the least effective Moriartys ever consigned to celluloid. But the special effects keep it popping, and if it turned but a fraction of its multiplex audience on to the original comic books, then it served some purpose.

The Masks of Death (TV: 1984)

Peter Cushing returns to the role of Sherlock Holmes fourteen years on from the brilliant 1960s television series; the sleuth is in semi-retirement by now (the film is set in 1913, with flashes forward to 1926) and offers up a charming, if occasionally upsetting, portrait of the existence that a real-life Holmes might have had to look forward to, once youth had faded and the old brain started to slow.

Bad-tempered, sometimes rude, and only occasionally prone to the savage deductive leaps that had once been his first instinct, this is Holmes on the precipice of life, rejuvenating himself one more time for an adventure that introduces new foes in the form of sundry high-ranking and absolutely nefarious Germans (the Great War would break out in 1914) and old adversaries, as Irene Norton *née* Adler steps back into his life.

An excellent movie was screened in the UK at Christmas 1984, when no less august a publication than *The Times* described it as "a peculiarly English combination of genuine horror and spirited comedy." But the unstated portents of Holmes's approaching death were not to be ignored. A follow-up movie, with Cushing as Holmes in *The Abbot's Cry*, was being discussed, but Cushing would never be well enough to make it. The grand old man of British horror, suspense, and mystery passed away at his home in Whitstable, Kent, on August 11, 1994.

Murder by Decree (movie: 1978)

No less than Holmes's manifold fictional encounters with Dracula, writers aplenty have tried to imagine just what might have occurred had Holmes been pitted against that other great predator of east London, Jack the Ripper.

Chronologically, they are a perfect fit. The first series of Holmes stories in *The Strand* were running at a time when London's Metropolitan Police Service was still struggling to restore public confidence in itself following the infamous deprecations of the Ripper. Just three years had passed since all of east London had been paralyzed with fear after becoming the happy hunting ground of an unknown, unseen, and ultimately uncatchable mass murderer.

The Ripper, as the media termed him, officially struck just five times between August 31 and November 9, 1888, after which it was generally agreed that the killer had left London, been jailed for another crime entirely, died, or otherwise been disposed of. But the killings did not cease, and whenever another especially grisly slaying was unearthed in the dark and dingy alleyways of Whitechapel, there was always one enterprising journalist willing to point the finger of guilt at the still-unapprehended Ripper.

In fact, as Conan Doyle set himself to penning his first stories for *The Strand*, one such murder, the eleventh in three years, was still on many people's minds. In February 1891, a woman was found with her throat slashed beneath a railway arch in Swallow Gardens, Whitechapel; and, while the police were swift to apprehend a suspect, his trial the following month was a farce. The man, James Thomas Sadler, was discharged because of a total lack of evidence, and one more unsolved murder was added to the Met's catalog of calumny.

Doubtless Conan Doyle was as distressed as any other Londoner by the law's continued inability to track down a killer whose cunning and stealth had seen him elude captivity which such apparent insouciance. Doubtless, too, he had heard the mumblings of those people who believed, in this case as in so many others of recent renown, that the only man who could capture the Ripper would be a real-life Sherlock Holmes.

That might even be the primary reason why Conan Doyle ensured that his fictional detective's cases rarely strayed into the kind of territory that the Ripperologists (the term had yet to be invented, but the mentality was certainly already in place) declared was Holmes's natural habitat.

Murder by Decree is the movie that places him there.

With Christopher Plummer a startlingly suave Holmes, James Mason as his bumbling but likable sidekick, and a supporting cast that includes David

Hemmings, Frank Finlay, Donald Sutherland, John Gielgud, and the radiant Genevieve Bujold, *Murder by Decree* opens with Holmes being approached by a Citizens Committee of concerned Whitechapel residents, begging him to investigate the murders that are benighting their streets. There have been three so far.

Holmes turns them down, only to reconsider when he learns of a fourth. From there, the movie spools out equally wild fiction, considered theory, and popular conspiracy, with the killer ultimately being traced to the highest echelons of British society and the royal household itself.

American Ripperologist Amy Hanson examined such theorizing in her article *Bloody Fodder for the Pen* in 1998 (since when, any number of other theories have naturally arisen): "By the late 1970s and 1980s it seemed everybody was publishing an opinion about the identity of the killer." Author Paul Begg had already explained, "When an historical event is used for fiction, the fiction can rapidly enter the popular imagination as fact. When the reality becomes submerged under fiction, it can often prove impossible to raise the truths from the depths." But not, continues Hanson, "from a lack of imaginative theories [that range] from the breathtakingly daring to the plain daft, for as long as new 'evidence' surfaces, it seems, new 'suspects' will continue to be found.

"*Psycho* author Robert Bloch tackled the 'whodunnit' question in *The Night of the Ripper* (Doubleday, 1984), which ties together all the then current biographical theories and brings in the likes of Conan Doyle and Oscar Wilde to help solve the puzzle." And, for fans of *Murder By Decree*, she cites Frank Spiering's *Prince Jack* (Jove, 1978), "a book that finally 'exposed' what the *Los Angeles Times* dubbed 'the royal cover-up, a kind of century-long Rippergate,' [to] represent . . . the zenith—or nadir?—of all the far-flung theories. Spiering compiles evidence proving that the killer was Queen Victoria's eldest grandson, Prince Albert—a distinguished addition to a company that includes such honorable members as the queen's physician, Sir William Gull; a Canadian racketeer, Dr. Neill Cream; and an early (if undoubtedly fictional) suffragette, Jill the Ripper."

Holmes, in *Murder by Decree*, was being modest, then. He unearthed only *two* Rippers.

Murder Rooms: The Dark Beginnings of Sherlock Holmes (TV: 2000–2001)

This series of five adventures eschewed Holmes entirely in favor of examining the crime-fighting exploits of . . . Dr. Joseph Bell, Conan Doyle's tutor during his days at medical school in Edinburgh. *Murder Room* does perhaps layer a few too many of Holmes's fictional attributes onto Bell's natural brilliance and can probably be counted upon to offend, or at least annoy, at least a few of Holmes's (and Bell's) most devoted admirers.

But watched from a purely televisual angle—thrilling at the manner in which Bell (Ian Richardson) brings an *almost* Holmesian ruthlessness to bear on what strike other people as intractable conundrums; enjoying Robin Laing's performance as the ideal student Conan Doyle; and losing oneself in the intricacies of mid-Victorian medicine, crime, and forensic investigation—*Murder Rooms* establishes period Edinburgh to be as great a player in the drama as London is in Holmes's own adventures.

True, the city is pocked by less instantly recognizable landmarks (at least to an international audience), but still its swirls and shadows are as gloomy and foreboding as you could hope for. Add to that a decided lack of squeamishness when it comes to both murder scenes and background color, and Holmes's "dark beginnings" are very dark indeed. And very highly recommended.

1994 Baker Street: Sherlock Holmes Returns (TV: 1993)

A couple of years before that other great British icon, *Doctor Who*, was transplanted to the streets of San Francisco for an (ultimately misguided) television movie, Sherlock Holmes was subjected to the same treatment—albeit with somewhat more enjoyable results.

A trauma-unit doctor, Amy Wilmslow, is offered the opportunity to buy a house, at an incredibly cheap price, from the widow of one of her former patients, a Mrs. Hudson. The house has been in her family for close to a century, since it was bequeathed to them by an eccentric Englishman known only as Captain Basil, whose one stipulation is that the electricity supply must be maintained without any interruption until January 1, 2000. At which point, inevitably, there is a short circuit and from out of the cellar staggers a mysterious figure who reveals himself to be Sherlock Holmes.

Preserved cryogenically since an otherwise fatal tussle with Moriarty in 1899, Holmes discovers that Amy is not the first to find his hiding place. Others have been there before her—descendants of Moriarty, who have stolen everything he had stockpiled to assist him with life after his planned resurrection in 2000. Amy agrees to care for him at her home at 1994 Baker Street, San Francisco, while Holmes sets about recovering the stolen property from Moriarty's grandson, a local crime kingpin named James Moriarty Booth.

It's a fairly lightweight tale but a thoroughly enjoyable one . . . certainly more so than the last time a preserved Holmes was de-iced, in 1987's *The Return of Sherlock Holmes* . . . and it is a matter of at least passing regret that the offer of a full series, depicting a rejuvenated Holmes practicing as a consulting detective in the twenty-first century, was never followed up. At least by any American concern.

But like the aforementioned *Doctor Who*, with its own premillennial setting, its own lovely local doctor and street smart sidekick, there was nothing to stop somebody else from taking the same basic concept and running with it.

Holmes would be back.

The Private Life of Sherlock Holmes (movie: 1970)

Billy Wilder's sensational Holmes pastiche is one of the lost classics of the genre. Not only was it absurdly overlooked at the time of its release, but the final print amounts to only a little over two-thirds of the original film. Conceived as a three-hour extravaganza based around four separate mysteries ("The Case of the Upside-Down Room," "The Singular Affair of the Russian Ballerina," "The Dreadful Business of the Naked Honeymooners," and "The Adventure of the Dumbfounded Detective"), it ultimately emerged with only the second and fourth of those vignettes still in place, and even they had been hacked.

Still, it remains a deeply atmospheric black comedy, with Robert Stephens and Colin Blakely resplendent as, respectively, Holmes and Watson, and an excellent supporting cast shrugging away the budgetary and scheduling problems that haunted the shoot. (Stephens even suffered a nervous breakdown during production, necessitating a ten-day break.)

Whether or not the cuts detract from the finished film is difficult to say—a full print has yet to be rediscovered (although some elements have been restored for DVD). But still it ranks high in any poll of the best noncanonical Holmes stories, while anybody wishing to catch more of the absurdly underrated Stephens should procure themselves a copy of *Lunch Hour*, a 1961 drama written by John Mortimer (of *Rumpole of the Bailey* fame) and directed by James Hill. Released in the British Film Institute's Flipside series of forgotten British movies, it could not be further away from Holmes if it tried. But Stephens's performance is just as superlative.

The Private Life of Sherlock Holmes was a worldwide success.

The Return of Sherlock Holmes (movie: 1929)

In this, the first Sherlock Holmes talkie, Clive Brook takes the leading role in the search for the killer of Captain Longmore, the father of Watson's newly acquired son-in-law, Roger. Moriarty turns out to be the guilty man, which should surprise nobody, and he also has a good go at killing Holmes.

Where the movie perhaps founders is in Holmes's apparent inability to actually make any deductions, preferring to rely on his ability to disguise himself as the quickest way to the end of the movie. Brook, however, caught the public imagination sufficiently to reprise the role three years later in *Conan Doyle's Master Detective Sherlock Holmes.*

The Return of the World's Greatest Detective (TV: 1976)

One of the most audacious updatings of the legend, *The Return* is the story of a Los Angeles motorcycle cop, Sherman Holmes (Larry Hagman), who is hit on the head by a poorly parked motorcycle while lying in a park reading . . . of course, the adventures of his near-namesake.

Recovering, he not only believes himself to be the original Sherlock, he has also acquired the kind of deductive superpowers normally associated only with being bitten by a radioactive sleuth. He is placed in the care of a social worker named Joan Watson, who encourages his delusion by dressing him in a cape and deerstalker, and when a murder mystery presents itself through the pages of the newspaper, Holmes is unstoppable.

Yes, it's silly. Yes, it takes way too many liberties with all that a serious scholar might deem holy. But NBC was confident in the TV movie. With Hagman (then best remembered for his part in 1960s sitcom *I Dream of Jeanie,* and *Dallas* still way off in the future) playing the oft-times comedic role with dashing aplomb, hopes that it might develop into a full-fledged series were high. It was not to be, however, and hindsight suggests that is probably for the best. A daft updating worked for one TV movie. Week after week of it would probably have been too much.

The Seven-Per-Cent Solution (movie: 1976)

Based upon Nicholas Meyer's 1974 novel of the same name, *The Seven-Per-Cent Solution* seeks to upend all we think we know about Sherlock Holmes by portraying him (although this only becomes apparent as the movie goes along) as a hopeless cocaine addict whose hatred of Moriarty is derived not from any criminal dealings the seemingly innocuous math tutor may be involved with, but from the man's role in the murder of Holmes's own mother. As a child, Sherlock witnessed his own father kill her, after catching her in bed with . . . Moriarty.

If that's not an attention grabber, nothing is.

Alan Arkin and Nicol Williamson contemplate the *Seven Per Cent Solution.*   *Photofest*

Hoping to free Holmes from an obviously dangerous delusion, Watson and Mycroft arrange for Holmes to visit Sigmund Freud, who promptly joins them in solving a mystery while continuing his treatment of the detective. Once Freud's work is completed, Holmes abandons his life as a consulting detective and takes up as an itinerant musician instead. Watson returns home with instructions to concoct a suitable tale to account for Holmes's disappearance. An account of his death at the Reichenbach Falls is duly published.

Sherlock Holmes (movie: 1922)

John Barrymore is Holmes in this 100-plus-minute silent movie, a film acclaimed as both the most accomplished of all the early attempts to give cinematic life to our hero and, sadly, decried as an extraordinarily overlong and overwrought melodrama that just . . . never . . . seems . . . to . . . end.

Loosely based upon the William Gillette stageshow, while also showcasing all the effects that modern cinematic technology could throw into the pot, a convoluted plot is not assisted by the fact that a complete print of the film has never been located; that which exists today was pieced together from a variety of sources, and an indeterminate number of sequences remain missing. Still, students of Holmes and cinema in general rejoice at its even partial survival. Just be warned, however. You will never get those 100 minutes back.

An un-Baskervillian hound on the scent of the *Seven per Cent Solution.*   *Photofest*

Sherlock Holmes (movie: 2009)

Robert Downey Jr. and Jude Law are unlikely to have topped many people's wish lists when it came to casting a new cinematic Sherlock Holmes one decade into the twenty-first century. Guy Ritchie, best known still for that sequence of brilliant British gangland movies that kicked off with *Lock, Stock and Two Smoking Barrels*, probably wouldn't have been high on any directorial dreamscape either.

But Law had appeared in the 1980s Jeremy Brett TV series, in the retelling of "Shoscombe Old Place"; Downey all but demanded he be cast the moment he learned of the movie, even overriding the director's initial intentions of starring a younger Holmes; and *nobody* films London quite as well as Ritchie.

Together, the trio not only struck box-office gold, with over $500 million in worldwide receipts. They also conspired to create the most action-packed Holmes adventure yet, a nonstop blur of vivacity and violence that may have thrown most past incarnations of Holmes to the wind but nevertheless maintained the spirit of the man.

His prowess as a boxer, for example, is alluded to in Conan Doyle's stories (who can forget his introduction to the manservant McMurdo in *The Sign of Four*—"Don't you remember that amateur who fought three rounds with you at

Alison's rooms on the night of your benefit four years back?"). Here, Holmes resorts to fisticuffs for fun, competing in East End bareknuckle bouts, and he has no compunction about striking out should the development of a case demand. Out of the ring, too, he bashes and batters his way through any number of sinister henchmen and violent thugs, and a monster-mountain hoodlum whose menace is oddly amplified by the fact he speaks only French.

But they are simply the outer rings of a Masonic-style government splinter group headed up by a murderous Lord Blackwood (Mark Strong), a devil in Victorian Voldemort frock coat whose grasp of trickery is almost as divine as Holmes's deductions. Who also happens along at precisely the same time as Watson is planning to move out and marry. The dysfunctions that are Holmes's daily wear, then, are twisted only around his displeasure at seeing his daily routine so disrupted, and every last character flaw that Conan Doyle laced so delicately around the man's genius is brought screaming into the daylight.

"There's quite a lot of intense action sequences in the stories," Ritchie remarked, noting that was something "that hasn't [always] been reflected in the movies." He spoke of allowing Holmes's "brilliance [to] percolate into the action," by allowing the detective to voice his intended blows and parries when preparing for a fight; and demonstrating, too, how his "intellect was as much of a curse as it was a blessing." Indeed, Downey's Holmes is thoroughly disreputable, utterly obnoxious, selfish to the point of boorishness, and so bound up in his own ego that even friendly bouts of verbal jousting with Watson are simply a demand for additional attention. In today's world, he would be a reality TV contestant; in his own, he creates that same environment around himself.

Such a forensic eye for his faults, of course, establishes him as an absolutely modern Holmes, at the same time as he remains cast unerringly into the foggy, shadow-strewn streets of Victorian London; and though the storyline itself was freshly written, the supporting characters include at least 50 percent of the Sherlockian touchstones you'd expect, from Mrs. Hudson to Inspector Lestrade, and on to Irene Adler (Rachel McAdams), elevated to virtually an equal par with Watson, at the same time as she is clearly working for another power entirely. A power whose name, she reveals in more or less her final scene, is Moriarty.

Moriarty would take his own center stage with more of the riotous same in the 2011 sequel, *A Game of Shadows*. Which was: faster, louder, darker, more dangerous, more littered with thrills and obsessed with explosions, but it really came nowhere close to its predecessor in terms of being a great movie. Too reliant upon set pieces, too content to tell tales with action, not words, *A Game of Shadows* pulls the viewer along by brute force, not brightness, with only the still-magnificent sets and the occasional Holmesian flourish (his developing interest in "urban camouflage," for example, which allows him to disguise himself as drapes or an armchair) to remind the viewer *who*, as opposed to *what*, he is watching.

Noomi Rapace and Robert Downey Jr. dance to Guy Ritchie's *Game of Shadows*   *Photofest*

Stephen Fry plays a suitably louche brother Mycroft; Jared Harris a delightfully sinister Moriarty. A conclusion set upon the dizzying heights of Reichenbach is certainly built to thrill. But whereas *Sherlock Holmes* repays repeated viewings, *A Game of Shadows* merely gathers dust.

Sherlock Holmes and the Baker Street Irregulars (TV: 2007)

Not, sadly, a remake of what was now the now quarter-century-old *The Baker Street Boys*, but a two-part mini-series that cast Jonathan Pryce as Holmes, Bill Paterson as Watson, and Anna Chancellor as the seemingly ubiquitous Irene Adler, and then more or less abandoned them to their own devices as the Irregulars set out on their own quest.

It wasn't, in all honesty, that great a series; 120 years on from Holmes's introduction, it would be hard for any creative team to truly scheme a new face for Holmes, while maintaining the old one for the fans. This is why Guy Ritchie and Steven Moffat's efforts, later this same decade, would prove so stunningly successful. Both were instantly recognizable, but both drew on Holmesian reserves that had not been done to death so many times before.

Sherlock Holmes and the *Case of the Silk Stocking* (TV: 2004)

The death of a woman presumed to be a prostitute (but who is actually a titled lady), suffocated with a silk stocking and then dumped into the Thames, leads

Holmes (calmly depicted by Rupert Everett) into a world of sexual fetishism that leans closer in places to author Chrissie Bentley's simultaneous Ambrose Horne mysteries than to anything in the traditional canon.

Of course its marketing as a Christmas treat for the family (it was broadcast on December 26, Boxing Day in the UK) ensures it remains strictly within the realms of decency, but with Holmesian erotica such a narrow and unplowed field, the story of a pair of footmen with foot fetishes, and Holmes's apparent and possibly intimate knowledge of a wide range of sexual perversions, certainly establishes this among the most risqué of all his cases.

The *Case of the Silk Stocking*—a light-hearted off camera moment.
© *Andrew Dunn/Wikimedia*

Sherlock Holmes and the Great Murder Mystery (movie: 1908)

Doctor Watson made his cinematic debut in this silent movie, although he could as easily have handed Holmes a copy of Poe's *The Murders in the Rue Morgue* and then gone back to bed. It is more or less the same story.

Sir Arthur Conan Doyle's Sherlock Holmes (movie: 2009)

An untold story of the great detective, related by Watson from some fifty years distant, and—had it actually occurred—neatly foreshadowing Conan Doyle's own *The Lost World*. Dinosaurs are at large, attacking a ship in the English Channel; killing a john in London's East End; chasing Holmes and Watson themselves.

But are they real dinosaurs, somehow transported to 1882 from a long-extinct world? Or are they rubber constructs designed by an especially imaginative supervillain? And does anybody even care? Had this movie appeared in the 1950s, in a world of drive-in movie lots ruled by cheaply produced, badly designed B-movies, *Sherlock Holmes Meets the Dinosaurs of Destiny* (as this clunker could, or even should, have been titled) would now be a cult classic. Released in competition with Guy Ritchie's *Sherlock Holmes*, on the other hand, it is simply sad.

The Strange Case of the End of Civilisation as We Know It (movie: 1977)

What do you do if the world was being menaced by the last surviving descendent of the criminal mastermind Moriarty? You would call in the similarly last surviving descendent of Sherlock Holmes, of course. And so Arthur Sherlock-Holmes, the grandson of the old Lion of Baker Street, is recruited by Scotland Yard and sets about defeating his ancestral nemesis once and for all.

His plan is brilliant. Or at least, it is when it is placed in the hands of John Cleese, returning to Sherlock four years on from *Elementary, My Dear Watson* and proving that his grasp on Holmes is as irreverent as ever. The best way to capture Moriarty, he decides, is to assemble every great detective in the world in one place and wait for the villain to strike. For how could he resist such a target?

And so, Columbo, Sam Spade, Hercule Poirot, Steve McGarrett . . . they all file into the Carlton Hotel. And they are all killed by Doctor Watson. Who is revealed to be Mrs. Hudson. Who is actually Francine Moriarty, and who then shoots Holmes in a cliffhanger ending that has never been followed up.

It's a stupid movie. The plot is absurd, the scripting is labored, the pacing is pathetic. We watch for the brilliance of Cleese, an attribute that he was eminently capable of bringing to even the most leaden of circumstances; for the familiarity of Arthur Lowe, playing the best comic Watson of all time; for the genius of Connie Booth (Cleese's then-wife) in the twin roles of Mrs. Hudson and Ms. Moriarty. None of them let us down. Indeed, the cast throughout do their best, and it's often really good. It's only when the movie ends that you sit back and wonder how any of them could have been persuaded to involve themselves in the first place.

A Study in Terror (movie: 1965)

Anybody with an eye for British acting talent in the mid-1960s will gaze on this movie with awestricken wonder. John Neville is Holmes, Donald Houstin is Watson. Frank Finlay, John Fraser, Anthony Quayle, Robert Morley, Barbara Windsor, Adrienne Corri, and Judi Dench all line up to either solve the case of or be the victims of the infamous Jack the Ripper. And Holmes is the man who must stop him.

Considerably less arch than the later *Murder by Decree*, made with its eye firmly on the gore-soaked horror then being turned out so masterfully by the Hammer

Barbara Windsor and Terry Downes in 1965's *A Study in Terror*.   *Photofest*

studios, it's a thrill-a-minute chiller, highlighted by grisly killings and stuffed with excellent portraits by that staggering cast. It even, on its American release, suggested Stateside viewers regard Holmes as "the original caped crusader," a tag that really should have garnered more mileage and respect than it has. Oh, and for scholars who consider such blood-and-guts nonsense to be far below their gaze, it is also the first movie to feature brother Mycroft. But of course, it would not be the last.

They Might Be Giants (movie: 1971)

A play staged in London in 1961 took a decade to reach the screen, with Joanne Woodward as Doctor Watson and George C Scott as Justin Playfair, a gent who dresses, talks, and generally comports himself as an ideal replica of Holmes, without actually being him.

Another of those movies that suffered as much at the hands of the editors as it would at those of the critics, rendering it both unsatisfying for the viewer and infuriating for its makers, *They Might Be Giants* is small fry in the overall sea of Sherlockian fiction, but as a portrait of delusion it is thoroughly engrossing—while also boasting one of the funniest one-liners in the cinematic history of Holmes. A New York cop walking up to Playfair, as he stands around in full Baker Street drag, shakes his band and exclaims, "Why, Mr. Rathbone, it's an honor—sit."

Without a Clue (movie: 1988)

Doctor Watson (Ben Kingsley) is the brilliant investigator here, and Sherlock Holmes is simply a failed actor, Reginald Kincaid (Michael Cane), whom the doctor hired to detract attention from his work, without ever imagining the fame that the creation would accrue. Watson's hopes of reclaiming the glory for himself come to naught, however, and though he had intended on retiring Holmes for good, a sophisticated forgery racket and the entreaties of the Bank of England force him to reprieve the monster one last time.

One of the best of all Sherlock-shaped comedies, *Without a Clue* also offers up one of the mature Michael Caine's most enjoyable roles. It is littered with loving references to the original stories, while also poking fun at one of the Conan Doyle creation's greatest failings: the fact that every utterance he makes is decreed by witnesses to be of the greatest import, another indication of his astonishing genius. Sometimes it's guesswork. And sometimes he's just plain wrong.

Of course *Without a Clue* is not the first tale to acknowledge this. Conan Doyle allowed his hero at least a fragment of infallibility on occasion, and good as this movie is, it still cannot touch one special moment in the BBC's retelling of "The Adventure of the Blue Carbuncle."

Holmes (Peter Cushing) has expounded his every deduction regarding the identity of the owner of the lost hat, a Mr. Henry Baker, growing more and more infuriating with every revelation, only for the hat's rightful owner to reveal himself as *Harold*. Nobody has ever extracted more merriment from a colleague's mistake than the ever-suffering Doctor Watson (Nigel Stock) does at that moment.

Young Sherlock Holmes (movie: 1985)

An oddly enjoyable movie that contrives to be both underwhelming and over-ambitious at the same time, it reveals Holmes (Nicholas Rowe) and Watson (Alan Cox) to have first met at boarding school. Holmes is the protegé of a schoolmaster named Rathe (a familiar name to fans of *A Study in Scarlet*) and in love with Elizabeth, the niece of a former master, now an inventor, named Rupert T. Waxflatter (played, incidentally, by Nigel Stock, such an indefatigable Watson for the BBC in the 1960s). Waxflatter, the boy has noticed, appears to be taking an inordinate amount of interest in a couple of mysterious local deaths, before falling victim to the same killer in his own right.

Was there ever a wilder Holmes than Gene?   *Photofest*

Written by Chris Columbus (who also penned period blockbusters *Gremlins* and *The Goonies*), directed by Barry Levinson, and co-produced by the Fonz, *Young Sherlock Holmes* is very much a child of its mid-1980s time, action-packed without too much regard for the niceties of the plot, and intent on showing where every last penny of its $18 million budget was spent.

An ancient Egyptian death cult lurks within a pyramid that is cunningly disguised as an East London paraffin factory; the late Mr. Waxflatter left a fully operational flying machine among his effects; and a computer-generated stained-glass knight turns in one of the era's most memorable SFX baddies. There is more than a taste of *Indiana Jones and the Temple of Doom* around the plot, and very little that even glances toward the ingredients one might expect from a true Sherlock Holmes story.

Utterly inconsequential, then, but thoroughly enjoyable all the same.

Young Sherlock: The Mystery of the Manor House (TV: 1982)

Predating the *Young Sherlock* movie by three years, an eight-part British children's show depicted a seventeen-year-old Holmes, home from boarding school to discover his parents are bankrupt and have moved to France . . . apparently without telling him that a rather unpleasant ex-army gent now owns the house. A surprise for Sherlock, but only the first of several that lie in wait for him.

It was a very well-made series; nobody watching at the time should have forgotten the so-atmospheric opening credits, with a pair of unidentified hands taking out an old time phonogram recording labeled "to be handed to Doctor Watson and listened to only after my death."

The voice of Holmes then explains how, following his retirement, he decided to preserve each of his earliest cases in this manner—cases "of which I have hitherto apprised no-one. The first of these adventures I choose to call . . ."

More were planned. Had a second series been commissioned, *The Adventure of Ferryman's Creek* was up next. Sadly, it was not to be.

18

The Multifaceted Case of the Alternative Detectives

In which we pop round to 221b, ring the Doorbell . . . and Nobody answers. Is there Someone else we could call instead?

In the world into which Conan Doyle placed Sherlock Holmes, there was just one man whom the detective considered, or at least described, as a rival, and that was the mysterious Mr. Barker. In fact, Holmes's precise description of the man was, "my hated rival upon the Surrey Shore," suggesting that Barker was not simply good at his job, he was actually excellent at it. "His methods are irregular, no doubt, like my own."

Other supposed detectives crossed his radar, of course. Occasionally he might utter an encouraging word about one of Scotland Yard's various inspectors—Lestrade, MacDonald and Hopkins—although one still got the feeling that he regarded them as generally incompetent. And when his attention was drawn to his own predecessors in the realms of fictional detection, he was utterly dismissive. Farewell, then, to Auguste Dupin and Gabriau's Lecoq.

The fact that Barker confined his operations to "the Surrey shore," meaning the south bank of the River Thames, probably accounts for why we do not hear of him more often. There is possibly a sighting in "The Adventure of the Empty House," when Watson describes "A tall, thin man with colored glasses, whom I strongly suspected of being a plain-clothes detective [who is] pointing out some theory of his own . . . while the others crowded round to listen to what he said."

Holmes does not interrupt during that first description. But when Watson encounters a similarly attired man during the course of his investigations into "the Retired Colourman," Holmes instantly recognizes the stranger: "a lounger who was smoking in the street . . . a tall, dark, heavily moustached, rather military-looking man"—who is wearing sunglasses. Possibly it is the same man; or maybe all private detectives of that time, Holmes aside, wore colored sunglasses. Conan Doyle does not elucidate.

Either way, Barker is adept enough at his profession for Holmes to have noticed him, and to even describe him as a friend—an honor that he dispensed upon precious few people.

If Holmes was reluctant to acknowledge his rivals, however, other authors have been only too willing to praise them, acknowledging their own debt to Sherlock Holmes as much by omission as by similarity. Indeed, so heavily did Conan Doyle's shadow fall across the detective genre during the first half of the last century, particularly in his British homeland, that at least two of the greatest fictional sleuths who arose in Holmes's wake were perforcedly exiled by their creators and given altogether more exotic (or at least unfamiliar) birthrights, simply to distinguish them from the Baker Street behemoth.

Agatha Christie's Hercules Poirot, for example, shared a great many of Holmes's distinguishing characteristics, all the way down to his epicurean attitude toward food. But he is so readily identified as a Belgian, and a somewhat roly-poly one at that, that the lineage is absolutely camouflaged. We must pity poor Georges Simenon, then, a Belgian author whose own pipe-smoking Holmesian genius, Jules Maigret, was forced to relocate to Paris to escape comparison with both Holmes and Poirot. But Ian Rankin's Inspector Rebus surely chuckled at his own subterfuge, making his nest in Conan Doyle's (and Rankin's) Scottish homeland, and disguising his Holmesian speech beneath the thick burr of what the critics quickly christened Tartan Noir. And so on.

Sherlock Holmes is more than a founding father in terms of literary detection, then. He is a blueprint, possessed of so many defining characteristics that it is all but impossible for a "respectable" detective to be devised who does not adopt at least one of his distinguishing features.

Mental instability, for instance. Holmes forever seemed to be on the edge, either coming toward it or stepping away from it, of a nervous breakdown. Inspector Borivka, created by the Czechoslovakian writer Josef Škvorecký, is a confirmed melancholic, while television's Adrian Monk suffers from an obsessive-compulsive disorder whose dictates Holmes could certainly appreciate.

Artistic sensibilities. Holmes appreciated art and played the violin. P. D. James's Adam Dalgleish writes poetry.

There are countless other examples, and perhaps it is duplicitous to accuse them all of being merely recoded examples of the same basic cipher. All human beings, fictional or actual, are created from a combination of essential characteristics, few of which vary from person to person. Why should detectives be any different?

Le Fabulous Case de la French Detective

Nevertheless, there are a handful of fictional sleuths who do step away from the Sherlockian norm, with perhaps the finest of them all being French author Maurice Leblanc's Arsène Lupin. And that despite the character having allegedly been created in direct response to an editor's suggestion that France needed her own Sherlock Holmes.

Lupin debuted in the magazine *Je Sais Tout* (*I Know Everything*—surely the best title of any periodical ever!) in July 1905, and superficially the detective was just one more chip off the same old block. But he also boasted his own unique traits. A secret lair in a rock stack on Normandy's beautiful Alabaster Coast. A demeanor that certainly placed him on the shabbier end of the social spectrum. And a parallel career as a criminal that echoed the exploits of Raffles, the gentleman thief dreamed up by Conan Doyle's brother-in-law E. W. Hornung (although Leblanc claimed never to have read those stories).

Lupin was also considerably longer-lived than Holmes. No faking his own death nor lengthy lapses into printed silence for our man. Leblanc was still writing fresh Lupin adventures, novel-length and oft-times gripping, a decade after Conan Doyle finally laid down his Holmesian pen, and that freshness was maintained in terms of content and storytelling, too.

The French detective was an immediate success, and while he was certainly aided by Conan Doyle's own comparative reluctance to keep Holmes in the public eye, there was also a sense that French readers applauded the opportunity to follow their own French detective. Particularly when he proved so delightfully capable of besting his English counterpart.

With an impertinence at which we can only marvel, Sherlock Holmes appears as himself in the 1906 story "Sherlock Holmes Arrives Too Late," only for Conan Doyle to register his unhappiness at his character being so flagrantly used and abused by Leblanc. An apology was issued, but how repentant was the author really? Just a few months and a swift reshuffling of letters later, the revised "Herlok Sholmes" (who appears in English translation as Holmlock Shears) reappeared in the six-part story "The Blonde Lady." In this tale,

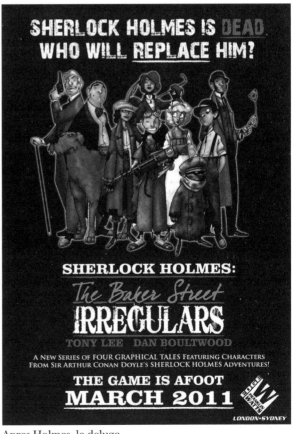

Apres Holmes, le deluge.

having been called to Paris to investigate a crime that Lupin himself committed, he appears to triumph when he ensures that the Frenchman is arrested. But Lupin has the last laugh, escaping from custody and making sure he is at the quayside to wave Sholmes and his sidekick, Wilson, off.

Immediately popular with Lupin's core audience, Sholmes reappeared in a new story, "The Jewish Lamp," in 1907, before the two tales were conjoined for the 1910 theatrical presentation *Arsène Lupin contre Herlok Sholmes* (*Arsène Lupin against Herlok Sholmes*). First produced at the Théâtre du Châtelet in Paris in 1910, the play has since been restaged on movie and television and enjoyed numerous theatrical revivals, as well. Indeed, if Lupin truly is the French Sherlock Holmes, then Sholmes is probably his own Moriarty.

Other writers have approached Holmes more directly, either by offering up fresh adventures for Conan Doyle's original sleuth (all the more so since the stories began to fall out of copyright in the late 1980s), or by taking favored aspects of the Holmesian prototype and creating—according to the reader's taste, as well as the author's intentions—pastiches, tributes, and even parodies of the deerstalkered detective.

The Remarkable Case of the Hellbound Holmes

As with straightforward fiction that merely glances toward Holmes, it would be a lifetime's occupation to catalog, let alone to read, every Baker Streetian irregularity. Likewise to chart the sheer breadth of those parodies, a range that commences, chronologically, with the American John Kendrick Bangs's *The Pursuit of the Houseboat*, published in 1897.

A sequel to his earlier *A Houseboat on the Styx*, this volume responds to Holmes's then-recent and still uncontradicted death by dragging the detective down to Hell to aid a spectral detective agency, the Associated Shades, in their quest for the titular houseboat—shades indeed of Alan Moore's later *League of Extraordinary Men*, as the likes of Julius Caesar, Nero, Walter Raleigh, Confucius, Shakespeare, the Emperor Napoleon, and Samuel Johnson all combine forces around him.

Over the ensuing decade, Bangs would incorporate several more Holmesian parodies into his books and other writings, including 1903's *Shylock Holmes: His Posthumous Memoirs*, and most audacious of all, *R Holmes & Co*, in which the writings of Conan Doyle's brother-in-law, E. W. Hornung, are likewise hijacked for the character of the gentleman thief Raffles, so that he and Sherlock might be combined into one conjoined kinsman, Raffles Holmes. Seldom recalled in the modern era, a sad fate that has befallen too many of his generation's (for want of a better expression) "lesser" authors, Bangs nevertheless retains all of his wit and imagination when read today, over a century on from his heyday.

Not so our next contestants. A favorite excerpt from Kenneth Grahame's *The Wind in the Willows*, published in 1908, skillfully embroils a distinctly Holmesian Ratty and a benevolently Watson-esque Mole in a snowbound quest for Mr.

Badger's front door; while J. M. Barrie, the creator of another timeless literary gem, *Peter Pan*, penned his own autobiographical Holmes parody in the aftermath of a doomed playwrighting experience that he shared with Conan Doyle himself.

In 1893, the two men conceived a musical comedy, *Jane Annie*, staged by the D'Oyly Carte, and its failure inspired Barrie to write "The Adventure of the Two Collaborators," in exquisite echo of Doctor Watson's customary style and littered with Conan Doyle's own eye for detail.

"I was (I remember) at the centre table writing out 'The Adventure of the Man without a Cork Leg,'" he writes, while Holmes "was amusing himself with a little revolver practice. It was his custom of a summer evening to fire round my head, just shaving my face, until he had made a photograph of me on the opposite wall."

A delighted Conan Doyle later declared Barrie's effort the finest Holmes parody he had ever read and even included it in his autobiography, *Memories and Adventures*. But others have proven equally adept.

Into this company, for sure, falls Robert Bloch, surely one of America's most distinguished twentieth-century crime and adventure novelists (and sci fi and horror and fantasy and seemingly anything else he turned his attention to). Bloch's "The Dynamics of an Asteroid" took its title from what is surely the most sought-after and discussed book in Sherlock Holmes's own redoubtable library, a mathematical treatise penned by Professor James Moriarty himself. A book, Holmes explains, "which ascends to such rarefied heights of pure mathematics that it is said that there was no man in the scientific press capable of criticizing it."

Clearly, Moriarty had other talents, too. For here he is, one hundred years old, explaining to a modern-day (the story was published in 1953) doctor how he was a big wheel in crime in the 1890s, how he survived a fight to the death with some detective or other, and how he wrote a book that was so far ahead of its time that he is still waiting for his genius to be recognized. At which point, sadly, he dies.

The Faithful Adventures of Solar Pons

August Derleth, the founder of the legendary Arkham House publishing company, was another dedicated Holmesian, spinning his yarns around a detective named Solar Pons (and his companion, Doctor Parker), who would sally forth from their home in Praed Street, near Paddington Station, to solve such mysteries as "The Adventure of the Circular Room," "The Adventure of the Tottenham Werewolf," "The Adventure of the Spurious Tamerlaine" . . .

Tale upon tale (many of which were published in *Ellery Queen's Mystery Magazine*), volume upon volume, Derleth published some half a dozen Solar Pons collections prior to his death in 1971; Basil Copper has continued the legacy in the years since then.

Where Pons differs from his prototype, however, is that he is not simply a parody of Holmes. Holmes himself lives and breathes in the same world as Pons; Derleth's detective is acutely aware of him, aware of his adventures; and he considers himself a fervent admirer of his predecessor; the Pons stories are set in the 1920s and 1930s, following Holmes's retirement.

Their methodology, however, is very similar. In "The Adventure of the Three Red Dwarfs" Pons painstakingly explains,

> You have only to use your eyes, Jamison . . . Those stains on your trousers are obviously bloodstains. The condition of your knees shows you to have been creeping about on the floor.
>
> The fact that you were creeping about on a floor where you stained your trousers with blood suggests that there has been a murder rather than a suicide, for in the latter case you would not have come to me. If there was so much blood on the floor that you could not avoid it in your examination of the body, I infer that the victim bled profusely, and that in turn leads me to suspect that a knife was used and drawn from the wound.

How Holmesian, too, is this fragment of dialogue from "The Adventure of the Proper Comma":

Pons: Tomorrow I will have you incarcerate me in Dr. Sollaire's sanitarium.

Parker: What? Pons, you aren't serious!

Pons: I was never more so.

Parker: But it is such a mad scheme!

Pons: Ah, I shall be mad as a hatter, if necessary. I have always had a fondness for Alice's table companions.

The Erotic Adventuring of Ambrose Horne

We compare Derleth's delightful approach with another long-running Holmesian parody, albeit one that is suitable only for readers of a XXX-minded disposition. Ambrose Horne, created in the early 2000s by author Chrissie Bentley, likewise inhabits a world where Sherlock is a living, breathing presence. But whereas Pons has only admiration for Holmes, Horne is distinctly unimpressed by his methods.

For Horne (and his aristocratic sidekick Lady H) investigates only the mysteries of the most intimate and sexually charged nature, a sordid underworld overflowing with devilish sex machines, uninhibited succubi, aphrodisiac potions, and so forth, the nature of which no respectable person would ever wish to see published in the journals of Doctor Watson.

"Yes, yes, he's brilliant," blusters Major Carpenter in "The Strange Case of the Confusing Corporal." "Everybody admits that. But having that preposterous little assistant of his, Watson or whatever his name is, write the cases up for the popular press is nothing short of shameless self-aggrandizement. Mark my words, he'll never work for this country's government again . . . and I don't care what Watson writes to the contrary."

And later, in "The Strange Case of the Coagulated Conundrum," Horne himself advises a Baker Street–bound client,

> You must do as you see fit, as I am sure Mr Holmes will. Certainly details of your loss [a priceless postage stamp] and, indeed, of any similarly valued items that have not been lost, will make a tasty filling for his assistant's next essay in the popular press, and I am sure you will meet many new acquisitive enthusiasts as a result. I wish you luck. And, should you then require a less voluble detective to assist you in any matters that might ensue from those meetings, I will be as willing to help you on that occasion as I am on this.

Horne, on the other hand, remains silent as the grave where his clients' wishes and requirements are concerned, lending his adventures an air of forbidden fruit above and beyond their already highly charged nature.

The Utterly Charming Adventures of the Twelve-Year-Old Schoolgirl

Detectives come in all shapes and sizes. Few, however, arrive packaged in the form of a twelve-year-old schoolgirl. Flavia de la Luce is the youngest child of decaying English aristocracy. She is also possessed of a ferociously analytical mind, a relentless curiosity, and a blazing yen for conducting strange-smelling chemical experiments in the deserted wing of the family manor house.

The creation of author Alan Bradley, Miss Flavia first stepped onto the literary stage in 2009, via *The Sweetness at the Bottom of the Pie*—a murder-and-more mystery that is just as intriguing as its title and whose cast of characters, for the most part, could have stepped out of any immediately post–World War II English detective novel. The fusty vicar, the frumpy busybody, the passing gypsy, the visiting entertainer, the mountebank bachelor, the nosy aunt, they're all here or hereabouts, and they go about their English ways with delectable English decorum.

So does Flavia. Or, at least, she tries to. But the village of Bishop's Lacey seems cursed to forever be visited by mysterious death, and with a local police force that, frankly, couldn't solve a crossword puzzle without looking at the answers. Flavia is fated to do their sleuthing for them. Or so she believes, and so, as her series of adventures goes on, she does.

Four further novels have followed that distinguished debut, and each bears its own utterly captivating title: *The Weed That Strings the Hangman's Bag*; *A Red Herring Without Mustard*; *I Am Half-Sick of Shadows*; *Speaking from Among the Bones*; and, in early 2013, *The Dead in Their Vaulted Arches*.

THE STRUGGLE OF SUPER-MINDS IN THE CRIME OF THE CENTURY!

The
Adventures of
SHERLOCK
HOLMES

Basil   Nigel
RATHBONE - BRUCE
            Ida   Alan
LUPINO - MARSHAL
A
20th CENTURY·   E.E.
FOX PICTURE
Darryl F.   Terry   George   Henry
KILBURN-ZUCCO-STEPHENSON-CLIVE

Accept no substitute! **CAPTION CORRECT? IMAGE CORRECT?**

Perhaps the confirmed Holmesian scholar will find it strange to step from the bustle of London to the calm of the country; from the mind of a mad genius to that of a precocious (if brilliant) child; from a Baskervillian hound to a bicycle named Gladys. In fact, doing so is strange. But in a literary world where detectives do now seem to fall into one of two categories— those that are obviously based on Sherlock, and those that are painstakingly not—it is a joy to read of one who actually is a little bit of both.

The Undocumented Cases of the Undiscovered Casebook

If Derleth and Bentley (who are by no means alone, though they remain ascendant, in their approach to Holmesian pastiche) choose to adapt the detective's technique for their own devices, other authors delve even deeper, into the archive that Holmes and Watson occasionally discuss, to extract those cases that are alluded to in the published works but have never been brought to light.

Sci-fi author Poul Anderson, for example, unraveled "the Singular Adventures of the Grice-Patersons in the Island of Uffa," a saga that Watson mentions in "The Problem of Thor Bridge"; John Dickson Carr set himself to untangling "The Adventure of the Conk-Singleton Papers."

The comedy troupe the Firesign Theatre investigated, albeit irreverently, "The Tale of the Giant Rat of Sumatra" across a 1974 album of that same title, with Philip Procter playing Hemlock Stones and David Ossman as his companion Flotsam.

Nicholas Meyer joined us in pondering the Arrest of Wilson, the Notorious Canary-Trainer (as mentioned in ("Black Peter"), "which removed a plague-spot from the East-end of London"; but whereas we can only wonder at what those canaries were trained to do, Meyer let us all in on the news with his 1993 novel *The Canary Trainer*. One clue, though. The novel is set at the opera in Paris, and Irene Adler is back. Maybe Watson was discussing a different East End. Or a different canary trainer.

Either way, Watson needs only allude to a case and somewhere, an author is inspired to unearth it. But what other marvels *do* reside in that legendary tin box that Watson introduced to us early on in the Thor Bridge adventure?

Around a hundred of these cases are at least mentioned in the published stories, and Watson is at pains to explain that "some, and not the least interesting, were complete failures, and as such will hardly bear narrating, since no final explanation is forthcoming. A problem without a solution may interest the student, but can hardly fail to annoy the casual reader."

Others, however, seem to have been pursued to completion.

We marvel, for example, at what could possibly have occurred in the strange case of "the Politician, the Lighthouse, and the Trained Cormorant (as referenced in "The Veiled Lodger").

We shiver at the tragic fate of Isadora Persano, "the well-known journalist and duellist, who was found stark staring mad with a match box in front of him which contained a remarkable worm said to be unknown to science" ("The Problem of Thor Bridge"). Or the Repulsive Story of the Red Leech ("The Golden Pince-Nez"), which of course begs the reader to wonder when stories about leeches are *not* considered repulsive, and how much worse must this one have been if even a medical man like John Watson chose to describe it thus?

There was "the Dreadful Business of the Abernetty Family," reminding us all that sometimes it is the most insignificant detail that needs to be examined. This case was brought to Holmes's attention by "the depth which the parsley had sunk into the butter upon a hot day" ("The Six Napoleons").

We contemplate the horror that assaulted the crew of "the cutter *Alicia*, which sailed one spring morning into a small patch of mist from where she never again emerged, nor was anything further ever heard of herself and her crew" ("The Problem of Thor Bridge"). Or another seafaring misadventure, "the loss of the British bark *Sophy Anderson*" ("The Five Orange Pips").

There were the adventures of the Paradol Chamber and the Camberwell Poisoning (both recalled in "The Five Orange Pips"); the adventure of the old Russian woman, and the singular affair of the aluminum crutch ("The Musgrave Ritual").

There were the singular contents of the ancient British barrow, referring to one of the prehistoric burial mounds that once littered the English landscape, a few of which have disgorged some of the country's most remarkable archaeological treasures; and, of course, "the arrest of Huret, the Boulevard assassin—an exploit which won for Holmes an autograph letter of thanks from the French President and the Order of the Legion of Honour" ("The Golden Pince-Nez").

Not to mention (deep breath): undisclosed services to the Crown for which Holmes refused a knighthood; the colossal schemes of Baron Maupertuis; the bogus laundry affair; the case of the Hurled False Teeth; the woman at Margate with no powder on her nose; the abominable wife of clubfooted Ricoletti; and many more adventures and escapades that transported Holmes to the farthest corners of the world.

There was that case involving the Netherland-Sumatra Company; the papers of ex-president Murillo; his work for the King of Scandinavia and for the reigning family of Holland; the unfortunate Mme. Montpensier; a commission for the Sultan of Turkey; and, of course, the Trepoff murder in Odessa.

What do you mean, you're not aware of the Trepoff murder in Odessa? Even the newly married Watson, who had understandably "seen little of Holmes lately" before they reunited to avert "A Scandal in Bohemia," had heard of that one. In fact, he "shared [it] with all the readers of the daily press."

Holmes traveled the world, then, in search of excitement, in search of fresh cases, in search of anything to keep that remarkable mind of his from atrophying to a state where he would be indistinguishable from any other mere human being.

But always he returned to London. For that was his home, that was his heart. And that was where all the greatest adventures invariably began, in the study of 221b.

But the longest and most thrilling adventure of them all was coming to an end. Not for Holmes, who was already immortal, but for Conan Doyle himself.

19

The Adventure of the Detective and the Ghost Hunter

In which Conan Doyle Dies, then Comes Back from the Grave, and we meet Harry Price, perhaps the One Man in England Qualified to Determine whether the Old Boy's Ghost was Really Walking

It was the sensation of the age. Sir Arthur Conan Doyle had been ailing for some time; few were surprised when a heart attack finally felled the grand old man of English letters on July 7, 1930, at Windlesham Manor, his home in Crowborough, East Sussex.

What was unexpected was the vehemence with which he apparently refused to remain in his grave.

The first "sighting" came within six hours of Conan Doyle's death, when his spirit manifested through a medium in the English Midlands. Within forty-eight hours, mediums as far apart as Vancouver, BC, and Wilkes Barre, PA; Paris and Milan; Sunderland and Sussex were reporting meetings with the departed Conan Doyle. From his office in London, the psychic investigator Harry Price registered no fewer than seventeen reports of the author's return within that same two-day span, and three years later, in 1933, he admitted, "today, my waste paper basket still gets jammed with newspaper clippings." In life, Conan Doyle had possessed a titanic presence. In death, he became practically Brobdingnagian.

If you have read this far, the chances are that you own at least one book by Sir Arthur Conan Doyle, be it a collection of the adventures of the redoubtable Sherlock Holmes or one of the equally enthralling adventure yarns he penned elsewhere in his career.

Few beyond the most devoted collectors, however, have paid much attention to the vast body of writing that Conan Doyle unleashed throughout the last twelve years of his life and that he himself claimed represented the ongoing development of more thought and research than he had ever expended on any other subject.

In 1916, at the height of the Great War, Conan Doyle publicly announced his "conversion" to Spiritualism, proving his zeal by all but exclusively devoting his energies to the subject until the moment of his own death—at which point, one presumes, he would have discovered precisely how reliable his beliefs really were.

His writing echoed his faith. Between 1918 and 1930, Conan Doyle wrote, edited, or translated some thirty books, fully two-thirds of which pertained to Spiritualism in some form or another.

To his public, still hungry for more tales of Sherlock Holmes, these books were an irrelevance; with few exceptions, they sold poorly, and many of them have remained out of print for decades. Indeed, by the late 1920s, Conan Doyle was reduced to publishing, or at least reprinting, the books under his own Psychic Press imprint, financing them with earnings from his other, more conventional writings (the last Sherlock Holmes adventures included).

Yet Conan Doyle's Spiritualist writings really are not too far removed from the tenets of Holmesian study. In other hands, it is true, his words might easily have formed a decidedly flimsy argument for Life After Death—Doyle rarely sought concrete proof that the events he witnessed were genuine. For him, his faith was sufficient. But these works offer a fascinating glimpse into the author's mind regardless. There is a distinctly supernatural angle, for example, to many of both Holmes's adventures and those of Conan Doyle's other creations, an angle that could never have been wrought so successfully had he not already been inclined toward Spiritualism.

Similarly, the faintly superhuman aspect of many of Conan Doyle's fictional heroes would also, through the light shed by his later writings, become clearer: Conan Doyle fervently believed in man's ability to rise above his customary station of pettiness, spite, and greed, and these qualities are frequently evinced in the heroes of his novels. This same belief was among the threads binding Conan Doyle's last books; it would also, perhaps ironically, become the theme of what was touted (by its publishers, at least) as his first posthumous work.

Thy Kingdom Come was a spiritual manifesto for man that Conan Doyle supposedly communicated from beyond the grave. In 1931, it was claimed, Conan Doyle appeared to a brotherhood of adepts living in a Himalayan retreat, in a state of considerable despair. As man advanced, the specter explained, and grew further apart from the spiritual beliefs that had once sustained him, the spirit world had fallen into stark decay. Like the slum reformers of Victorian England, Conan Doyle was now on a heavenly mission to restore humankind to a state of spiritual grace . . . if not for its own sake, then for that of the Other Side.

The Himalayan Brotherhood relayed Conan Doyle's dilemma to "a certain occult brotherhood in France," who in turn recruited a medium capable of summoning Conan Doyle to her side, and a copy typist who would dutifully record his words. *Thy Kingdom Come*, Conan Doyle's recipe for a better world (and a healthier Hereafter), was the result.

Doyle himself was a devout supporter of "posthumous authorship," devoting one chapter of his final book (at least as a living author), 1930's *The Edge of the Unknown*, to an impassioned defense of similar efforts purportedly dictated by Oscar Wilde and Jack London. However, even he argued for some "internal evidence of the author's identity," and sadly, *Thy Kingdom Come* offered little.

Contemporary reviews described it as nothing more than generic spiritual-ist mumbo jumbo, only lightly disguised by the lofty pretensions of its alleged authorship, and seated in his office at the National Laboratory of Psychical Research, Harry Price doubtless consigned his copy of this slim volume to the same jammed wastebasket as the news clippings. He knew, as all the author's other friends and fans surely knew, that Conan Doyle would hardly have resorted to such overly mystical means in order to get any "message" across. Painfully aware as he was of the skepticism that his beliefs aroused, Conan Doyle would never even have ventured to the Himalayas. He would found a far more mun-dane route than that.

Discussing Conan Doyle in his own autobiography, 1933's *Leaves from a Psychist's Case-Book*, Price wrote, "there is not a spiritualist living with the same dynamic personality, driving force, dogged grit, tenacity of purpose, fighting qualities, large-heartedness, and world-wide prestige that the great High Priest of Spiritualism possessed."

Yet Price, reveling in his role as the prince of real-life Ghostbusters, would also admit that his relationship with Conan Doyle was often strained, occasion-ally hostile, and sometimes downright appalling. They were both explorers in the psychic field, Price explained, but they were "diametrically opposed" in their beliefs.

Whereas Price was convinced that even the most inexplicable phenom-enon had an animistic cause and devoted much of his career to unmasking the fraudulent mediums and all-round charlatans who preyed on the gullible public's psychic appetite, Conan Doyle championed the most unworthy cases, often flying in the face of even hardnosed evidence of duplicitous chicanery. (The aforementioned Cottingley Fairies are a case in point.) Such evidence was frequently furnished by Price.

Price was everything Conan Doyle was not, with one exception. He, too, was a prolific author, and one whose writings are today as revered by students of the supernatural as Conan Doyle's are by fans of detective fiction. Over the course of three decades spent painstakingly researching the psychic world, Price wrote some two dozen books, and several hundred essays and magazine articles, all devoted to documenting, in the most ruthless scientific terms, the phenomena in which Conan Doyle placed his faith.

In stark contrast to the often pitiful fate of Conan Doyle's books on psychic subjects, however, Price was a born best-seller. Naturally cynical though it is, the reading public is nevertheless captivated by "true" tales of the supernatural, and even Price's driest paragraphs possessed the innate ability to captivate and thrill.

Whether his audience was a team of earnest fellow researchers, in the sterility of a lecture hall, or a roomful of housewives in a church hall in the sticks, Price could lend the dullest tale a sparkling luminescence. An uneventful night spent in a distinctly unhaunted house became a masterpiece of suspense; an unembroidered legend became a Homeric epic; and once on the trail of a fraud or a trickster, of course the gathering of insignificant clues could not echo anyone but the Sherlockian sleuth himself. By the time Price got round to finally exposing the charlatan, the audience would be utterly spellbound.

Trickery, knavery, downright dishonesty, Price was exposed to every guile in the fraudster's book and might even have invented a few more himself. A skilled conjurer, he knew precisely what could be accomplished by sleight of hand and a roomful of mirrors. Attempting to test the veracity of one family who claimed their home was haunted, he turned common wine into thick black ink, just to test their reaction, then threw "spectral" stones across the room to see what they would do. If their house wasn't really haunted before he arrived, they would certainly think it was when he left!

Conan Doyle detested Price's methods but could not help but admire his tenacity—high praise indeed from the creator of that most tenacious detective of all. Yet the passion that unquestionably united—but simultaneously divided—these two great minds belied the fact that under other circumstances, their lives could scarcely have been more dissimilar.

By the time Price was born, on January 17, 1881, Conan Doyle was already a young man of twenty-two, on the verge of completing his medical studies at Edinburgh University. While Price encountered his first poltergeist at the age of fifteen, when he spent the night in a so-called haunted manor close to the family home, Conan Doyle had been conjuring fictional spirits from blank pages for close to half a decade.

And by the time Price made his first appearance in print, with a numismatic handbook, *The Coinage of Kent*, published by his local (Sussex) historical society, Conan Doyle was already the highest-paid author in history. It is, then, pure coincidence that the two should have stumbled upon the themes that would ensure their subsequent fame—and immortality—within weeks, maybe even days, of each other.

In January 1888, the seven-year-old Price watched enthralled as "The Great Sequah," an itinerant magician and illusionist, performed for a curious crowd on a cold London street. That same month, the Southsea-based MD Arthur Conan Doyle received the first in what would become a tidal wave of plaudits for his novella *A Study in Scarlet*, published the previous month in *Beeton's Christmas Annual*. The story, of course, marked the literary debut of Sherlock Holmes.

Deception (for what else, after all, can conjuring tricks be described as?) and detection—two worlds that are poles apart but are inextricably linked regardless. It was indeed a wry fate that decreed that having made these subjects their own,

Price and Conan Doyle should reverse their roles for the rest of their lives. While Price, through his relentless pursuit of psychic jiggerypokery, would one day rival Holmes himself, Conan Doyle, with his childlike credulity, would prove as easily impressed as the Great Sequah's young admirer.

It was bitter irony, too, that decreed that Conan Doyle should emerge as the champion of the psychic world at precisely the same time as Harry Price erupted as its earthly nemesis, in the aftermath of the Great War of 1914–18 and the massive revival in Spiritualism wrought as millions of bereaved families sought to come to terms with the loss of their loved ones on the killing fields of France and Belgium. It was Price's campaigning against the obvious charlatans unleashed in this revival that first brought him to public attention—and opprobrium.

Conan Doyle's induction into the upper echelons of Spiritualism was considerably smoother, if no less controversial. At first, his pronouncements on the subject were regarded as simply the latest hobby of a notoriously butterfly mind; over the years, Conan Doyle had unleashed his passions upon a myriad themes, passions that threatened at times to consume him whole. But they had passed; in 1916, when he publicly averred his support for, and belief in, the afterlife, it was assumed that this, too, would pass.

It didn't.

Conan Doyle's first Spiritualist book, *The New Revelation; or, What Is Spiritualism?*, was published in 1918, a document not only of his beliefs, but also of his own "conversion" to the cause:

> When the War came, it brought earnestness into all our souls and made us look closely at our own beliefs and reassess their values. In the presence of an agonized world, hearing everyday of the deaths of the flower of our race in the first promise of their unfulfilled youth . . . I seemed suddenly to see that this subject with which I had so long dallied was not merely a study of a force outside the rules of science, but that it really was tremendous, a breaking down of the walls between the two worlds, a direct undeniable message from beyond, a call of hope and guidance to the human race at the time of its deepest affliction.

This confession staggered an audience raised on the cold objectivity of Holmes, on the reasoned understanding of Watson, the clinical ruthlessness of Moriarty. So did Conan Doyle's next sentence. "The objective side of it ceased to interest . . . . The religious side . . . was clearly of greater importance."

There is no doubt that Conan Doyle was sincere in his beliefs; just as there was no doubt that, if he continued down this path, he would one day cross swords with Harry Price. The only real surprise was that it took so long. Not until 1922 did the two men publicly take up arms against each other, when Conan Doyle rushed to the defense of the spirit photographers Ada Emma Deane, whom Price was then thinking of investigating, and William Hope, whom he had already denounced. "It was," Conan Doyle admonished the researcher, "very wrong to try and ruin a man [Hope] who had long years of fine psychic work behind him."

Spirit photography is, as its name suggests, the act of photographing spirits, an art that, as the camera itself approached the centenary of its practical invention, was seen by many as the next logical progression in the development of the science.

Over the years, a great many photographs have been published that appear to show a figure or object that was not there when the picture was taken. Never, however, were so many produced as during the early 1920s, after Conan Doyle included a discussion of the subject in his second Spiritualist volume, *The Vital Message*.

Over the next few years, spirit photography became little short of a national pastime, as amateur cameramen from all walks of life raced to capture their own spooky images on film, and in 1922, Conan Doyle contributed to a new (but today little known) book on the subject, *The Case for Spirit Photography*.

A wonderful book, as much for the unflagging belief of its (otherwise obscure) contributors as for the almost foolish credulity of many of their opinions, it is also noteworthy for the sustained attack on Harry Price that Conan Doyle launched from its pages.

William Hope, Doyle insisted, remained above reproach, an unselfish man whose only wish was to turn his inexplicable gifts to the service of others. He charged only for the cost of his materials (which, naturally, were more expensive than those a "conventional" photographer might require), and in return, he brought hope and happiness to all who consulted him. Price, on the other hand, was nothing more than a base skeptic, the very premise of whose work, under "controlled laboratory conditions," was frequently as fraudulent as he claimed his victims to be.

In fact, the vogue for spirit photography faded as quickly as it had arisen. Even as Conan Doyle continued to vouchsafe its veracity, the infant art was finally sent to an early grave by the unmasking of its greatest practitioner, the aforementioned Ada Emma Deane. And this time, Harry Price wasn't involved.

Ms. Deane's fame rested on her ability to photograph the dead warriors whose spirits accumulated around the Cenotaph, a newly erected war monument in London's Whitehall. Price had attempted to arrange a controlled sitting with this redoubtable talent, but failed. In November 1924, however, editors at the newspaper *The Daily Sketch* were studying one of her photographs when somebody noticed something familiar about one of the wraiths.

The photograph was enlarged, and suddenly the whole picture became clear. The face was that of a famous soccer player! So was the one beside it; so were another and another. Within a matter of days, *The Daily Sketch* had exposed the wretched woman's trickery and the public's taste for her trade was finally exhausted. Conan Doyle, on the other hand, continued to support her long after members of even his own persuasion began doubting her credentials.

Price, too, was on the attack. Smarting from Conan Doyle's published assault, he found himself giving a lecture to a psychic research group in Hove, just a few miles from his foe's old medical practice in Southsea. There, to the delight of the assembly, Price revealed how Conan Doyle, on a recent trip to New York, had visited the famed American psychics Eva and William Thompson, a well-known duo whom Price himself had already written off as nothing more than "a rather entertaining vaudeville act."

During the course of their seance, the Thompsons "brought back" Conan Doyle's now-departed mother, a display that allegedly reduced their illustrious visitor to tears, copiously shed while he embraced the figure. Three days later, the Thompsons were unmasked as fakes, but had Conan Doyle even commented upon the affair, much less explained his emotional outburst? No, he had not; in fact, it would be May 1924 before Conan Doyle finally broke his silence, when he somewhat belatedly informed Price that not only had he *not* hugged the spirit, he had known the whole thing was a put-on from the start.

The pair clashed again over the author's support for the Cottingley Fairies, but it was the summer of 1925 before they met in person in Paris. Despite the bitter words that had passed between them, both privately and in print, their meeting was cordial; recording the event in *Leaves from a Psychist's Case-Book*, Price recalled that when Conan Doyle accused him of "medium-baiting . . . I suggested that his great big heart was running away with him and that he was no match for the charlatans who . . . battened on his good nature." The two men "parted good friends once more."

The truce was not to last, however. In January 1926, while Conan Doyle gave his first, and vehemently anti-Price, speech as the newly elected president of the London Spiritual Alliance, Price himself was standing two floors below, hosting the opening of his National Laboratory of Psychical Research, an organization that apparently stood against everything the alliance represented. The fact that the alliance (and therefore, Conan Doyle) was the laboratory's landlord only amplified the forthcoming flashpoints.

Mrs. Deane and her phantom footballers remained a bone of contention between the two men. The half-decade-old Thompson incident, too, would spark a major confrontation, after a reporter mistakenly referred to one of Price's earlier lectures (in which Conan Doyle was again ridiculed) when reporting on a more recent one (in which the author was not even mentioned).

Price seemingly needed only put pen to paper, something he did with increasing regularity as his fame as a spirit basher spread, for Conan Doyle to launch another broadside against what he demeaningly referred to as "his anti-Spiritualist articles." Gently or otherwise, the books that flowed from Conan Doyle's pen as the 1920s progressed abound with assaults upon Price's name, character, and occupation, a campaign that climaxed with Doyle's last book, the aforementioned *The Edge of the Unknown*, and its viperishly veiled opening sentence: "who was the greatest medium-baiter of modern times?"

Contemporary logic, and Price's own (allegedly not inconsiderable) vanity, vouchsafed just one response: Price himself. Conan Doyle, however, cited the American escapologist Harry Houdini, then rubbed further salt into his adversary's wounds by refraining from even mentioning Price's name, or that of his laboratory, anyplace in the book. A reasonable parallel might be a history of rock 'n' roll that doesn't mention Elvis Presley.

Price's protests, against both his own ill-treatment and that of his work, were in vain; letters flew between Conan Doyle and Price on a daily basis, reaching a crescendo of sorts when Price, apparently trying to make amends, informed his adversary, "a representative of a big group of American newspapers called upon me and asked me what I thought of you. I was tempted to tell them . . ."

He intended it as a joke, but this new overture was no more successful than any other he had employed during the course of this tempestuous relationship. Back in 1923, Price had asked Conan Doyle to contribute a preface to his latest book, a favorable study of one of the few mediums in whom Price himself had the utmost faith, Stella C (*A Page of Psychic History*). Conan Doyle "begged to be excused."

In this latest battle, he begged to be rid of Price altogether, and yet they did reconcile, and just in time. Conan Doyle was not long for this world, and over the course of his last few months, he and Price finally kindled the friendship that their undeniably deep mutual respect should have nurtured years before.

One reason for the cessation of hostilities was Price's increasing absorption into a new case, one that continues to enthrall ghost hunters (and debunkers) even today. Price was first alerted to what would become known as "the most haunted house in Britain" in June 1929, when he was commissioned by the *Daily Mirror* to investigate "a most unusual poltergeist case that was disturbing the inmates of a country house somewhere in the Home Counties."

Price was on the scene within twenty-four hours, not imagining for a moment that Borley Rectory would not only cement his name in the national consciousness, it would also dominate the last two decades of his life.

Price's enthusiasm knew no bounds, and the public lapped it up. Two books on the subject, *The Most Haunted House in England* (1940) and *The End of Borley Rectory* (1946), became best-sellers. He published over a dozen articles on the subject and gave as many talks on British radio. With other authors since adding their own observations and theories, there are now as many books on Borley as there were ghosts in the place to begin with. And there were an awful lot of ghosts.

Borley was everything Price dreamed a haunted house should be; between October 1930 and October 1935, Price estimated that upward of two thousand poltergeist phenomena were experienced at the rectory. Mysterious lights shone through the night; bells rang, footsteps echoed. Coins and medals flew through the air. When *Life* magazine dispatched a photographer to Borley, the ghosts obligingly raised a brick off the ground for the cameraman's personal benefit. Unknown writings appeared on the walls. Heavy objects were hurled at the occupants, and when Borley burned to the ground on February 27, 1939 (an event that the spirits had predicted precisely eleven months beforehand), spectral figures were seen passing through the flames. Even today, with every last physical trace of the rectory having disappeared, it remains an eerie site. Harry Price was in his element.

Throughout the hauntings' most active phase, Borley was home to Lionel and Marianne Foyster, with Marianne's son (by a later marriage) Vincent O'Neil himself becoming a much-regarded expert on the hauntings. O'Neil recalled, "Sir Arthur never really knew about Price's latest project, passing away shortly before Borley first hit the headlines." But still O'Neil enjoyed imagining what might have transpired, if only Conan Doyle had lived to witness, and perhaps even join, his most favored foe in an investigation of the phenomena.

The shadow of the Sherlock!   *Photofest*

"Would [each] man have stared into the other man's eyes looking for clues as they prepared for a joint seance? Both were members of the Society for Psychical Research and were accustomed to all manner of supposed paranormal events. Whether from the touch of a ghost, or the tension between two dedicated spiritualists, the electricity the two would generate during a seance together would be something to behold!"

Sadly, imagination is all anybody has to cling onto, with even fiction failing us here. Amid all the "new" adventures with which sundry modern authors have felt obliged to saddle Sherlock Holmes, a visit to Borley must certainly have crossed somebody's mind. Yet only one, Trevor Hall, has made the connection, using the rectory as the setting for a privately published 1986 novella, *The Last Case of Sherlock Homes.*

Unfortunately, what could have proven an excellent exercise in supernatural deduction emerged instead as a mundane (if complicated) murder mystery, with the reader's disappointment compounded by the Holmes of the title not even being the real thing! Hall invented an illegitimate son for the great detective, and it is he who seeks to solve the case.

There can be little doubt, however, that had Conan Doyle lived, Price would have done his utmost to recruit the old man to the Borley cause. He might even, in his own way, have done so.

On October 7, 1930, Price invited one of Conan Doyle's own favorite mediums, Mrs. Eileen Garrett, to his laboratory, for the express purpose of contacting the three-month-deceased author. The séance was a success. Some forty-five minutes into the sitting, Garrett's spirit guide, an Arab named Uvani, announced a visitor. Moments later, a second "voice" announced, "here I am, Arthur Conan Doyle. Now, how am I going to prove it to you?"

Price smiled; "were this the real Conan Doyle," he later wrote, "he would know that I should require absolute proof of his identity." The spirit's terse welcome fit the bill exactly.

The séance lasted for over an hour, and not once, Price later marveled, did his visitor step out of character. Indeed, documenting this extraordinary afternoon in both *Cosmopolitan* magazine (January 1931) and his own *Leaves from a Psychist's Case-Book*, Price, having dismissed the standard accusations of fakery, seemed convinced that he had witnessed a genuine manifestation. Indeed, one subsequent event might even prove his point.

During a séance staged at Borley in 1932, one person present claimed to have seen the spirit of a recently deceased "well-known psychic researcher." Respect for the dead man's family apparently prevented the publication of his name at the time, but Conan Doyle, one of the few men in that profession whose features were well known enough to be recognized by a stranger, certainly fits the bill.

Unfortunately, we will never know for certain, but if it was Conan Doyle, what could be more fitting than that he should choose to visit the house that was so bedeviling his old adversary?

Appendix

Arthur Conan Doyle Bibliography

Sherlock Holmes novels

1887   A Study in Scarlet
1890   The Sign of Four
1902   The Hound of the Baskervilles
1915   The Valley of Fear

Sherlock Holmes short story collections

1892   The Adventures of Sherlock Holmes
1894   The Memoirs of Sherlock Holmes
1905   The Return of Sherlock Holmes
1917   His Last Bow
1927   The Case-Book of Sherlock Holmes
1928   The Complete Sherlock Holmes Short Stories

Professor Challenger Stories

1912   The Lost World
1913   The Poison Belt
1926   The Land of Mist
1927   The Disintegration Machine
1928   When the World Screamed

Fiction

1879   The Mystery of Sasassa Valley
1885   The Surgeon of Gaster Fell
1889   Micah Clarke, his statement as made to his three grandchildren
1889   The Mystery of Cloomber
1889   Mysteries and Adventures
1890   The Captain of the Polestar and other tales
1890   The Firm of Girdlestone: A Romance of the Unromantic

1891   The White Company
1892   The Doings of Raffles Haw
1892   The Great Shadow
1892   Beyond the City
1893   The Gully of Bluemansdyke (reissue of Mysteries and Adventures 1889)
1893   The Refugees: A Tale of Two Continents
1894   An Actor's Duel and The Winning Shot
1894   The Parasite
1894   Round the Red Lamp: Being Facts and Fancies of a Medical Life
1895   The Stark Munro Letters
1896   The Exploits of Brigadier Gerard
1896   Rodney Stone
1896   Uncle Bernac: A Memory of the Empire
1898   The Tragedy of Korosko
1899   A Duet, with an Occasional Chorus
1900   The Croxley Master
1900   The Green Flag and Other Stories of War and Sport
1901   Strange Studies from Life
1903   The Adventures of Gerard
1906   Sir Nigel
1908   Round the Fire Stories
1911   The Last Galley: Impressions and Tales
1918   Danger! and Other Stories
1922   Tales of Long Ago
1922   Tales of Pirates and Blue Water
1922   Tales of Adventure and Medical Life
1922   Tales of Terror and Mystery
1922   Tales of Twilight and the Unseen
1922   Tales of the Ring and Camp / The Croxley Master and Other Tales of
the Ring and Camp
1928   The Dreamers
1929   The Maracot Deep and Other Stories

Verse

1898   Songs of Action
1911   Songs of the Road
1919   The Guards Came Through and Other Poems
1922   The Poems of Arthur Conan Doyle, collected edition

Nonfiction

1900	The Great Boer War
1901	The Immortal Memory
1905	The Fiscal Question
1906	An Incursion into Diplomacy
1907	Through the Magic Door [essays on books]
1909	The Crime of the Congo
1909	Divorce Law Reform: An Essay
1911	Why He is Now in Favour of Home Rule
1914	The German War
1914	Civilian National Reserve
1914	The World War Conspiracy
1914	The German War
1915	Western Wanderings
1915	The Outlook on the War
1916	An Appreciation of Sir John French
1916	A Visit to Three Fronts
1916	The British Campaign in France and Flanders, 1914-1918
1917	Supremacy of the British Soldier
1918	Life After Death (A Form Letter)
1918	The New Revelation: or, What Is Spiritualism?
1919	The Vital Message
1922	Spiritualism: Some Straight Questions and Direct Answers
1921	The Wanderings of a Spiritualist
1922	The Case for Spirit Photography (with others)
1922	The Coming of the Fairies
1923	Our American Adventure
1923	Three of Them: A Reminiscence
1924	Memoirs and Adventures
1924	Our Second American Adventure
1924	The Spiritualists Reader (editor)
1924	Leon Denis: The Mystery of Joan of Arc (translator)
1926	The History of Spiritualism, 2 vols.
1927	Pheneas Speaks: Direct Spirit Communications
1928	A Word of Warning
1928	What Does Spiritualism Actually Teach and Stand For?
1929	An Open Letter to Those of My Generation
1929	Our African Winter
1929	The Roman Catholic Church: A Rejoinder.
1930	[A Form Letter]
1930	[A Second Form Letter]
1930	The Edge of the Unknown

Plays

Bibliography

Accardo, Pasquale J. (1987). *Diagnosis and Detection: Medical Iconography of Sherlock Holmes*. Madison, NJ: Fairleigh Dickinson University Press.

Baring-Gould, William (1967). *The Annotated Sherlock Holmes*. New York: Clarkson N. Potter.

Baring-Gould, William (1962). *Sherlock Holmes of Baker Street: The Life of the World's First Consulting Detective*. New York: Clarkson N. Potter.

Barnes, Alan (2011). *Sherlock Holmes on Screen: The Complete Film and TV History*. London: Titan Books.

Blakeney, T. S. (1994). *Sherlock Holmes: Fact or Fiction?* London: Prentice Hall & IBD.

Dakin, David (1972). *A Sherlock Holmes Commentary*. Newton Abbot: David & Charles.

Duncan, Alistair (2008). *Eliminate the Impossible: An Examination of the World of Sherlock Holmes on Page and Screen*. London: MX Publishing.

Duncan, Alistair (2009). *Close to Holmes: A Look at the Connections Between Historical London, Sherlock Holmes and Sir Arthur Conan Doyle*. London: MX Publishing.

Green, Richard Lancelyn (1987). *The Sherlock Holmes Letters*. Iowa City: University of Iowa Press.

Hall, Trevor (1977). *Sherlock Holmes and His Creator*. New York: St. Martin's Press.

Harrison, Michael (1973). *The World of Sherlock Holmes*. London: Frederick Muller.

Jones, Kelvin (1987). *Sherlock Holmes and the Kent Railways*. Sittingborne, Kent: Meresborough Books.

Keating, H. R. F. (2006). *Sherlock Holmes: The Man and His World*. Edison, NJ: Castle.

King, Joseph A. (1996). *Sherlock Holmes: From Victorian Sleuth to Modern Hero*. Lanham, MD: Scarecrow Press.

Klinger, Leslie (2005). *The New Annotated Sherlock Holmes*. New York: W. W. Norton.

Klinger, Leslie (1998). *The Sherlock Holmes Reference Library*. Indianapolis: Gasogene Books.

Mitchelson, Austin (1994). *The Baker Street Irregular: Unauthorised Biography of Sherlock Holmes*. Romford: Ian Henry Publications.

Redmond, Donald (1983). *Sherlock Holmes: A Study in Sources*. Quebec: McGill–Queen's University Press.

Rennison, Nick (2007). *Sherlock Holmes: The Unauthorized Biography*. London: Grove Press.

Riley, Dick (2005). *The Bedside Companion to Sherlock Holmes.* New York: Barnes & Noble Books.

Riley, Peter (2005). *The Highways and Byways of Sherlock Holmes.* London: P. & D. Riley.

Shaw, John B. (1995). *Encyclopedia of Sherlock Holmes: A Complete Guide to the World of the Great Detective.* London: Pavillion Books.

Sinclair, David (2009). *Sherlock Holmes's London.* London: Robert Hale.

Smith, Daniel (2009). *The Sherlock Holmes Companion: An Elementary Guide.* London: Aurum Press.

Tracy, Jack (1988). *The Sherlock Holmes Encyclopedia: Universal Dictionary of Sherlock Holmes.* London: Crescent Books.

Weller, Philip (1993). *The Life and Times of Sherlock Holmes.* Simsbury: Bracken Books.

Wexler, Bruce (2008). *The Mysterious World of Sherlock Holmes.* London: Running Press.

Index

THE FAQ SERIES

Armageddon Films FAQ
by Dale Sherman
Applause Books
978-1-61713-119-6.........$24.99

Lucille Ball FAQ
*by James Sheridan
and Barry Monush*
Applause Books
978-1-61774-082-4......$19.99

The Beach Boys FAQ
by Jon Stebbins
Backbeat Books
978-0-87930-987-9...$19.99

Black Sabbath FAQ
by Martin Popoff
Backbeat Books
978-0-87930-957-2....$19.99

James Bond FAQ
by Tom DeMichael
Applause Books
978-1-55783-856-8....$22.99

Jimmy Buffett FAQ
by Jackson Quigley
Backbeat Books
978-1-61713-455-5.......$24.99

Eric Clapton FAQ
by David Bowling
Backbeat Books
978-1-61713-454-8......$22.99

Doctor Who FAQ
by Dave Thompson
Applause Books
978-1-55783-854-4....$22.99

The Doors FAQ
by Rich Weidman
Backbeat Books
978-1-61713-017-5.........$19.99

Fab Four FAQ
*by Stuart Shea and
Robert Rodriguez*
Hal Leonard Books
978-1-4234-2138-2.......$19.99

Fab Four FAQ 2.0
by Robert Rodriguez
Hal Leonard Books
978-0-87930-968-8..$19.99

Film Noir FAQ
by David J. Hogan
Applause Books
978-1-55783-855-1......$22.99

Grateful Dead FAQ
by Tony Sclafani
Backbeat Books
978-1-61713-086-1.......$24.99

Jimi Hendrix FAQ
by Gary J. Jucha
Backbeat Books
978-1-61713-095-3......$22.99

Horror Films FAQ
by John Kenneth Muir
Applause Books
978-1-55783-950-3....$22.99

Stephen King Films FAQ
by Scott Von Doviak
Applause Books
978-1-4803-5551-4.....$24.99

KISS FAQ
by Dale Sherman
Backbeat Books
978-1-61713-091-5.......$22.99

Led Zeppelin FAQ
by George Case
Backbeat Books
978-1-61713-025-0.......$19.99

Nirvana FAQ
by John D. Luerssen
Backbeat Books
978-1-61713-450-0.....$24.99

Pink Floyd FAQ
by Stuart Shea
Backbeat Books
978-0-87930-950-3..$19.99

Elvis Films FAQ
by Paul Simpson
Applause Books
978-1-55783-858-2.....$24.99

Elvis Music FAQ
by Mike Eder
Backbeat Books
978-1-61713-049-6.....$24.99

Rush FAQ
by Max Mobley
Backbeat Books
978-1-61713-451-7........$24.99

Saturday Night Live FAQ
by Stephen Tropiano
Applause Books
978-1-55783-951-0.....$24.99

Sherlock Holmes FAQ
by Dave Thompson
Applause Books
978-1-4803-3149-5.....$24.99

Bruce Springsteen FAQ
by John D. Luerssen
Backbeat Books
978-1-61713-093-9......$22.99

Star Trek FAQ
(Unofficial and Unauthorized)
by Mark Clark
Applause Books
978-1-55783-792-9......$19.99

Star Trek FAQ 2.0
(Unofficial and Unauthorized)
by Mark Clark
Applause Books
978-1-55783-793-6.....$22.99

Three Stooges FAQ
by David J. Hogan
Applause Books
978-1-55783-788-2......$19.99

U2 FAQ
by John D. Luerssen
Backbeat Books
978-0-87930-997-8...$19.99

The Who FAQ
by Mike Segretto
Backbeat Books
978-1-4803-6103-4....$24.99

Neil Young FAQ
by Glen Boyd
Backbeat Books
978-1-61713-037-3........$19.99

Prices, contents, and availability
subject to change without notice.

HAL•LEONARD®
PERFORMING ARTS
PUBLISHING GROUP

FAQ.halleonardbooks.com